Orphaned,
NOT WANTED

by Constance Abel

Orphaned, Not Wanted

Trilogy Christian Publishers A Wholly Owned Subsidiary of Trinity Broadcasting Network

2442 Michelle Drive Tustin, CA 92780

Orphaned, Not Wanted

Cover design by: JP Staggs

For information about special discounts for bulk purchases, please contact Trilogy Christian Publishing.

Manufactured in the United States of America

10 9 8 7 6 5 4 3 2 1

Library of Congress Cataloging-in-Publication Data is available.

ISBN: 978-1-68556-665-4

E-ISBN: 978-1-68556-666-1

Dedication

I dedicate this book to everyone who has ever been orphaned or felt "not wanted" and those who found themselves homeless and loveless. It is in times like these, one discovers the importance of a true relationship. Relationships can be defined in many ways, such as a relationship between siblings, father and son, parents and children, or husband and wife, are defined as "true relationships." A true relationship is one of selflessness, one without prejudice, one that sees the heart and not the person, and one that gives to meet a need. A relationship that looks past the fault to see the need. In a true relationship, love is not an option but an obligation. Incidentally, just maybe you know or have known of someone who has lived a life of silence but overcame, and you can testify of their triumph and victory. It is possible that your testimony of their victory will propel change and bring awareness to another's silent cry for help. Just imagine what it would feel like to rescue an endangered child or person from harm's way.

In honor of Sharon Matthew and all the children, young adults, and those who have aged out of the system yet are living a life of silence, forced to live a life of abuse, shame, neglect, and trauma, abandoned and lonely. This book is dedicated to you.

Acknowledgments

It would be remiss of me to take credit for any written word in this book. I must say without hesitation, "To God be the glory!" Over twenty years ago, in a dream or vision, after successfully chasing the devil into the home of a family member, God said to me, "Give Me the glory." From that day to this, I do not fail to give God the glory. This book is from God's heart to mine. Also, I want to thank my very dear friend Ms. Jay whom God used to encourage me "to write it down."

Acknowledgments

I would like to thank [illegible]

Table of Contents

Table of Contents

Table of Contents

Table of Contents

Preface

After our team of missioned-minded Jesus-loving men and women from different ethnic backgrounds and students of Christ for the Nations (CFNI) decided to open an Independent Placement Agency to place children transitioning from the Department of Child and Protective Service (DCPS) into Christian homes, our goal was to secure their future by placing them with foster parents who would love them unconditionally. After receiving all the necessary programs and certifications, we discovered that the final requirement was $10,000.00 required by the State to open such a facility. After reaching out to friends, family, church, and society as a whole, we were suddenly chosen to become ambassadors for the ministry to Ghana, West Africa; our responsibility was to assess the needs of the local schools in Kumasi, Ghana. Also, while in Kumasi, we met some of the people and children we had only heard about and saw firsthand their desperate need for food. Our primary goal was to provide the orphanages with corn, milk, rice, and flour. But the needs were far greater than what we could provide. Not only was this an indescribable experience, but humbling and life-changing.

We met with the village council and chiefs, who, without hesitation, gave us fair warning of exploiting them by making broken promises. Their distrust of Americans was very obvious and understandable. The chiefs had two plans to ensure our integrity. First of all, they expected us to be truthful and to respect their exceptional hospitality and gratitude as their way of displaying their trust and accepting our assistance and support. Secondly, they suggested that their ambassador should go to the States along with us, just to make sure we kept our promise to support their Village. Of course, we agreed; however, we had no idea what they really expected of us, not until they requested that one of the women on our team should volunteer to become their ambassador to the United States. Apparently, women in leadership played an important role in that culture. Prior to our visit to the villages, we were invited to their local museum.

As it happened, all the artifacts on display were nostalgic and full of history, all pieces on exhibition were from ancient Africa, and one, in particular, was the Queen Mother's stool, or throne. Our guide was asked to sit on the royal stool, but she refused because it was too sacred, but she insisted that I sat on the sacred stool. Therefore, with poise and a straight back, I sat on the sacred Queen Mother's stool. Unfortunately, that episode was the premise of the argument used by the women on our team that I should be the ambassador. With much resistance but to no prevail; therefore, I was forced to accept the honored position as the village ambassador to the States. A feeling of uncertainty left me feeling very nervous, but our primary goal was to aid and assist in whatever way we could. Once again, I reminded myself—it was not about me but the children.

Introduction

On that day, after arriving to work, a dear friend, Ms. Jay stopped by the office just to visit, and I shared with her the audio-visual being downloaded into my mind about this person, whom I could actually hear her thoughts and experience her emotions: emotions that were happy, but very sad at the same time. I shared that it started while getting ready for work, how it continued while driving to work, then stopping, sort of an intermission during the company's weekly meeting, only to resume shortly after the meeting with the character struggling with a decision that would eventually end in death. Her decision left her with mixed feelings. After sharing that information with Ms. Jay, her eyes filled with tears; while wiping her eyes, she said, "Write it down!" You see, Ms. Jay felt a deep calling for fostering, and hearing the vision only confirmed what she felt so strongly about. Instantly it became very clear to me that the story being downloaded into my mind and heart was also a calling and an assignment. As I began to write, the words came effortlessly as I recalled every word from the very beginning of her story.

Afterward, midway through her story, I began to empathize with the character. Her thoughts became my thoughts, her dreams, my dreams, her hopes, my hopes. It was all too real; even her deepest desire to belong burned within my heart. Although my training with the Department of Child and Protective Services somewhat prepared me for the most unspeakable and unbelievable treatment as well as abuse of children of all ages, seeing all the scares and bruises hidden underneath their clothes left me angry and hurt for those children. Even though well trained, nevertheless, I was not prepared for the raw emotions experienced by Sevella. Her story allowed me to feel what I had not felt in any of my certification training. As I lived through Sevella's experience, I now understand their silent cry. It was then her story became my story.

Oftentimes we understand orphaned as someone who has been tragically separated from their parent(s). However, a child can become orphaned when a child has been abandoned, deserted, separated from their abusive parent(s), and placed in foster care. Even more so when one or both parents decide to abort. Believe it or not, even the unborn is orphaned; the only difference between the child taken from the parent by Child Protective Service and the aborted child is the intervention process. You see, the abused child becomes the responsibility of the State: on the other hand, the aborted child goes straight into the arms of our Heavenly Father. The Psalmist states, "When my father and my mother forsake me, then the Lord will take me up" (Psalm 27:10, KJV).

Prologue

"Sevella… Sevella… Sevella." She turned in her sleep from one side to the other, Sevella, Sevella. Suddenly she raises up on both elbows. Before sitting up, she looked cautiously around the grossly dark room. Carefully, she turned over on her belly, then slid off the bed until her feet finally touched the floor. Reaching out into the darkness as she takes small steps toward the bedroom door until her hand finds the knob. She slowly turned the knob from right to left before attempting to open the door, but it did not open. She turned the knob from left to right and again pulled the knob to open the door, but it did not open. She slowly places her right ear to the door and listens carefully for that softly spoken voice. For several minutes, she leaned against the door, listening carefully, but the voice did not call out to her. At this point, she slid down on her knees; placed her ear to the door while still holding the doorknob, listening very carefully, but could not hear the voice.

Again she stood, turned the knob from right to left, and left to right before pulling with all her might, but the door would not open. Frustrated, Sevella turned to look behind her, only to be welcomed by the darkness of the room. In spite of her two failed attempts to open the door, Sevella remained positioned, one hand on the knob and the other reaching out in the darkness, hoping to find her bed. As she looked from one direction of the room to another, she noticed the darkness covering every inch of the room. After unsuccessfully searching for the bed, Sevella placed her back against the door and slid down slowly until her little bottom touched the floor, and there she stayed until she was awakened by another voice, "What are you doing? Get off of this door! What, did you not learn your lesson last night?" The door was pushed with such force that Sevella fell forward on her face.

Surely I thought you would learn your lesson after being sent into this room without a meal, but I guess I was wrong. It was then the large hand grabbed Sevella by the wrist and flung her onto the small cot just as the back of her head hit the wall. The pain was unbearable, and Sevella began to cry, but the sternness of the warden's voice silenced her. As tears filled her eyes, Sevella fought back the tears as she wiped vigorously one side of her face and then the other. Shortly afterward, the warden turned, walking quickly toward the door as Sevella began to tremble all over as fear tugged at her heart. She waited patiently for the warden to return with the strap. Sevella stared at the walls, and for a brief moment, she noticed that there were no windows, just walls.

Her Story

Her name is Sevella Thorn, and this is her story.

As she sat on her couch, peering through the small holes in her lace curtains and the slightly opened blind, sitting very still and very focused, just across from her home was another beautifully designed home; however, her attention was not on the design, on the contrary, she wasn't really sure why this place on her couch became the only place in the home that allowed her to dream, and hope for a better life. Apparently, it was too early for anyone to be outside, and there was no one in sight, but that did not bother Sevella. She continued to peep out of her window, sitting very still, patiently waiting. Suddenly, the front door opened, and there they were, holding hands and smiling before getting into their car and slowly driving away until out of sight. She then closed her blinds, moved away from the window, walked through the dimly lit living room, and went into her bedroom; after resting, she prepared for her busy day and evening.

Once again, she sat on the couch for one last glance across the street before rushing to get everything ready for work. While walking out of her front door, she stopped briefly, looked over her shoulder for one last glance, then rushed one block away to the awaiting taxi. Once at work, Sevella busied herself with Neal's to-do list. First instruction was for her to contact him right after she looked over the list. Feeling very agitated, Sevella pushed the list away and turned toward the window, speaking in a whisper,

"For once, I wished Neal would take me and my work seriously! The only thing he seems to be concerned about is his "so-called clients." Once again, her thoughts were on her neighbors as she stared aimlessly out of the office window. Momentarily deep in thought, without warning, the images of her first trip to Florida brought back the fear and torment of her attacker, images that usually occur in a reoccurring nightmare.

Between the busyness of the day and constant ringing of the phone, Sevella began to feel some relief from her memory of that night and was grateful that the memory could only frighten her and no longer hurt her. Meanwhile, the ringing of the phone startled her. Now pulling herself together, hoping the nervousness she felt would not be so obvious when answering the phone. Quickly, she picked up the receiver. "New Ventures, LLC," sighing loudly. Immediately, the caller responded, "Sevella, Sevella, what's wrong? What's has happened?" Sevella now realized that her sighing was too loud. Thinking fast, she said, "I haven't really had an opportunity to complete the list; I've just arrived at the office, and may I remind you that I'm an hour early and I haven't had my coffee." For a few seconds, there was silence on the other end of the line before Neal continued, "To conclude, I need for you to complete both lists; following that, I need for you to return each call to our clients and give them the itinerary for the investors' meeting tonight. In addition, you will be hosting the meeting." With that being said, the next thing Sevella heard was the dial tone.

In spite of Neal's rudeness, Sevella was thankful for her first job, learning early on to ignore her boss's rudeness, and was grateful that he hired her. After working for several years, Neal allowed her to be a house sitter for one of his investment properties. Moving out of the third homeless shelter into a place she could call home was similar to her first Christmas. "My very own place to stay, even though it comes with a *For Sale* sign," she whispered, turning back to the window. Shaking her head in order to focus, she grabbed the to-do list, and from that point on, she was determined to be the best receptionist ever. Remembering her coffee, she walked slowly to the break room and prepared the pot of coffee, knowing the day would be a long one. "I will not put up with this any longer, and I hope his clients notice how professionally I'm dressed and keep their hands to themselves. What if I told Neal what happened in Florida? Will he believe and help me, or will he take sides with my attacker and fire me?" The smell of her fresh, peculated coffee interrupted her thoughts.

Simultaneously glancing from the clock to her list, she quickly rushed into Neal's office and grabbed the PowerPoint. She then rushed into the conference room at the same time, looking over the list and noticing the time Neal would be arriving from Florida as well as all the other demands. Stopping abruptly to take a deep breath before exclaiming, "Wow! Why didn't he mention this list first? What if I had not seen it? I truly believe he's looking for a reason to fire me. First, his constant rudeness; lastly, the forgotten list." Once again, she is experiencing that familiar insecure feeling. "Of all the important things I could be doing, it appears my real job description is to host those evening meetings while dodging the improper advances and touches of his clients."

Once home, she sat down on the couch, parted the curtains, slightly opened the blinds, and once again, she sat staring at the home across the street. A few minutes later, a car drove into the driveway as she watched and waited. One door opened, then the other. They quickly joined hands, walking through their gate, and disappeared into their home. Momentarily squirming uncomfortably, all the while feeling like a peeping tom and desperately wanting to stop the foolishness, yet, there was joy, unexplained, as she looked forward to watching them come and go. She summed up her actions as watching love stories, whispering, "And watching love stories is no crime," as she slowly closed the blinds. After several months of observing the couple, Sevella discovered that she was pregnant. Frightened, she immediately reflected back on the night in Florida. After returning to her hotel room, she was viciously attacked. All this took place after Neal, without her consent, loaned her to Ellor to assist as his Personal Secretary.

Although Neal hired her as his receptionist, he pretentiously promoted her to executive assistant for this particular business venture. Sevella remembered how frightened she was, and angry with Neal for sending her away without warning. She screamed out, "Now look what has happened!" Devastated, frightened, and desperate, she immediately contacted Neal and informed him of her need to take off work, unwilling to give a justifiable reason other than confessing her assault. "After all, I fear being accused of lying; compared to Ellor and his important clients, I considered myself a nobody, and I couldn't risk losing my job," she whispered through her sobs.

My Heart's Desire

After her discovery, Sevella began to look through the yellow pages for information on abortion clinics. After what seemed like several hours of searching, she finally called Neal back, requesting a specific time to be off work. Neal was reluctant; he agreed hesitantly but congratulated her for a successful trip to Florida and a successful meeting with their clients. "I'll be in touch," said Sevella before hanging up. Now she was thinking, *I am more than a receptionist, and Neal knows that; he's just too cheap to acknowledge it. Even so, I don't want to press my luck, plus my focus should be on finding a doctor, making an appointment, and getting this done as soon as possible.* Sevella began to contact as many abortion clinics, which proved to be very difficult, but finally, she had three contacts that appeared to be a good source. At this point, she considered what type of questions to ask and what answers she would receive but realized she had to move quickly in order to rest before returning to work. Momentarily, Sevella entertained the thought of motherhood, but quickly dismissing the thought, she turned her attention to the investors' meeting wishing she had been more persistent, but Neal wouldn't hear of her having the whole day off.

Without a doubt, the meeting would eventually turn into a party, with the guest mistaking her for an escort. "Being pregnant and working in an environment like that would be impossible." Now laughing while speaking out loud, "At that moment, she recalled the conversations with the receptionists at each clinic as she began to focus on the task ahead of her, yet her desire was to someday have a family of her own. *But not today,* she was speaking to herself as she looked over her list of chosen clinics. After exhausting all of her options, she became more agitated at this unplanned interruption in her life; with the only solution being abortion, she began to remember the mother of one of her foster parents, Miss Timothy, for the most part, was very kind. She remembered when times were difficult. Miss Timothy was always kneeling down on her knees and praying. As Sevella knelt on her knees, she whispered,

"Well, this is a difficult time for me. I could lose my job…" now remembering to bow her head, it was then she didn't know what to say. At the same time struggling to recall Miss Timothy's prayer: only to remember Miss Timothy's invitation, "I rejected her invitation to pray. Instead, I would just look away and ignore her. Okay, my problem is, I've never ever prayed. Now that I think of it, no one has ever taught me to pray. Looking away was my excuse. Now, please hear me (tears running down her cheeks). I know it is wrong, but I cannot be responsible for or even know if I can care for this child; it is out of the question. Please, help me!"

Reoccurring Nightmares

As the hour approached for the scheduled office meeting, Sevella prepared, wishing she had that whole day off, but Neal quickly reminded her of the business meeting. "That's probably why he didn't protest a couple of days off. No doubt he has something planned," she complained as she opened the door and embraced the quietness of the neighborhood. Once again, Sevella glanced over her shoulder, looking toward the house directly across from her home and noticing a light in an upstairs room. The streets were clear yet dimly lit, now walking slowly down her steps, quietly opening and closing her gate as the streetlights cast her mysteriously shaped shadow on the sidewalk. Only the clicks of her heels revealed her presence; being careful to stay out of sight and unnoticed by suspecting onlookers, she walked with head down one block to the taxi. Taking careful steps, one at a time, hiding behind the shrubs that lined the sidewalk until she could quickly slip into the back seat of the waiting taxi. Undoubtedly, breathing a sigh of relief as she wondered about the couple's happiness as the taxi sped silently out of the neighborhood.

As time quickly passed and right at five in the morning, as the night passed and dawn appeared, the taxi dropped her off in the same place. In the same manner, she walked home, taking one meticulous step at a time until she reached her home. Slowly walking through her gate up the steps, opening the door, before entering, she stopped, looking down at the welcoming mat. It was then she began to feel her life had come to an end, "Nonsense, everything I do from this time forward depends on me carrying out my plan and returning to work right away." With that being said, Sevella walked into her home without turning on any lights. Instead, she went into the living room, shivering, but not from the chill of the weather but from the memory of the night of her attacker. She slowly sat on the couch near the window, opened the curtains, then slightly opened the blinds as she arranged her body to see the entrance of the house across the street, only to fall into a deep sleep.

Shortly after falling asleep, she's awakened by the pain in her neck; now the sun is rising. She peeps through the blinds just in time to see her neighbors getting into their car and backing out of their driveway before disappearing out of sight. She closed the blinds, pulled the curtains together, stretched out on the couch, and quickly fell asleep. Almost instantly, she began to dream of the couple across the street. In the dream, they were walking out of the house, but this time they were not alone, but there was a child with them. She woke up with a jolt; and grabbed her neck to shield the pain as she considered the day her neighbors moved into the neighborhood, "I've never seen them with a child. Why am I dreaming about them with a child, better still, why am I dreaming about them at all?" At other times, Sevella's sleep would be interrupted by the reoccurring nightmare of her fighting off her attacker, forcing her to revisit that horrible night in Florida over and over again, "Except for this morning," mumbled Sevella, the nightmare has been replaced by a dream of the couple across the street."

New Life Together

Suddenly, and refreshingly this time, the nightmare was replaced by the dreams of her neighbors. Sevella recalled the first day with her neighbor; she enjoyed watching as they moved into their home. Next, as they held hands, smiling at one another as they came and went, and she did this for almost four months, yet there was never once a child to be seen. She finally concluded that dreaming about the couple was by far a more pleasant experience than waking up fighting the covers off her face. Imagining they had everything a newlywed couple could possibly dream of. *After all,* she was speaking to herself, *they always looked so very happy!* Finally, she glanced at the clock, realizing she had only slept an hour; with that thought in mind and forgetting her own problem, she began to reposition herself on the couch until the pain in her neck reminded her of the uncomfortable sleeping arrangement; therefore, she slowly stood as she walked into her bedroom, first siting then positioning herself on her bed laying on the opposite side of the pain hoping to get some pain-free rest.

Waking up to the brightness of the sun shining brightly through her bedroom window, as it reflected from the picture on the wall into her face, she realized that she had missed breakfast entirely and slept until noon. After springing out of bed, it was then she realized that Neal had given her time off. Now mentally calculating every move and making mental notes of the busy day ahead of her while experiencing minimal excitement, she began to contact her chosen clinics to set appointments. "In order to choose the right clinic,

I must remember what my fourth foster mother taught me. She would say, 'Sevella always asks questions; only dummies refuse to ask questions.'" Laughing as she remembered the expression on her foster mother's face when she said, "dummies." Rubbing her aching neck, Sevella stood in the mirror, touching her stomach, and speaking to her image, "Now I understand why knowing is better than guessing. Therefore, I must ask as many questions of each doctor as possible to get an understanding of what my options are and how realistic my physical and mental expectations are. Most importantly, abilities after returning to work."

Since Neal had his own plans, he decided to grant Sevella's requested days intending to reschedule her on weekends in order to make up for her time off. However, Neal has yet to share this information with Sevella. Every day for three months, she feared her attacker would inform Ellor, blaming her, and eventually telling Neal, and finally losing her job. At the same time, being very upset with Neal, "I know without a doubt Neal would have taken the attacker's side, ignoring all the hard work and long hours I put in, not to mention my tiny wages. So what? I have worked tirelessly since I returned, working nonstop morning and evening; that should at least earn me some type of merit. After all, if he had never sent me off all alone, this would have never happened. It's all Neal's fault!" At the same time, quietness filled the room; after the extended silence, Sevella began again to speak to her image, "Wait a minute!" As she reflected on her neighbors' closeness as they held hands, smiling at one another. Suddenly, she realized that she was smiling, too! Feeling very foolish and a little apprehensive as always for secretly spying.

Abortion Information

Shortly after that, she asked herself, *Why am I intruding on their privacy?* At the same time, she knew stopping cold turkey would be difficult. *My strange and wonderful infatuation with my neighbors is the only time I feel real joy and the only vision of happiness I've ever known. After all, it makes me happy to see them happy! Is that so wrong?* Once Sevella arrived at her first appointment, two things caught her attention; the first was the clinical smell that greeted her at the door, the second was the overfull waiting room; thirdly, the unfriendly receptionist. *Wow!* she thought. *The one thing I've learned early in life is how to be courteous. Even though waiting to be adoptive proved to be pointless, only to age out with no hope of future parents, no place to go. The one thing I learned was to be courteous, hoping someone would help me. Completely on my own since sixteen, I can remember how kind some of the homeless people were and how unkind others would be.*

Now totally engulfed in thought and completely distracted, "At the time, I wouldn't allow anyone to tic me off, I treated them kindly, and that kindness kept me safe and alive while living on the streets. Anyway, what could her problem be? She's working; I'm sure she has a roof over her head and food to eat. So why is she so rude? I was taught by one of the Foster Care Case Managers, "Regardless of the situation, your attitude speaks volumes and will determine whether or not those potential adopted parents return for you." In spite of the experience, Sevella was determined and excited about getting it over with. Arriving at her final appointment, Sevella received a very polite reception. The office was decorated in a rustic but soft, inviting mixture of gold and blue tones; "Very inviting," she said to the receptionist. After meeting with the receptionist, her meeting was successful; without a doubt, this would be her chosen clinic. "Yes, this is the one; although each doctor's visit was brief, I'll call them tomorrow to schedule my appointment."

Right after her conversation, she carefully considered her options based on all the information gathered; her mind was pretty much made up. Also, she knew her time off would be a week, including the weekend. "Tomorrow, I'll rest before I make my appointment. No, I need to use this time to get it done, so on second thought, I'll rest afterward. For the most part, I've found the doctor that can do the surgery!" Now feeling really excited, at the same time even more excited about the short time she would be off work. She then remembered, "Tonight's investors' meeting will be without me; therefore, I can rest until I schedule my appointment for noon tomorrow. Neal previously informed me that he would take my place on the next trip to Florida; therefore, I can have the whole weekend off to recover." As Sevella was leaving the clinic, she noticed on the small table in the foyer brochures with information regarding abortion. She then picked up a brochure and began to glance through it quickly, noticing some key points with additional information and details on abortion.

Not Wanted

Upon meeting each doctor, Sevella listened very carefully as each one shared an overview of the process. "But no one had explained this part to me," she said as she placed the brochure in her purse. Once she flagged a taxi, Sevella sat back, closed her eyes, and relaxed until the taxi woke her. After arriving at the corner near her home, she quickly rushed from the taxi; later that evening, and before preparing for bed, she began to ponder how she would look or act once she returned to work. "Never mind," she spoke to her image in the mirror, "I will look and act normal, and Neal will not be the wiser. Especially since he never knew what really happened in Florida! Once he returns from his trip, he'll be too busy giving orders to notice anything. Yes, everything will be back to normal." Although apprehensive about the surgery the following morning, she was still excited and couldn't wait to check her account to see what Neal had deposited; or withheld from her living expenses. Sevella wanted to be sure she could pay the expense before calling and making her appointment.

Unlike other mornings, Sevella bypassed the window; instead, she opened the brochure and began to read. She felt she needed to get as much information as possible before setting her first appointment. As she read through the information, "Most importantly, I can then finally go back to work problem-free! My plan is to just stay off my feet or maybe get some other things done; it depends," she boasted. Now positioning herself on the bed, feeling very eager, she quickly opened the brochure and began to read, paying close attention to every detail. Slowly turning each page, suddenly she gasped and quickly shut the brochure while covering her mouth to shield the gasp, speaking to her image in the mirror, "These pictures are unbelievably grotesque!" She yelled out, "Could this be true?" Taking a deep breath, she slowly opened the brochure, looking straight ahead, then slowly looking down at the page, momentarily closing her eyes as if to make the images disappear, but the images were indelibly impressed upon her mind. Briefly, she covered the pictures with the palm of her hand; she then began again to read; it was hard to concentrate because the words were as explicit as the pictures.

As soon as her nerves allowed, Sevella unwillingly began to focus on words, hoping to understand clearly the process and how the fetus was eventually removed. "This cannot be true; this has to be fake. Besides, it is only a mass of tissue, and that is all!" She shouted as she stared at the words on the page. Suddenly she realized that tears were running down her cheeks onto the brochure. As the tears dropped onto the page, she remembered two very painful words, "Not wanted!" As she remembered those very harsh and painful words from classmates and foster siblings, the same words now echoed in her mind. She whispered, "All I have ever heard was, 'You are not wanted,' from foster siblings and classmates. Now, here I am saying the same words to the child in my womb!" Overwhelmed by a feeling of rejection, accompanied by a feeling of anger directed toward her attacker, the doctor, for placing such information in his office, made her feel physically ill. She spoke through her sobs, "What on earth was the doctor thinking?" Now enraged at the very idea of that office freely giving out such information, she threw the brochure on the floor, realizing it was all too difficult to process.

Too Soon

"Of course, I would choose the clinic with the professional receptionist. After all, it appeared the best choice." Now, feeling betrayed, at the same time very nauseated, wishing she had made the first appointment with the impolite receptionist. "At least," still looking at the brochure lying on the floor, she reasoned, "I could have had it done right away at the first clinic, right then and there, but that smell. Forget the smell; they were ready to do the job right then and there and without question," still feeling very angry for being taught so well to get details and be informed. Instead of being well informed, she was now indecisive; she walked from the bedroom to the kitchen, then into the living room, and finally, over to the couch. As she sat down, she whispered, "You are not wanted." Now seriously thinking about what she read, Sevella decided to wait a couple of days and return to the first clinic and get everything taken care of, hoping she would not have to make a second request for time off. Also, hoping that both the images and the words she read would be less important by then.

The next day Sevella was still indecisive; therefore, instead of making the appointment, Sevella decided her work schedule would keep her busy and take her mind off the appointment until she felt more positive. She then thought, *I don't need to take off work; after all, it is too soon to make a decision. I am just being hasty. For the most part, whoever wrote the brochure could be wrong about everything.* All of a sudden, her mind went back to the couple, and she smiled as she imagined how it would feel to be in a relationship with someone that really cared and loved her. "I believe their lifestyle may just be the lifestyle I've been dreaming of and someday will be mine." After living most of her life in and out of foster homes and the orphanage, Sevella wondered, *Could it ever be a reality for me?* She had not seen the couple in a few days; now, she wondered how they were doing. She laughed out loud, saying, "How are they doing? Focus, this is about me!" In that brief moment, she realized that watching the couple gave her hope, hope that someday she would have a similar life.

Momentarily turning to look at the house across the street, whispering, "Otherwise, I would never believe that such a life could ever be possible for me." Meanwhile, Sevella returned to work to welcome a very hectic schedule, but she decided to keep a low profile so Neal would not know right away about her return. As the days passed slowly by, Sevella knew she had to make that appointment; by then, her schedule at work only grew tighter. Meanwhile, Neal was calling every five minutes, and eventually, Sevella answered a call. Much to her surprise, the caller was Neal, and Sevella, instead of Naomi, answered the phone. After the initial shock, Neal quickly welcomed Sevella back, at the same time giving her his arrival schedule. One day she decided to request a few days off to visit a very sick friend. As she walked closer and closer to Neal's door, her heart felt as though it was going to pound out of her chest. As she knocked on his door, she could hear him talking on the phone, so she peeped in and then walked in as he motioned for her to have a seat.

The Timing

Thereafter, as he hung up the phone, he said, "Hey, that outfit is fitting a little snug; she then looked down and responded, "Yes, I guess it is fitting a little tighter than usual." Now feeling very agitated at putting off the appointment, she decided to visit the clinic the following day. Sevella then explained, "Neal, I'm sorry to have to ask this question. May I have two weeks off? I need to visit a very sick friend. Most likely, I will need to stay awhile." Neal looked puzzled as he stared at Sevella. Suddenly a knock on his door interrupted their conversation; a young lady entered, greeting Neal, then walking quickly over to shake his hand. Neal smiled as he motioned toward Sevella and introduced Kathy the Temp. Sevella's heart sunk as fear paralyzed her. She attempted to shake Kathy's hand while looking toward Neal as he spoke up, explaining, "I know, I know, you want to know what is going on. Well, this was supposed to be your time off. Remember? Guess what, you are officially free to visit your friend. Whatever the case, everything is working out for you. At least before your next planned trip to Florida, by the way, it was also going to be a surprise. I guess I am the one that is surprised since you returned to work without notice."

Gradually releasing Kathy's hand, still looking at Neal, then realizing her arm was still suspended in midair, now feeling embarrassed, as she slowly let her arms down to her side. Strangely enough, Neal appeared to be moving in slow motion as he prepared to take his seat. As he began to explain to Kathy her job descriptions, answering frequent calls from Florida, compiling documents that must be faxed at intervals while Naomi assisted her in getting familiar with the office. Suddenly Neal realized that Sevella was still standing but motionless. He stood as he walked toward her with his hands extended toward her saying, "You must think that I am a heartless workaholic, but yes, by all means, take some time to visit your friend, you have trained Naomi well, and hopefully in a couple of weeks when we meet back in the office, you'll have some good news regarding your friend's recovery. However, I do have one request since you will not be going to Florida. Could you work a couple of days before you take your leave, just to make sure the office is running smoothly? After all, I think the timing is perfect."

At that very moment came a call from Naomi. "Mr. Nest, line 1." A moment later, Neal continued, "Consequently, I have to meet up with a new potential investor, and I'll see you when I get back. How does that sound?" Sevella nodded her head, smiling and clearing her throat, "Well, since you will be out of town, I'll work alongside Naomi and Kathy until Kathy is familiar with the dynamics of the office; that way, I'll feel better about visiting my friend." Neal stood, walking toward Sevella, grabbed her hands slightly, squeezing them before continuing, "I don't mean to be impolite, but if I didn't know how diet conscious you are, I would say that you've put on several pounds." Sevella threw her head back in an attempt to laugh, but she couldn't pull it off; instead, she frantically fought back the tears. Quickly turning to walk out of the office, while responding to Neal's remark, "Well, I guess you will have to increase my wages so I can afford to replace my too-small wardrobe."

I'm So Confused

Trembling from head to toe, Sevella slowly opened the door to walk out, but suddenly Neal called out to her, saying, "Oh, by the way, you will be paid for your time off; that's part of my surprise. Consider it a paid vacation, so while you are off, go and buy yourself some new clothes." Without turning around, Sevella managed to say in a hearty tone, "Wow, thanks, Neal! Enjoy your vacation in Florida!" After a week of training Kathy and preparing Naomi to manage the office and continue to train Kathy, Sevella decided to follow through with her original plan to have the abortion before Neal's return. "Knowing Neal, he could either return earlier or stay longer than planned; therefore, it will all work in my favor; two weeks and I'm back at work." Once she made it home, she stood in front of the mirror and screamed, "What is going on? I should not be having this problem!" Now angry at losing track of time, "After all, none of this would have happened had Neal accompanied me on the first trip to Florida." Still staring in the mirror, she then whispered, "I wonder if it's too late. Have I waited too long? I'll just work until a day or two before Neal returns; after all, I couldn't possibly leave now."

"Besides, I'll just stay away until the baby is born." At that moment, Sevella was shocked at the words that came out of her mouth. "What! What did I just say? Did I just decide to have this baby? Was it the images in the brochure, the overwhelming pain of feeling unwanted, or both? Did I decide when I postponed the appointment, waiting much later than I planned? Wasn't I supposed to get this done immediately?" Now staring in the mirror at her budging midline, she remembered Neal's words and shivered. "If I didn't know better, I would say that you are putting on weight." At that moment, Sevella knew that she would not go through with the abortion. Now totally confused with her sudden decision to do what she really needed to do, now feeling overwhelmed and frightened with the idea of being responsible for anyone other than herself, she then collapsed on the floor in tears as she cried out, "I know what it feels like to be not wanted!" Later that evening, while still lying on the floor and feeling very weak and too tired to cook, Sevella decided to go out for something to eat. She screamed while getting off the floor, "I can't work for Neal like this! What will his so-called clients think? I wonder if they would be interested in pawing a fat pregnant lady."

Up until that time, Sevella never thought much about her income. Suddenly she' was forced to consider, "My only income is from Neal if that's terminated." Now worried, the thought caused her to feel very nauseated. "I'll have to find another line of work. I'm so confused! I've just gotten my job back." Sevella quickly changed into something loosely fitting as she contemplated her conversation with Neal for a leave of absence, thinking, *I need to get out and go somewhere to clear my head.* She called a taxi while considering the cost of a taxi compared to the bus as she traveled to the east side of town and noticed a Breakfast Bar restaurant. She asked the cab to stop and let her out at the restaurant. Before entering, Sevella caught her reflection in the large window and was reminded, at the same time, of her horrible past as a child and her attacker in Florida.

Wetness on My Cheeks

After opening the door to the restaurant, she found an empty booth. Shortly after sitting down, she was greeted by a very polite waitress; after her order, the waitress was off to another waiting customer. While sitting very still and feeling hopeless, a feeling she was well acquainted with, she then looked down at her budging midriff before looking through the large window and seeing her reflection. Then she noticed the passing cars and how the wet street became a very large mirror reflecting the cars as they drove past the breakfast bar. Startled by the waitress and realizing the wetness on the streets mirrored the tears running down her cheeks. Refusing to look up at the waitress, Sevella looked down as the waitress placed a hot cup of coffee on the table. At the same time, Sevella was looking in her purse for a tip. After receiving her coffee and still avoiding eye contact with the waitress, Sevella turned toward the large window, looking past her reflection as she took a sip of her coffee, suddenly thinking of the incident that left her in this situation and what a mess her life had become.

As she began to reflect back on the night, she was attacked and remembered trying to be discrete; as she and Ellor left the late meeting and headed back to their hotel rooms, it was obvious that Ellor had a little too much to drink. Every now and then, he would stumble, but it wasn't so obvious. It was then Sevella decided to walk slower so Ellor wouldn't have to keep up with her, hoping he would make it to his room before he fell on his face. Meanwhile, Sevella was trying to be as professional as possible, and one embarrassing fall and Ellor would be the laughing stock of the company, and her career would come to a sudden end.

"Surely, Neal would blame me. Of course, it would be my fault for not making sure Ellor made it to his room without falling down drunk." As they exited the elevator, Sevella began to talk to Ellor to keep his focus. "I'm sure after I call Neal and give him my report, he will be excited to follow up with you, Ellor." Ellor unlocked his door; without looking back, he walked into the dark room, slowly closing the door behind him. "Good night!" Sevella whispered as she headed to her room.

Meanwhile, she was thinking, *Should I tell Neal about Ellor's condition? No, I'll just leave that for Ellor to do. If he wants Neal to know he can't hold his liquor, let him tell. After all, this trip is all about impressing Neal's investors and showing how professional I am to Ellor and his staff.* All the while, Sevella was hoping, in spite of Ellor's condition, he would remember to give Neal a good report, how serious she was about making a good impression for herself and Neal. Even though she didn't agree with this working arrangement, and although it meant pretending to be excited when she was actually frightened of being there alone, not having any support from Neal unless it was by way of telephone. Determine to exemplify an attitude of professionalism. *After all*, she thought, *I've been in this type of situation all my life. This trip to Florida is no different from a trip to another foster home. I can handle it.* Just then, a large truck passed a standing pedestrian and splashed water all over him; the yelling startled Sevella, bringing her back to the present situation, "That horrible man!" she screamed, "What happened? I was living my dream life before that horrible night! Now my life is a living nightmare."

I Need a Job

At the end of that conversation with herself, the sound of someone's voice startled her. Now focusing on the reflection of the waitress returning with her order, overwhelmed with embarrassment for not knowing how long the waitress had been standing there, blaming her inability to forget that horrible night; every wakening moment of each passing day was consumed with thoughts of her attacker. *And today is no difference,* she said, speaking to herself. Still attempting to hide her tears, Sevella apologized for being so preoccupied. The waitress could see that there was something wrong; just as she was about to ask if she could help; Sevella interrupted her without really knowing what would come out of her mouth; Sevella spoke in such a low tone that the waitress had to lean down and forward to hear Sevella's words. Now listening very carefully, she heard, "I need a job but not right away, but maybe in a month." The waitress responded in a lower tone, "You need a job?" Sevella nodded her head, indicating her answer would be yes. The waitress noticed the outfit Sevella was wearing; now, speaking to herself, *this person wasn't dressed like someone who needed a job, especially a waitress job.*

Occasionally looking at Sevella's image, then at the top of her head, the waitress stood looking down at Sevella, then asking quizzically, "Have you ever worked as a waitress?" Sevella responded, "No, but I know how to serve; serving others is what I do." Not long after, from the back of the room, a very loud thunderous voice yelled, "Sam! What's the hold-up?" Quickly, turning with a jolt, both Sam and Sevella looked in that direction of the voice just as Sam hurried toward the serving window, revealing only the face and head of a very bearded man, looking as though he had tasted something very bitter. *Sam*, Sevella said, speaking to herself, *must be short for Samantha.* Again the thunderous voice, "Hey, you need work?" Interrupting Sevella's thoughts, she waited before turning nervously, wiping her spilled coffee from her hand, and then the table. Almost afraid to turn to look toward the counter window, finally turned to see the man's head and now shoulders as he looked in her direction; but, in that moment, everything in her wanted to yell back, "No, no, and no again!" But Sam spoke up before Sevella could respond, "Isn't that what I just said, Jack. Are you hard of hearing?"

In turn, Sevella realized that Jack would become the next Neal in her life. Meanwhile, she is still wiping the spill that is no longer there. After another quick glance in Jack and Sam's direction, speaking to herself, *Once I get the job, that man with the loud thunderous voice and Sam is someone I will soon get to know.* Again Jack yelled out to Sevella, "Sam tells me you need a month; well, after that, you can start work. Your shift will start at 6 a.m., be sure to be on time." Now feeling frightened at the prospect of explaining to Neal why she was requesting an extended leave of absence is another hurdle. *No!* she said, speaking to herself. *I can continue working for Neal at least until he returns in a month. Yes! That's it! I can make this work. I'll just work evenings for the office and mornings for Jack. That way, I can stop working for Neal and start working for Jack before I really start showing.*

Facing Neal

"Hereafter, I can request an extended leave of absence, and the Diner is where I'll be, and there I'll remain until I give birth." As soon as she started work for Jack, Sevella realized that, eventually, she had to face Neal and request a longer leave of absence. "That's it! I'll call Neal and give him an update on my friend's condition, letting him know the progress of my friend's recovery, hoping the frequent updates will hold my job until I return." Once she arrived at the office, she explained to Naomi and Kathy her plan to remain for at least another month and then leave when Neal returned. After speaking to the staff, she picked up the receiver and dialed Neal's number. "Hello." Holding her breath, Sevella waited before answering, "Hello, is anyone there?" Now feeling very nervous, Sevella managed a hearty greeting, "Hello, Neal! How are things going? By the way, I've decided to wait until you return before visiting my sick friend, but if I have to leave before you get back, I will keep you posted." There was a moment of silence, then speaking in a mumbling tone, "That's great! I was worried about leaving the girls without supervision. Now I need to get to the meeting, and I'll see you when I see you." Even though Sevella blamed him for the whole horrific situation, she hoped if the story leaked, she would be able to explain her side of the story. "If push came to shove, I hope Neal will side with me."

"Not a moment too soon," she spoke into the receiver, "now I can get this vacation time off without an explanation. I wonder, if my stay is longer than planned, will he hold my position? No problem, I'll recommend that Neal keep Kathy's temporary service just in case my stay was extended." Four months later, Sevella was feeling discomfort in her lower stomach but ignored it, thinking, "I've spent too much time on my feet; that must be the problem. The next day, as she cleared the tables, the pain returned but was more intense. Sam noticed Sevella holding her back and decided to tell Jack she was taking Sevella to the hospital. "No problem. I thought it was a mistake to keep her on after her belly grew, but she's a hard worker. Besides, we will be closing in an hour. Tomorrow is a holiday; go ahead. I can manage until closing." Immediately, Sam helped gather Sevella things and hailed a taxi to the county hospital. Once inside, Sam realized that this would be her first experience helping someone in labor.

In addition to all of the excitement, a feeling of apprehension engulfed Sam as she approached the nurse's station, thinking, "My sister would know what to do." Sam turned, asking Sevella, "What's next?" Sevella smiled. "This is going to take a while. Why don't you go get something to eat and bring me something?" Sam agreed, waving to Sevella until she entered the elevator. Sevella, now terrified, had to think fast. She didn't want her attacker to find out he had impregnated her, so she gave the name of one of her make-believe friends, hoping that information would keep her safe. After Sam returned, the nurse gave her a note from Sevella, explaining, "Since there seemed to be complications, and only relatives will be allowed to visit, please don't wait all night. Just go home, and I'll call no later than tomorrow with room information the moment they allow me to have visitors. Please, don't worry, I'm fine; just problems. The seventh month is a little early."

Is It Time?

Sevella knew that none of that was true, and she felt uncomfortable having to lie to Sam, but that was her least problem. Afterward, the nurse spoke up, "You'll be fine, you have been experiencing discomfort since the seventh month is a little early, but you are having this baby tonight; therefore, we have taken you into the delivery room, and please don't worry, everything is going to be alright." Sevella noticed the nurses' heads together as they examined her, but she was preoccupied with her own thoughts and wasn't aware that the discomfort meant that she was actually in labor. Suddenly another sharp pain, Sevella attempted to speak through the pain, clasping the side of the bed, asking, "What... the delivery room... Is it time?" Now the pain was so sharp that Sevella fought to hold back the scream, now holding her breath to prevent the scream from exiting her throat. The nurses squeezed her hands, instructing, "Miss Nix, when you feel pain, just breathe through your mouth until the pain stops."

As a result of the breathing, the pain slowly subsided; it was then Sevella remembered a time similar to this moment, but it was more of a dream than reality. The place was familiar, but not the hospital; there was a woman, but the rest was vague. There were images, or mostly shadows, so nothing about the dream made sense. "Ms. Nix, can you hear me? You've giving birth to a beautiful baby boy, just beautiful." The voice seemed to be very far off, and the faceless person only had a head and not shoulders. Now feeling very frightened, Sevella began to cry, but someone began to comfort her, saying, "Now, now don't you worry. Everything is going to be alright." Sevella squeezed the hand holding hers; before dozing off, she repeated, "Everything is going to be alright." In the meantime, Sam was calling but was unable to get in touch with Sevella. Whenever she asked for Sevella, she would get the same response, "Ma'am, are you sure you have the right hospital?" Unable to get any information, Sam decided to wait for Sevella's call.

Once awake, Sevella was told that she had to have a c-section, and the baby was premature but healthy. It was then Sevella remembered someone telling her she had a son, so she asked, "It's a boy?" The nurse smiled and said, "Yes, and he is beautiful!" Still smiling, the nurse suggested, "You might want to get your family to come and take pictures. Suddenly, Sevella remembered Sam and said, "Yes, I do. When will we be dismissed? I need to call and let them know." The nurse, now looking very serious, asked, "You mentioned that your purse was stolen, and that's why you had no Identification. Is that true?" For several seconds Sevella stared in confusion at the nurse's statement. "I don't remember saying that." Thinking quickly, *Oh, that's right, my purse was returned but nothing else.* The nurse responded sympathetically, "Good luck with that. Replacing licenses, credit cards, and social is a real headache. By the way, your doctor will discuss your time of dismissal." With that being said, she hurried out of the room.

Do You Mean Prostitution?

In that moment, fear entered Sevella's heart as she imagined how difficult taking care of a baby would be. Another nurse came into the room holding the baby wrapped in a blue blanket and handed him to Sevella, saying, "He is so beautiful!" Afterward, sharing instructions on care, cleaning, and feeding. Sevella interrupted her, asking, "Is there a book I can get on care, cleaning and feeding." The nurse smiled and said, "There are books on postnatal care, and I just happened to have one here for you." Once Sevella was alone with the baby, she quickly read through the book, only the information wasn't exactly what she needed. Now looking at the baby and the little bracelet on his arm, Baby Nix. Tears now running down her cheeks, Sevella kissed the baby on the head and said, "You are beautiful, and welcome to my world, a world not so beautiful." As the sunset signaled the closing of an old life for Sevella, but the beginning of a new one with Baby Nix, Eventually, the nurse returned to carry the baby to the nursery. Finally, the day came for her dismissal, and Sevella had to come up with a story that Sam would believe. Finally, the day for her dismissal had arrived, and Sevella still didn't know what to tell Sam.

Not long after, the nurse returned, instructing Sevella, "Miss Nix, you may want to call someone to pick you up. Remember, you'll be dismissed today." The nurse was taken aback at Sevella's facial expression. Sevella realized she was frowning, something one of her foster parents always punished her for. "I was just wondering if the baby and I could wait in the lobby for our ride." Now smiling, the nurse responded, "I don't see a problem with that. Just let your ride know to be here before we wheel you done." After several hours had passed, Sevella's newfound friend and co-worker picked her and the baby up from the hospital and carried them home. As they entered the neighborhood, Sam gasped, whispering, "Wow!" Now holding one hand to her face as they walked into the house. Sam turned from left to right then, finally, in a complete circle as she looked around, moving in slow motion, "Beautiful, it is so tastefully decorated, and you have antiques and paintings." Suddenly Sam realized that she and the baby were still standing in the doorway, so she apologized as she slowly closed the door behind her.

Meanwhile, Sam was taking a tour while still whispering, "What about your boss, and what boss are you talking about?" Stunned at what just came out of her mouth Sevella managed to say, "Oh, I meant my former boss, the one I couldn't keep working for because I was pregnant." Now looking at the sleeping baby, both Sam and Sevella began to walk slowly toward the bedroom. Once in the bedroom, they both walked over to the crib as Sam laid the baby down. Sam then turned and pointed toward the living room, then slowly and quietly walked back into the living room. Sam, now looking very confused, sat down. Finally, Sam asked, "Do you want to start from the beginning?" Sevella walked over to the couch but did not sit; instead stood looking out of the window at the couple's house across the street. She then looked at Sam, saying, "I'm not saying my boss was a bad guy, but I worked in corporate, and my job was demanding and involved a lot of traveling and…" Sevella's thoughts cause her to drift off. "Traveling and what?" Sam demanded. "Some entertaining, which I will no longer be doing."

In the meantime, Sevella turned and walked toward the bedroom, peeked in, and walked back to the living room, still standing, before continuing, "As soon as I became very uncomfortable with all the sexual advances of certain clients, I would go into the bathroom and cry, and that would somehow help me through the next few hours of the meetings. Once I returned to the meeting, I noticed that particular client had left the meeting. My boss would keep me busy with copying documents and taking notes, as well as explaining our company to potential clients, so that helped me keep out of sight long enough to be forgotten by that awful man." Sam then pulled Sevella down beside her as she attempted to further explain her uncomfortable situation. "I was hired as a file clerk; then he had this wild idea to have these investors' meetings, inviting his clients and their guest. One particular client that I remember seeing only once insisted that he needed an escort and would I fill in." Jumping to her feet, Sam demanded, "Do you mean prostitution?" Now, Sevella was pulling Sam down to sit as she stared in shock, waiting for Sevella to answer.

At that very moment, they heard a sound coming from the bedroom. Quickly jumping to their feet and rushing to the crib, only to see the little frame lying completely still. Again they heard the sound of a cat's meow, and both started to laugh as they walked quietly back to the living room. Sam sat, but Sevella remained standing, now looking very serious. She continued, "Before he hired me, I really needed the job. Eventually, the business began to grow, and my boss, at times, would introduce me as his Executive, you know to look and sound important to our potential investors. For a long while after that, my responsibilities kept me very busy and mostly out of sight. Next, the opportunity to travel for the company…." Now holding both hands in the air, Sam demanded, "Stop! I understand, and I know that it can be difficult to work in corporate, and I think it is great, but I don't recommend you go back. By the way, what does the father think about you working under such… well… conditions?"

"First of all," Sevella spoke but paused before continuing, "because…" Now shifting uncomfortably as she searched for an answerer that would make sense. "He works there also, but in a different state, so he doesn't know what I have to put up with, and we don't see each other or talk much because our schedules are so hectic. I knew taking care of a baby may create a problem, and that's why I started working in the diner." Sam, now looking sympathetically at Sevella as she placed her right arm on Sevella's shoulder, "I didn't mean to pry. I'm so sorry. You have gone through so much, not to mention having to be all alone throughout the delivery. For days I tried to reach you, but I wasn't a relative, so I couldn't get in touch, but I'm here now, and I'll be here whenever you need me." As they turned to walk back into the bedroom, Sevella struggled with the words to explain to Sam what happened in Florida but decided against taking that chance.

Orphaned

Prior to Sam's arrival at the hospital, Sevella was considering sharing with her that she was orphaned; rehearsing how she would explain the upscale neighborhood, speaking to herself, *Also, I need to explain why I lived in such an elaborate neighborhood; starting with I never really had a home of my own, didn't have one when I started working for Neal, and It was his idea to have me stay on the property just in case a prospective buyer wanted to see the home. Should I tell her now?* Sam whispered. "Are you okay? I know this is all new to you, but believe me, you will get the hang of it. My sister has three, and she was so protective of her at first, but after the last two, she has become a Mom of the year! Trust me; I believe you will make a great mother. After that display of wisdom, I am going to get out of here and let you get some rest." Sam grabbed both of Sevella's hands and squeezed them gently, saying reassuringly. "Sevella, everything is going to be okay; you'll be fine!" Finally, Sevella was alone and feeling very tired. Suddenly, the same fear she felt when they told her she could take her baby home came back, but more intense. She stood and walked slowly over to the crib, noticing the baby lay motionless.

At that very moment, her heart rate increased, and she felt faint. From time to time, she would hold her finger under the baby's nose to test for breathing as she stood watching him while he slept. She noticed how very tiny his little frame was, and he looked so helpless. In that moment, she began to feel desperate, so she picked up the Bible Sam took from the hospital after saying, "The Bible is now yours, Sevella, because you paid for it when paying the hospital bill." Now laughing out loud but quickly covered her mouth to silence the laughter. Still smiling, she hesitantly opened the Bible. Feeling very embarrassed at not really knowing where to start or what to read. When she looked down at the words and began to read, she noticed the Bible story was about two women, one with children and one without; the women with children made fun of the women without children. "I would think that the women with no children had it made, and the women with all the children had all the problems."

All at once, Sevella blurted out, "Work!" Again covering her mouth but speaking in a whisper, "I can return to work, but four months later! What will Neal say, and will there be tons of questions? On second thought, I was supposed to call and give him an update. Matter of fact, I can still call; that's right, the baby came early! On the other hand, I'll call with an update on my friend's miraculous recovery, and I can return much sooner than scheduled. I'm sure Kathy will appreciate an extra week or two added to her pay." In that moment, the baby moved with a jerk. Sevella placed her hand over her mouth, watching as the baby moved again, kicking his legs and waving his arms. "The sound of my voice wakes him up. Oh my, I haven't once thought about how to fit him into my plans to return to work. Oh boy, I'm right back where I started. I need to first figure out what to do with the baby. I know, I'll call Sam; she has a sister, maybe her sister will babysit. That's it!" For the most part, Sevella was convinced that her babysitting problem was solved until her focus was again on Neal, "But how can I explain my silence? Doesn't matter; I'm going to call and beg if I have to."

Painful Memories

Afterward, Sevella broke into tears after reflecting back on the painful memories of never having anyone to call Mom or Dad in her time of need; the very thought of having to be there for the baby seemed to paralyze her, vigorously shaking her head from left to right mumbling, "Get a grip on yourself," but the reality of returning to work for Neal also meant several more trips to Florida. As she made several attempts to convince herself, speaking softly, "I'm not the one to run away from my responsibility, and I will not run away now. My income is the only reason I'm going back. The money would be just enough to take care of my needs and the baby's, even though going back could be very harmful once my secret is exposed." Now recalling the conversation with Sam, Sevella sat motionless for several minutes before getting up and slowly walking into the living room and slowly sitting on the couch. Instead of looking out of the window, her attention was on the little blue book on the coffee table, speaking softly, "I must be realistic; once I return to work, my schedule will be so rigorous I will barely have time for myself. How will I work this baby into my schedule with all the traveling that is expected of me?"

Just as Sevella positioned herself on the couch, feeling tired and now very weak, in that moment, she realized she hadn't eaten since that morning. Also, she knew her strength was important for taking care of the baby. "He will soon be awake and wanting to eat." So Sevella tipped into the kitchen and poured a bowl of cereal and milk, whispering so as not to disturb the baby, "I wonder what happened to the lady with no children?" Turning and tipping quietly but quickly to the living room to her Bible on the coffee table but couldn't remember what page she stopped on. Now tipping back into the bedroom past the crib to the dresser, grabbed the blue book, "The Gideon Bible; he must be the author of the book," she said as she opened the Bible, noticing the older Bible belonging to Miss Timothy was very old compared to the little blue book, as she tipped quietly past the crib back into the kitchen, closing the bedroom door behind her.

Previously, Sevella recalled that she was midway through the book as she quickly began to flip the pages, and then a word caught her eye; she noticed that someone was telling the woman to stop being a drunk. She continued to read over that chapter, and that's when she realized the woman was only praying. She quickly tried to find the story in the blue book but became overwhelmed and quickly dropped to her knees, remembering Miss Timothy praying for her, so she silently asked, "Please, tell me what to do because I don't know what to do, please tell me what to do!" At that moment, she wasn't sure if her words were the right ones to say, so she continued to turn pages in the blue book until she found her place. She continued reading the story; after reading further, she realized the woman was talking to a man, and he told her she would get what she asked for. Now curious to know the answer to the question, Sevella kept reading until she read the part where the lady had the baby and named him Samuel. "Therefore," now standing and walking into the bedroom and looking down at the baby, she continued, "not only have I not given you a name, but I didn't complete the certificate of birth, the whole missing ID thing, I need to get it back to the hospital pronto!"

Samuel

Obviously, the wristband read only, "Baby Nix." Since she hadn't considered a name for the baby. Pretending to be overly concerned with her stolen Identification. Once again feeling horrible for lying to Sam and the records department, she slowly walked out of the bedroom again, closing the door behind her before sitting down at the kitchen table, staring aimlessly at the form, thinking, *I have lied to everyone, Sam, the hospital staff by telling them that my purse was stolen and that I had no ID.* Angry at her hopeless situation, she yelled out, "No, I did not lie!" Before covering her mouth, thankful she had walked out of the bedroom, closing the door behind her. Now listening for a whimper, she whispered, "I have not lied! My purse was left in the conference room and returned to the front desk. That horrible man found my purse, took my hotel key, and tossed my purse. So what? I gave a made-up name to the register; I had no choice." All of a sudden, she had an idea, "That's it, Samuel, that's what I will name him, Samuel!" She filled out the form while finishing her cereal but, at the last minute, decided not to place the envelope in the outgoing mail; she didn't want to open the front door and wake the baby. "I know; I'll just wait until tomorrow morning."

At that moment, Sevella remembered and began to complain, "Another roadblock!" Now what? I can't think; I'm too tired, and I need to rest in order to clear my head before the baby wakes up." After making herself comfortable on the couch, without any effort,

Sevella quickly fell asleep. While asleep, she dreamed of the couple across the street, and they were walking to the car as usual, but once again, they were not alone. Sevella woke up quickly and sat straight up, realizing she had not yet mailed the certificate. After a while, she remembered to wait until the following day. Now wondering about the dream and the couple with the child. Without a second thought about her next move, Sevella knew exactly what she had to do. She quickly dressed Samuel and placed everything the hospital had given her; all the clothing, blankets, bottles, diapers she received from her baby shower, and anything else she received from Sam, Jack, and her customers, placing everything in a large box.

After a period of time, she reconsidered what she was about to do but quickly proceeded with her original plan, as she methodically arranged each piece of clothing according to his schedule before centering Samuel in the middle. Sevella then rushed across the street to the home of the couple, and not once did she consider that someone could be watching her, as she had so often watched her neighbors. The few yards across the street seemed like miles, quickly opening the gate and finally reaching the third of six steps. Stopping, she looked over her shoulders before climbing to the last step and putting the box with the child in front of her neighbor's door, speaking silently, "Thank goodness, Samuel is resting quietly." Suddenly, feeling absolutely horrified, Sevella knew that she would have only a few minutes to get back across the street and into the house before her neighbors drove into their driveway, so she quickly ran through the opened gate, running back across the street, and could not wait to get inside.

I Am Not Ready

Following that moment of madness, she quickly rushed across the street, almost tripping before opening her door and slamming it closed behind her. Uncontrollably she began to cry, her body trembling profusely as she ran to her bedroom, falling on the floor with her arms feeling numb as she fell to her knees, folding her arm on the bed, laying her forehead on her arms, suddenly noticing the pain in her chest, but her main concern was a very unfamiliar pain in her chest as she cried out, "Samuel, Samuel, oh, Samuel!" In time, I know this will someday make sense to me, but for now, I need to rush to the window, open it and watch out for Samuel. Before she could complete her sentence, a sense of relief came over her as she began to console herself, "That's it! Now I can return to work free of worries, but the relief was short-lived." Therefore, she cried bitterly, at the same time trying to convince herself, screaming aloud, "I'm not ready, I'm not ready!" Now whispering, "I'm just not ready." Still feeling as though her heart had vacated her chest, Sevella cried herself to sleep. However, her sleep was interrupted as she was suddenly awakened with a jolt, and ran to the window, and was shocked at the lateness of the day, as her neighbor's car wasn't in the driveway: also the box was gone and no longer in front of the door.

Eventually, the pain she felt is now mixed with an overwhelming feeling of helplessness; thoughts of something awful happening to Samuel left Sevella feeling as though a giant hand had gripped what was left of her heart and finished ripping it out. At that very moment, a paralyzing fear seemed to be choking her. She couldn't swallow; now holding her throat, crying, "What's wrong with me? I need to know what has happened to Samuel. That's what's wrong with me. I can't get him back, but why can't I?" she asked, still looking out of the window. Crying uncontrollably as the tears continued to run down her face. Suddenly she ran into the living room and stood over the couch looking out of the window, but her view was only of the front door and the driveway. She then rushed to the front door, but she stopped before she opened it, still reasoning, "All I need is for them to drive up, and then I'll quickly rush over and demand to know where is the baby?" In that moment, she realized her actions would only raise questions. "Terrible, terrible mistake," she whispered. "I'm not being reasonable. I'm overreacting. Besides that, my actions would only expose my identity."

Once Sevella calmed herself down, she slowly walked into her bedroom, still pondering her mistake; it was then her thoughts went back to the couple, asking herself, "Is it really possible, really, that someone else could have taken Samuel? No, I don't believe that!" Now feeling totally exhausted, she sat on the bed, and as she looked around the dark room, she decided to lay her head on the pillow opposite the pain in her neck, but it was so painful she couldn't get comfortable; therefore, she began to cry bitterly remembering that same feeling each time a couple chose another child instead of her, and the river of tears each time she wasn't chosen or adopted, once again being rejected left her broken-hearted. Now her heart was breaking into many tiny pieces, not because she has been rejected, but because Samuel has been rejected by her as more tears streamed down her face.

Unrecognizable Pain

Earlier the next morning, Sevella was awakened by the rising sun shining in her face along with the throbbing pain in her neck; slowly sitting, she then attempted to move her leg, but her legs had fallen asleep from hanging off the side of the bed, and she screamed in pain as she stretched one leg and then the other. All the while holding on to the bed until she was able to stand. Sevella glanced over at Samuel's crib as she remembered her first encounter with foster adoptive parents. She then looked at her image in the mirror and noticed the puffiness around her eyes, thinking, *I was once accepted into a home complete with siblings, the adoption was absolute, and my adoptive parents knew it was absolutely going to happen. So much so that they gave me a certificate with my new last name, saying to me, "Get used to it because it will be permanent!"* Now, wiping the tears from her face, Sevella recalled that day with a smile, saying, *I remember the very words I spoke; I remember saying, "Once the adoption is complete, I'll belong to someone."* Those words were still fresh in her memory, whispering as she walked closer to the mirror, *But it never happened, did it?*

Now vigorously rubbing her brows as if to rub them off, recalling that day as though it was yesterday, "Sure you do; the happiest time in my life never happened; that's right, it never happened. No, while waiting for the adoptive process to be completed, we received the news that six family members had lost their home to a fire and were arriving and needed a place to stay. Afterward, it was finally decided that family came first." For this reason and in sheer agony,

Sevella threw herself across the bed, weeping silently but bitterly, speaking through her sobs, "Even worse, that chain of events placed the adoption on hold and me packing up and being sent back to the orphanage. Since they were the closest to having parents, it felt as though my parents had died, but even that pain is no comparison to the pain of losing Samuel. I am hurt; I may never see Samuel again." Sevella remembered the day she left her adoptive home; the feeling of rejection left her broken as she packed her few items, taking them out of the bag and placing them in her new suitcase, her very own possession, walking slowly out of the front door, never looking back, refusing to let them see her brokenness, and her tears as they dropped from her eyes onto her new blue dress.

At this point, not only were her legs stiff and painful, but her heart was experiencing a new and unrecognizable pain. After the pain in her legs subsided, she glanced at the clock and realized that she had fallen asleep from sheer exhaustion; Sevella then slowly crawled into bed and instantly fell into a deep sleep but was soon awakened by sounds coming from across the street. A voice was loudly calling out, voices that could be clearly heard from her bedroom. She quickly ran to her bedroom window, not trying to shield her image. Therefore, could easily be seen by her neighbors. This particular view was of her neighbors' garage. Suddenly she realized that they had always parked in their driveway. "Why now?" she asked as she continued to stare at the activity in her neighbor's driveway. She watched once again as the sound of joy echoed as her neighbor's husband rushed to his wife. After the husband walked to meet his wife, both walked toward the open garage and smiled as usual before getting into the car.

Deep Regret

Now literally screaming at her neighbors, "This isn't normal for you! It's actually very abnormal," as she strained to hear clearly. Now questioning every unexplainable move, gesture, and behavior of the couple, but unable to make sense of it all. "Why are they parking in the garage? Next, the uncharacteristic laughter, especially before sunrise. Look, I have analyzed every movement from the time you moved into this neighborhood up until now, and your actions this morning are not like you at all! I should know. I've watched the two of you long enough to know your behavior." Desperately searching with her eyes from the front door to the gate, from the gate to the driveway, for something, anything that would indicate Samuel's presence, while still trying very hard to see into the open garage for any signs of his existence. Again Sevella spoke to her neighbors, "Where is he? Why is there no sign of Samuel?"

Following that feeling of deep regret, Sevella was once again experiencing an unfamiliar pain in her heart, and she began to cry as if Samuel had died. "Not knowing is tearing me apart. Why all of a sudden were those people parking in their garage, and where have they hiding him, possibly in the garage? Nonsense! At first, I was just happy to see them; now I am not so happy," she said as she pressed her nose against the windowpane in order to get a better look. Again she thought of the cheerful tone in her neighbor's voice as she continued watching and hoping to see any indication that they had found Samuel. Sevella couldn't stop thinking how very cheerful the wife sounded as she called to her husband, "Was it having Samuel that made her so happy? Had Samuel eaten? Is he alright? What could have happened to him?" Now feeling sick in her stomach, she rushed to the bathroom. Afterward, she stood looking in the mirror. "That's what I get for thinking more of myself and my work than Samuel!"

Not Kittens or Puppies

The day before their discovery, Lawrence and Catheryn were driving home from the Center; on that particular day, they decided to go shopping for items of clothing to donate to the Center. After leaving the shopping center, they drove home in silence. After entering their driveway, Lawrence turned off the engine, but neither moved; instead, they sat quietly until Lawrence spoke up, "Honey, I know this is a tender subject, but I must admit I actually enjoyed shopping for those smaller items." Catheryn turned slowly, staring at the steering wheel before responding in almost a whisper, "I know, me too." Once again, silence filled their space as Catheryn reached for the door handle, suggesting, "Should we get out of the car, or will we be spending the night? I think we spent more time than planned at the mall." Now smiling, Lawrence took Catheryn's left hand and gave it a reassuring squeeze, "Don't worry, we will be shopping for our own baby boy or girl one day. Just wait and see. Remember, the doctor said it just takes time." Catheryn opened the door before responding, "Yes, I know, and it's been four years," but she made sure she closed the car door before Lawrence heard her doubtful remark.

The following morning Catheryn was gathering the bags of items to take to the car. "Lawrence, why on earth did you bring the bags into the house, only to take them back to the car." Stopping short of walking out of the front door, Lawrence looked over his shoulder, asking, "Honey, what can I carry?" Frowns in her brow, Catheryn responded, "All of this! After all, you brought it into the house." Lawrence hesitated before saying, "There she is," looking confused, Catheryn responded, "There is who?" Lawrence gave Catheryn a smack on the cheek before saying, "My girl's spunk." Realizing that her behavior the night before must have been that of sheer gloom. Catheryn promised, "The next time we go shopping, I promise to leave you in the car," Now, laughing as she kissed him on the cheek, now leaning forward, Lawrence responded, "Oh, I guess you're trying to say I was bad company." They both laughed as they hurried to the car.

The following evening as they drove home, instead of dropping by the Center, they decided to take the clothes to the center the following weekend, meanwhile discussing how happy the parents would be to receive the new clothes. They were still discussing plans for the next day when they walked up to their steps and noticed the very large box. The first thought was someone had dropped off their abandoned kittens or puppies. They both shared the same concerns before opening the box, thinking, *How many? We could easily get attached, and that would create a huge problem since we could only keep no more than two out of the liter.* All of a sudden, a different sound came from the box, and judging from the sound, they weren't kittens or puppies. Lawrence turned wide-eyed to Catheryn. "It may be just one." Catheryn is now focused on the sound, whispering, "Honey, I don't think baby puppies or kittens sound quite like that." They carefully removed the box cover, and their curiosity was replaced by shock. Caught off guard, Lawrence jumped backward and almost fell from the top step. Catheryn quickly grabbed him by the right arm until he could get his balance. Following Catheryn's question, Lawrence's anxiety was now replaced by relief, nodding.

Child Protective Services

A moment later, they are staring back and forth from the box to one another, "Oh, my, Lawrence, it's not kitten or puppies. It's a baby!" cried Catheryn as she clapped her hands over her mouth. Lawrence looked over into the box and gasped, saying almost breathlessly, "A baby, it's a baby!" They began to glance to the left and right, finally turning and looking across the street at the houses behind them, again glancing to the left and to the right. There was no one in sight. The street lights were on but were dimly lit, making it easy to see if someone was looking from their opened window or door. After that, they quickly picked up the box, opened the door, and rushed inside before the baby's cry could be heard by the neighbors. Once inside, they shut and locked the front door behind them; after the crying stopped, periodically lifting the lid, Lawrence slowly sat the box on their round coffee table. For several minutes they sat in silence, staring at one another before deciding to remove the lid, and clearly, in shock, Lawrence hesitated to completely remove the lid. By then, the baby was sound asleep. Lawrence whispered, "Whoever was responsible for abandoning this tiny baby made sure there were plenty of holes in the box." Catheryn whispered, "Absolutely."

Once again, silence filled the room while both sat thinking, *Had we not decided to come straight home, someone else may have discovered the baby.* Finally, Lawrence shared his thoughts with Catheryn. "It might have gotten pretty warm with all those clothes, not to mention the baby's crying...." Now breaking her silence, Catheryn agreed, laughing nervously, "Our timing was perfect." Lawrence, now looking puzzled, asked, "Or was it planned?" Once again, Lawrence and Catheryn were thinking the same thought as both reached for the baby to remove him from his box. After half an hour of holding the baby, Lawrence spoke in a very peculiar tone, suggesting, "Maybe we should call into work, leaving messages requesting personal time off tomorrow. I don't think this problem has an immediate solution. Also," now hesitating a few seconds, Lawrence continued, "I, I think we should call the police or Child Protective Service." Catheryn turned toward the clock on the wall, disagreeing, "No! I mean, no, we can't do that. Look at the time. Surely, the Department of Child and Protective Service (DCPS) is closed."

Up until that time, Catheryn believed Lawrence would agree; however, Lawrence slowly shook his head from left to right, but Catheryn insisted, "Plus, the poor thing has been through so much already. Can we just wait until the morning?" Eventually, Lawrence gave in, firmly suggesting, "It would be the right thing to do; therefore, we'll wait until morning before contacting Child Protective Services." Suddenly, Lawrence turned to Catheryn, "Hey, I know we can call Chuck!" Stunned at the sudden burst of excitement, Catheryn was now looking up from the baby, asking, "Who?" Turning to look at Catheryn, Lawrence reminded her, "You know Charles Miller, my friend, he works as a Child Advocate, and he's an attorney." It was then Catheryn confessed, "I'm afraid... and nervous. I can't really explain why." Now, staring at the baby in Catheryn's arms, Lawrence was also experiencing a few of the same emotions as he watched Catheryn cradle the baby. He wanted to discuss a forbidden topic, a topic he personally refused to discuss.

How Can I?

Now desperately searching for the words to say without confusing Catheryn. Lawrence stood, looking down at her as she made these weird sounds while cuddling the baby in her arms. Now clearing his throat, "I was just thinking," but stopped when he noticed that Catheryn never looked up at him. Now thinking to himself, *How can I bring up the subject of adoption, and why am I even thinking of adoption when I was the one who refused to discuss the subject? I know. I can hint at it.* Suddenly he realized he didn't have the courage as they sat watching the baby sleep. Catheryn was now looking up and noticed that Lawrence was in deep thought. "Honey, what's wrong? Are you thinking what I'm thinking?" Not able to look into Catheryn's eyes, Lawrence kept his gaze on the baby. Speechless, instead of answering, he responded with a question, "What are you thinking?" Now voicing her concerns, "Do you think someone has been watching our home or us? I don't know what I'm saying, but could it be possible, or was our house randomly chosen?"

Following Catheryn's question, Lawrence's anxiety is now replaced by relief. Nodding his head, agreeing, "Yes, of all the homes in this neighborhood, why ours?" Purposely avoiding eye contact with Catheryn for fear that she would read his mind and see the hope stirring in his soul. Suddenly Catheryn spoke Lawrence's thoughts, whispering the word "Hope." In that moment, Lawrence's heart was beating at an unprecedented rate. Therefore, he quickly turned to face the window to hide his emotions. Catheryn sat smiling as the baby stretched arms and legs, then laughed quietly as the baby resumed his peaceful rest. Lawrence smiles, speaking silently, "This abandoned child has aroused in my heart feelings of hope and love; I never thought it possible for a child not of my own making. If I could have just considered adoption when Kat first suggested it, maybe by now, we would be parents; instead of waiting four years trying unsuccessfully to get pregnant. "

As it happened, Lawrence was in such deep thought that he did not hear Catheryn call. Therefore, she stared at him in silence, thinking, *Surely he's angry.* Meanwhile, Lawrence was thinking, *It has been a very painful experience; being childless has caused me so much pain, now all of a sudden, we find a baby on our steps.* Suddenly, Lawrence spoke up out of sheer frustration, "But this is someone else's baby, and we can't keep it!"

Why Didn't You
Tell Me?

In contrast, Sevella was still feeling guilty for having fallen asleep and was not keeping a watchful eye on Samuel; now, this sinking feeling of uncertainty and the horrible thought of speaking to Neal about her job made her feel nauseated. "You're just tired, scolding herself silently while wiping the tears from her eyes. Again glancing up, noticing her reflection in the mirror, "What's even worse; is knowing that someone out there wants me dead, most likely a client that I could easily encounter at any one of Neal's meetings. Oh, but not if I kill him first. Nonsense! Well, only in self-defense, if it comes to that." Clearly shaken at the thought of Samuel missing, Sevella decided to contact Neal, "Do it right now! What if I'm fired?' She scolded and reasoned while deep in thought. Afterward, she dialed Neal's number, "New Ventures, LLC. May I help you?" but Sevella was too deep in thought to respond. After a long pause, Sevella again heard, "Hello," Sevella apologized and asked to speak to Neal. After briefly speaking with Kathy, she was transferred to Neal; hurriedly rushing through their conversation, Neal promised Sevella that her position had not been filled.

"Consequently," Neal began, then hesitated… "By the way, we will be starting a new company, one that needs a Professional Assistant, someone that is qualified with a Degree in Business Administration…." Sevella interrupted him, asking, "Well, what part do I play in this, or will I have an opportunity to apply for this new position?" Neal considered her question before answering, "I guess I can at least give you first choice. One thing, how many words can you type?" Before answering, she nervously cleared her throat, then spoke firmly, "You'll have to test me." As she waited for Neal's response, Sevella remembered helping her foster mom, an office manager for a very large legal firm, and the long hours helping with, typing and proofing her documents. Finally, she asked, "Agreed?" Neal responded, "Oh, sure, I thought you hung up." Sevella said to herself, *On the contrary, you weren't listening as usual, so preoccupied and never paying any attention to me.*

Now standing and looking into the receiver, Sevella recalled the last conversation with her foster Mom; she remembered her saying, "Sevella, your typing is very accurate, and you've picked up speed. I would say that qualifies you as a typist." The sound of Neal loudly shuffling papers caused Sevella to respond in a loud tone, "At least sixty-five words a minute." Now standing to his feet, Neal exclaimed, "No way! You mean to tell me you can type? Why didn't you tell me?" Carefully choosing her words, "You advertised for a receptionist. You were too busy giving orders regarding the accurate filing of your documents, telling me what you expected of me and what you would not put up with, all while insisting that I follow instructions. In other words, you never asked." At that moment, Neal yelled into the receiver, sounding very excited, "Woman, do you know how much more money you could have been making?" Sevella was now feeling very annoyed and answered in a much lower tone, "Never mind." At the same time, feeling very relieved, thinking, *Just as I needed a job, then I really, really need it now.*

Dream Home

Shortly afterward, Neal was speaking to Kathy in the background, sounding very annoyed; then returning to his conversation, Neal continued, "Yes, we are going into the big times. Apparently, you made a big impression on Ellor and his investors. His clientele has doubled since you were his acting assistant." Momentarily in shock after hearing the name *Ellor*, unexpected fear gripped Sevella's heart as she began to reflect on that horrible night in Florida. Ignoring her silence, Neal continued, "Now that I know you are qualified, there is no need to test you; of course, you know this means more responsibilities?" Still preoccupied with her own thoughts, Neal waited for Sevella's response, at the same time; the background noise of papers being moved about, drawers opening and closing, interrupted her thoughts of that night in Florida. For a moment, she listened carefully, waiting for a response from Neal. "What did—?" Before she could ask her question, Neal interjected, "Now that I know your qualifications, I'm confident you can hold down the responsibilities and duties of an Executive Secretary. By the way, Ellor gave your work rave reviews, and I know now that you will be an asset in getting my business off the ground!"

As a result, her thoughts of that horrific night were now replaced by excitement, now asking in unbelief, "Did you say promotion?" Thinking back to when Neal first hired her, "After all the years, I worked for just enough to buy a good meal, and I was happy to be able to do that," Sevella sensed a feeling of anger rising up as she remembered her struggles just to get bus fare to work. "I could have been making more money and moved out of the homeless shelter a lot sooner than I did. Nonetheless, I recall being very appreciative of a place to stay, a bed of my own, and finally, an address. Still, with more money, I could have afforded my own room and board." Still deep in thought, Neal continued his discussion, unaware that Sevella wasn't listening. "Not to mention the many, many times I wanted to buy new clothes but didn't have the money. More time than I could remember, I hinted around for a raise, but he would say, 'I have to pay the mortgage and other expenses on my investment property that I'm thinking seriously about making you my property manager.'"

Eventually, the sound of movement on Neal's end interrupted Sevella's intense thoughts. Neal continued, "Maybe, just maybe, I could work something out with you to become the new owner of that investment property." As if waking up from a dream, she asked in total disbelief, "New owner, finally my dream home." Now considering his own admission, Neil quickly added, "In other words, well, for now, let's just focus on one thing at a time." Sevella started to question him but realized getting it all in writing would be more practical. As Neal silently went down his list; Sevella waited patiently for him to return to their conversation; remembering the day Neal offered her a place to stay, he proudly announced, "I know just what to do; I will use a portion of your pay to help remodel my investment property, and when it's finished and sold, we will split the profit. Isn't that great?" Speaking aloud, Sevella responded sarcastically, "You think so?"

Assault

Now understandably angry and in disagreement at that ridiculous offer, as was the day he made it, but she was in a tough predicament, and disagreeing wasn't an option. Therefore, she didn't hear Neal when he again suggested, "Alone with your new position as Executive. I think you should consider yourself an investor. Since you are acting house sitter and property manager, how about you consider buying the home?" Now sitting, Sevella said excitedly, "New owner!" Suddenly, Neal excused himself to answer the other line, later coming back sounding more like himself, insisting, "Whatever the case, I need to hear from Naomi. I'll be out of town for another three weeks, and Kathy's term ends next week. If Naomi doesn't show up, I'll be one person short. If Naomi does show up, then we can sign off on Kathy's time card, Sevella. I really need you to step it up." Sevella accepted happily, saying, "I really appreciate and thank you for hiring me back after such a long period of absence." As Sevella prepared to ask about Naomi, Neal spoke up first, "Sevella, call me in the morning," suddenly, she heard a click. She spoke into the receiver, "That's right, just rudely hang up; that's so like Neal, thoughtless and selfish!"

The following morning she was awakened with a jolt and obviously shaken from the bad dream of her attacker pulling her by the arm. Sitting straight up in bed, she suddenly remembered; it all started after the call from Ellor. Sevella is now remembering an assault at one of the foster homes. As she held her head between the palm of her hands, hoping to block out the impending images following an unfair and unwarranted punishment caused by a boy who slipped into her room to share his grapes, only to make an attempt to sexually assault her. Due to his threat, she cooperated, but she screamed. It was that scream that summoned his father, who heard her and came into the room just in time. Afterward, the boy lied, telling his father, "Dad, she stole the grapes!" Therefore, she was punished severely. Shaking herself as if to shake off the horrible memory, but all of a sudden, that awful night in Florida overshadowed the memory of the first assault.

It was then she remembered Neal's instructions to call him. Sevella rushed to the phone and quickly dialed. "Hello!" said Kathy, sounding very excited. "Hello to you!" said Sevella. Kathy continued, "After you hung up from talking to Mr. Nest, he told me the good news. Aren't you excited?" Now remembering her last conversation with Neal as his Executive, Sevella gradually began to smile, admitting, "After Ellor called, I wasn't sure what to expect, I could anticipate the worst, so I was waiting to continue my conversation with Neal. Thank you for confirming what I hoped would happen...." Before Sevella could finish her statement, a call came through, and Kathy quickly switched lines. While waiting for Kathy to return, before long, she heard the shuffling of papers. "Hello, Kathy. Are you back?" Neal, surprised to hear Sevella's voice, asked, "Who is this?" Both were surprised at the other because Kathy transferred the call without making the announcement. Neal then asked, "Sevella, are you there?" Sevella was still trying to figure out what happened. Finally, she answered, "Neal, yes, I'm here, but I didn't know you were there." After a moment of silence, Neal quickly asked, "Well, do we pick up from where we left off, or did we settle everything?"

A New Investor

Rarely was Neal's behavior unpredictable. Once she figured out what was behind the whole change of behavior, she could determine what Neal was really up to. Placing her hand on the receiver and whispering, "I never really believed he would actually follow through on his promise, but ten years later, he's promising to work out a deal for me to eventually own the home!" Her thoughts were interrupted after hearing Neal repeatedly saying, "Hello, hello, are you still there?" Now smiling because of the promotion and raise, Sevella responded, "Neal, where else would I be?" Now complaining, "You know, you could have just come on in to work. By the way, I'm sure you know by now this place is a mess. Enough talking. I'll see you hopefully this morning." Ignoring Neal and speaking to herself, *I can take it easy and let Kathy do all the heavy work.* Before long, she heard a click after that the dial tone. "Yes, just like Neal, Mr. Rude, and never a goodbye." The jolt from the dream and the excitement from the raise and promotion left Sevella feeling exhausted.

As she slowly placed both hands behind her head, laying back on her pillow, she whispered, "Yes, and most importantly, I have to take it easy until my next doctor's appointment; thanks to Sam for recommending her sister's doctor. That way, before I return to work. I can complete my final postnatal examination. In that moment, she realized the butterflies in her stomach, and she crossed arms over her head, the way she would do when placed in a really nice foster home, "Now I'm actually being recognized for what I can do, and no longer for what I am." She pinched herself to make sure she wasn't dreaming a very welcome and wonderful dream. "I can't believe all this good news!" squealing as she bounced up and down on her bed. However, in that same instant, she was reminded of Samuel, and suddenly that disturbing feeling replaced the butterflies. Looking into the mirror, "No, this can't be. I must find out what has happened to him. In the meantime, I can't let what happened to Samuel cause me to lose focus; therefore, I must believe that he is safe."

Not long after, she's reminded of Neal's offer, "In case Neal is just being Neal and changes his mind about selling me this house—that's okay. From this point on, with a promotion and a raise, I can afford my own place." Once again, that disturbing feeling in the pit of her stomach was back. "Better still, once my salary is actually increased, I will discuss a contract for sale: why on earth am I thinking about this house? I really need to know what has happened to Samuel." After calling for a taxi, she quickly began to prepare for work; rushing from one room to the other, finally dressed, she grabbed her bag and keys rushing out of the front door, only to look behind her to the house across the street as the taxi pass her and stopping at the appointed address. After getting into the taxi, Sevella began to mentally organize the office, knowing that Neal's idea of clutter was him having to figure out what goes where. Not long after arriving at the office, she was greeted with unexpected confusion. First, the unorganized, very long to-do list, and next, a note to contact Miss Allen regarding Mr. Kingsley's itinerary. Concluding with a call from a Florida Investigator, no name but regarding Naomi Pratt.

Not Normal

At that very moment, she felt dizzy. "Wow, my first day back at work, and it feels more like I've already put in a full day." As she prepared for a busy day, she suddenly remembered that Sam has given the phone number to her sister's doctor. "That's it! I need to schedule appointment for my six-week checkup. That's probably why I feel so dizzy and tired; my six-week checkup is due in a month or so. Also, I've been given a prescription for something. I need to be more serious about my health if I'm going to perform professionally. The next thing on my to-do-list is to schedule an appointment with that doctor. Oh, no! I can't use the same name at the hospital; I'll have to use another play name and pretend to have had a miscarriage. Afterward, that one final doctor's visit, and I'll be done." After making the appointment, Sevella repeated the nurse's words, "Miscarriages and birth are no difference. The body has to adjust to not being pregnant, and therefore you will have to take it easy." Now sitting after standing throughout the morning, she said, "I guess this extreme tiredness is one of those systems."

Along with her responsibility at the office, she now had to focus on getting back to her normal weight, "That's right! It's time I get back to my normal life and focus on returning to my normal schedule." All though Sevella was very familiar with organizing large amounts of documentation and numerous files, she realized her workload would double, "In spite of the extra work, I must remain focused; the point is, I must be efficient." On the contrary, it was Neal who appeared confused as he made every attempt to give instructions, only to discover the task was completed. As Sevella moved to the next task on the list, Neal continued to get in her way. After a while, he realized Sevella was sufficient, and he could trust her to manage the difficult task without his supervision. With the new position came Mr. Kingsley and a new group of clientele who no doubt signed up with the company during her absence.

After a few days of none stop and long hours of work, her new job description now involved keeping everything moving until Neal's return from his next trip to Florida. "On the other hand, normal life," she said, laughing out loud. "What exactly is my normal life? Not normal has been by normal, and not normal has been my life's description for as long as I can remember. The only normality in my life at this point is a baby created by a horrible creature, but even that is not the normal way to start a family." Momentarily, feeling helpless and very angry, along with that unwelcoming feeling of fear, she declared, "That man deserves to die, and in the beginning, I believed his baby also deserved to die!" With that thought in mind, tears began to fill her eyes as she spoke aloud, "As for Samuel, I know what I feel is not normal. How could it be? Although I have no idea where Samuel is, I believe with everything in me that the couple across the street found him." Now moving away from the piles of files on her desk, she walked over to her office window, saying, "My life from this moment will consist of waiting until I finally see some sign of Samuel's existence."

It Appears She's Vanished

Following the first long and hectic day, Sevella promised, "This I will do; every evening, and morning, until I see Samuel, I will sit on that couch waiting." As her words echoed, she looked around as her fears once again began to overwhelm her. Again thinking about that horrible night in Florida as she stood alone with the instructions left on Neal's to-do-list, "Just when the good news should have brought a lasting joy, I'm now struggling with Samuel's abandonment and that feeling of uncertainty," Suddenly, "ring-ring," startled, Sevella quickly answered the phone, "Yes, hello!" Neal began by saying, "Incidentally, I should have prolonged Kathy's assignment and postponed my trip before bringing you back into the office. How is your friend? Is she okay? Will there be any future incidents?" Obviously caught off guard, Sevella quickly remembered, "Don't worry about that; everything's fine!" Of course, Sevella had forgotten all about her fabricated excuse to take off from work. Occasionally holding her hand over her chest. Meanwhile, Neal continued, "That was my main concern; as for my plans, and since you've proven to be efficient at your new position, I'm leaving it up to you whether or not to keep Kathy until we hear from Naomi."

Up until that time, Naomi's whereabouts were of little concern to Neal; however, at that very moment, Neal spoke without thinking, "Oh, by the way, one more thing; I had planned to promote Naomi from receptionist to your Assistance, but it appears she's vanished, and since then I have not heard a word from her. It has been a couple of days since we spoke." After that, Neal was silent. Sevella, raising her voice, asked, "Hello, Neal, are you still there?" There was a rumbling noise on the phone; Neal continued, "The thing is, I can't seem to locate her since our last investors' meeting." Again silence on Neal's end, but before Sevella could utter a word, Neal spoke almost in a whisper, "I think she might have been hired by one of my competitors." Sevella wanted to scream at Neal for being so selfish, but tears were running down her face, and she didn't want Neal to know just how angry she'd become. The following day was full of more adjustments and many mistakes made by Kathy the Temp. Finally, Sevella approached her, suggesting she take a break.

Before Sevella could take her place, the phone lines lit up simultaneously, "Hello, hold please, hello, hold please," returning to the first call, "yes, may I help you?" Kathy watched in amazement as Sevella mastered one call after the other. Once all calls had been sufficiently directed to its prospective voicemail, Sevella turned to Kathy, asking, "What's your expertise?" Kathy responded, "Computers, boy, you really know how to handle those calls!" Sevella smiled and asked, "What was your job description with your last employer?" Kathy responded rhetorically, "Am I fired? Well, internet technology was my last job description and preferred profession." Sevella smiled at Kathy as she considered her next move. "Kathy, I'm really going to need your expertise in accounting and data entry, also occasionally filling in for the new receptionist. I know that your expertise will soon pull you from this position, but while you're here, we'll take advantage of your IT skills. Do you think working in accounting will be a problem? Can you handle that?" Smiling before responding, "Yes, of course!" said Kathy.

One Night of Horror

Before continuing, Sevella noticed several documents addressed to Ellor and was unable to focus on her conversation with Kathy. Finally, she managed to speak clearly in spite of her nerves, "I'll have Neal approve another Temp to handle the phones, but right now, those documents in accounting are our first priority." Once Sevella was comfortable with leaving Kathy with data entry, she contacted Preferred Temp Service and exclusively requested Dorothy Meese for full-time office management. An hour later, Dorothy walked through the front door as Sevella skillfully managed several calls. Therefore, Dorothy immediately releases her; Afterward, Sevella rushed into her office, attempting to calm her nerves. After work, she was emotionally drained, and once she made it home, she went straight to bed. The weeks to follow were more organized, but she couldn't shake the uneasiness she felt since seeing those documents. After three weeks in Florida, Neal returned from his trip but mostly kept to himself, only to respond to incoming calls.

While meeting with Kathy and Dorothy, Kathy motioned for Sevella to look at the entrance to the main offices. Turning quickly, only to see Neal standing in the entranceway between the lobby and the main offices. Getting up quickly, she followed Neal to his office and was surprised when Neal closed the door behind them but stopped quickly, turning and asking, "What did I do wrong?" Confused, Sevella asked, "What do you mean?" Neal places both his hands in his pockets before answering, "You replaced Kathy. Why? Never mind, you don't have to explain. I did ask for Dorothy, but Kathy was sent instead." Despite Neal's cautiousness, Sevella realized something was wrong; therefore, before responding to Neal, she motioned for him to sit, just as Dorothy directed a call to his office. While waiting for Neal to complete his call, Sevella began to reason with herself, *Maybe those documents were from a recent meeting; that is it, he just returned from Florida, and those documents had to be from that trip.*

Once he was sitting down, he occupied himself with the call. Sevella then remembered an evening in one of the foster homes while watching her foster brother and sister open Christmas gifts. Although she didn't have a gift to give, she enjoyed the atmosphere of laughter and surprised looks after each gift was unwrapped. However, the thought of having to leave that family shortly after the holiday left her feeling very sad; therefore, she couldn't continue to celebrate and excused herself, rushing off to her room only to cry herself to sleep. Now looking at Neal's slump shoulders, frown on his brow; in that moment, Sevella began to focus on Neal's body language as he talked to the person on the phone. Similar to that Christmas night, the excitement of her new position was being overshadowed by that horrible night in Florida as she tried to imagine what could have happened to cause Neal to look so defeated. Otherwise, she would bring up the documents from Ellor but feared the worst. She then pretended to busy herself with managing the office as Neal busied himself with the call from Florida.

Never Adoption

Occasionally Catheryn would glance up at Lawrence, momentarily glancing at the sleeping child and again at Lawrence, each time he appeared to be in a trance, but this time she's starring intensely at him, wondering, *What did he just say? Did he say what I think he said? Has he had a change of heart and feeling exactly what I'm feeling?* Still standing with his back to Catheryn, Lawrence dropped his head as if he was praying, but his emotions were getting the best of him, and actual tears were running down his cheeks onto his blue shirt, making patterns as they dropped systematically one after the other. As it happened, the baby began to squirm, and Catheryn's attention was once again on the baby. While she was cradling the baby, she silently considered Lawrence's outburst. "Is he suggesting that I alluded to adoption, did I? Of course, I didn't." New tension filled the room; Catheryn finally got the courage to respond, whispering, "Honey, maybe we had better unpack the rest of his things; it's been almost two hours now. I don't know about you, but I'm getting hungry. Goodness knows when the baby has last eaten. Don't you think we need to eat before he wakes up?"

Obviously embarrassed by his outburst, Lawrence didn't respond right away; he was still trying to get past speaking his thoughts out loud. Nodding in silence, now being very careful not to reveal the hope behind the outburst, he smiled but avoided eye contact with Catheryn, who was now staring lovingly at the little bundle in her arms. Since Catheryn's earlier suggestion to unpack the box, Lawrence began to remove the neatly arranged items, again thinking out loud, "It seems to me the person was laying out clues for the baby's schedule." Meanwhile, Catheryn was remembering a time when they were patiently waiting for the doctor's report and hoping that the pregnancy test results were positive. However, hopefully, the test results were all the same—negative! Regardless, the doctor assured them that there was still hope. "In spite of the doctor's reassurance," Catheryn responded silently, "now four years later, after being very hopeful, until hope has disappeared."

In that moment, Lawrence began speaking, but his voice cracked, "On the other... hand," now attempting to clear his throat, he continued, "all of a sudden and out of nowhere, we find a baby on our doorstep." At the same time, wishing the beautiful baby was their very own, even if it meant adoption. In that moment, Catheryn thoughts were on every negative pregnancy report they received but managed to put on a brave face. Angrily speaking her thoughts, "Well, time has not been very kind because we are now celebrating our fourth wedding anniversary, and still no baby." By this time, Lawrence is in the kitchen wiping tears from his eyes, at the same time looking into the fridge, only hearing the sound of Catheryn's voice but didn't really understand what she said. During the same time, Lawrence remembered secretly looking at pamphlets on adoption, unknowingly, that Catheryn was also secretly looking at pamphlets, as well as reading numerous books. Apart from their discussion with adoptive parents at the Center, each of them refused to openly discuss the subject with each other. Lawrence once said reassuringly, "Matter of fact. We're well able to produce our own children. Therefore, discussion closed, never adoption!"

A Cruel Joke

As Catheryn looked through the remaining items in the box, she was hoping to find a note of instructions. "Great," she whispered when she discovered that there wasn't one. "Okay, no problem. We will figure it out." Again cradling the baby, asking, "Where will you sleep? We were expecting someday, but not today, so we are not prepared." Momentarily considering the spare bedroom, she quickly changed her mind, speaking aloud, "No, we would not hear you cry; we will just save that for when you are old enough to sleep in your own room." Panic struck at her spoken words, and she desperately hoped that Lawrence was too preoccupied to hear her conversation. As fate would have it, he heard every word. However, he began to open and shut cabinet doors to distract any attention from his eavesdropping and, at the same time, hoping adoption was possible. By the time they had finished their meal, the covers in the dresser drawer and the makeshift baby bed had begun to move, and the baby began to cry, this time louder and louder. Once over the initial shock, both Lawrence and Catheryn jumped to their feet, rushing to the baby's side, only to stare in complete confusion.

Immediately Catheryn began to pray, "Lord, help us, show us what to do!" Catheryn quickly takes the baby from the drawer and grabs the milk formula, shaking the baby while carefully reading the instructions. She then calmly turns to Lawrence, "Honey, I need you to take those bottles and place them in hot water; they need sterilizing. While I quiet him, next take this formula and place it in a bottle. After feeding him, we will bathe him and get him ready for bed." Momentarily speechless. Finally, he shouted, "Honey, did God tell you all of that in that short while?» She smiled as she held up her finger to silence Lawrence, then she measured the formula and poured it into the bottle. Afterward, she tested the milk's temperature. Lawrence exclaimed, "Wow, look at you! I'm impressed!" Although her nerves were jumbled, Catheryn slowly and carefully placed the nipple in the baby's tiny little mouth while Lawrence watched in amazement. She explained, "The answer to my prayer was, 'He's a person just like you, with needs just like yours.' The rest I remembered from watching TV."

As she watched the baby sucking the bottle and occasionally falling asleep, Catheryn fought back the tears and the urge to share with Lawrence her deepest hopes of adoption. At the same time, the feelings of joy are now so overwhelming; both avoided eye contact for fear of being found out. Shifting her gaze from the baby but looking straight ahead, Catheryn spoke quietly, "This child has been abandoned, or someone is playing a cruel joke on us. Especially…." Lawrence now turned and walked over to the kitchen window, speaking in an angry tone, "Who would do such a thing? Who would abandon a baby? I am still waiting for that positive pregnancy report, but never in my wildest dream did I expect to find a baby on our doorstep. Remember that day, honey? We stopped at the park to recover from another negative pregnancy report. I would think a place where mothers strolled their babies would be a likely place to find an abandoned baby, or better still, across the street on the steps of Community Center, but never on our doorstep."

Do You Remember

After recalling that particular day, Catheryn whispered, "Yes, I remember. I remember pleading with you while pointing in the direction of the center to go inside and look around." Meanwhile, Lawrence was staring at the baby as he lay asleep in Catheryn's arms. Lawrence began speaking, but Catheryn was distracted, "That same day, the director walked up and introduced herself, Mrs. Kennie, remember? For some reason, she mistook us for volunteers." Again, Catheryn was motioning for Lawrence to lower his voice as she stood to lay the sleeping baby in the drawer while directing Lawrence into the living room while leaving the kitchen door open. After sitting and directing Lawrence to come away from the kitchen door, saying, "Yes, I remember Mrs. Kennie and the program, although I knew when you placed your hand on my back, you were directing me toward the exit, but my feet were frozen in place. I was amazed and shocked that she thought we were there to volunteer." Lawrence was distracted, but Catheryn continued, "I excitedly greeted Mrs. Kennie, then turned to you with a pleading stare while you purposely avoided eye contact, similar to what you are now doing."

After hearing "avoided eye contact," Lawrence turned toward Catheryn, explaining, "I seriously wanted to say no, and run for the exit, but those pleading puppy eyes finally won me over, and I finally gave in. Remember?" Catheryn looked up just in time to see a look in Lawrence's eyes that she hadn't seen before but quickly looked away before Lawrence noticed her gaze. Instead, she questioned him, "When Mrs. Kennie motioned toward her office and invited us in, and after explaining the program, you were not yet convinced, but you changed your mind. Why was that?" After processing that particular day, Lawrence hesitated before continuing, "Well," began Lawrence. After a brief period of silence, he continued, "Because you had pretty much accepted for the both of us. Anyway, as it turned out, following that discussion, we spent many hours throughout that year volunteering and working with the children. Twice a month to serve food, play games, or just sit and read stories, and to be honest, I have enjoyed every moment of it."

Now feeling trapped in his own body, Lawrence was wondering, *Could I be the problem; should I admit it to her? Better still, I should confess that I want to adopt this baby. It seems likely that my outburst could be a clear indication that I have mixed feelings.* After bathing the baby and getting themselves ready for bed, Lawrence was preoccupied as he stood staring at the baby before carefully placing the blanket over the baby's tiny little body. Slowly walking over to the drawer, Catheryn leaned over Lawrence's shoulder and whispered, "He's asleep, and we need our rest before the next feeding." Startled by Catheryn's voice, Lawrence turned to ask, "What do you mean next feeding?" Catheryn laid her head on the pillow and whispered, "Two a.m. feeding, now good night."

A Blessing in Disguise

As a result of all the excitement and confusion, both fell quickly asleep. The following morning, they were surprised when waking up, and the baby was quiet. Thinking the worst, they jumped out of bed and rushed to the drawer, only to see the baby turning his head from left to right and waving his little arms in the air. "How long has he been awake?" asked Lawrence. "Aren't babies supposed to wake up screaming at the top of their lungs?" Catheryn picked the baby up, whispering, "Yes, but not…" stopping herself, then continuing with a laugh, "Not this one!" Too late, Lawrence had already silently completed the sentence, "But not ours." While Catheryn changed the baby, Lawrence went downstairs to prepare the formula. After reading all the instructions for the formula, he placed the bottle into the hot water. In the meantime, Catheryn and the baby were headed downstairs. As she walked into the kitchen, Lawrence proudly handed her the bottle. "I tested it, but you had better make sure." As Lawrence watched Catheryn feeding the baby, he suddenly remembered a particular certificate on Mrs. Kennie's wall, the one for foster and adoption.

Suddenly he gasped, now looking into Catheryn's surprised face, he whispered, "I can't get over this whole ordeal; someone has chosen to leave their baby on our steps." Previously, as newlyweds, they were hoping to eventually buy a home but were waiting for the right time. Catheryn chided in, "Just think, all the while we were driving to the center, we saw no signs of this neighborhood ever existing. This community was carefully hiding off the freeway behind the most beautiful shrubbery and trees, not to mention several feet of wrought iron fence, shielding the most beautiful custom-built homes we have ever seen. Besides…" Catheryn began to reposition the baby while Lawrence watched in silence. Catheryn continued, "Before denying…." Interrupting and holding his hand up in Catheryn's direction, Lawrence argued, "On the contrary, I wasn't really lost, but I hadn't driven this way before." After several minutes of reminiscing, Lawrence noticed Catheryn signaling for him to take the bottle as she placed the sleeping baby in the drawer, as they looked on in silence.

From time to time, both would glance over to the drawer while rushing to prepare their breakfast and eat before the baby woke up. After breakfast, they tipped into the living room and began their conversation. Catheryn placed her arm inside Lawrence's as she sat on the couch; she whispered, "Right then and there, we said at the same time, I think we should buy this home." Now laughing together as Catheryn threw her arms around Lawrence's neck, saying, "Hey, this was the best-kept secret, and I am so glad that you missed your turn. Otherwise, we never would have found it!" Now frowning and smiling at the same time, Lawrence commented, "Well, I do remember one thing in particular, and that was that serious look on your face; just before you changed the subject…" Since they were standing near the baby, Catheryn suggested, "You are talking too loud," while laughing at Lawrence's facial expression. Lawrence then whispered, "By the way, we both thought it was a waste of time to sacrifice two of four weekends, but after the first session, it turned out that the center was exactly what we both needed to get us through those tough times."

New Parents

A moment later, Lawrence placed his hand on Catheryn's arm, saying, "Even before moving to this neighborhood, we both eagerly looked forward to driving those ten miles one way to spend those few hours working with the children." Again the baby moved, now whispering; Lawrence admitted, "It was when my friend Charles Miller suggested we get more active in the Volunteer Program; that's the only reason I began to get more involved. Actually, that day, the truth is I disagreed with Miller because of something else he had suggested. Therefore, I was in deep thought, and that's why I made the wrong turn that led us to our dream house." Catheryn, now looking at Lawrence with a wide grin on her face, "You know what is so strange?" Without waiting for an answer, and before Lawrence could respond, Catheryn squeezed Lawrence's hand and said, "I really didn't want to get more active either, giving up two of my weekends just to sit and read to the children, but you know how persuasive an attorney can be."

It was in that moment Lawrence realized what he had to do; now sitting with head slightly tilted, looking past Catheryn toward the baby, he stood up, picked up the phone, and contacted the office of Miller & Miller. After speaking to Charles, Lawrence turned to Catheryn and whispered, "Charles advised us to contact Child Protective Services and report this unfortunate incident; afterward, they will know what to do next." However, Catheryn wasn't in agreement, so she continued discussing the center, purposely avoiding calling Child Protective Service. Within an hour, Charles called back and referred them to another attorney by the name of Stan Helm, a Family Court attorney. After speaking with Attorney Stan Helm, Lawrence explained their situation and that they were returning home when they discovered the box on their step with the baby inside. Before ending the conversation, Mr. Helm promised to contact each entity involved with the case before getting back to them. Immediately after hanging up, Catheryn suggested, "I want to take him to an emergency and have him examined."

At the same time, Lawrence was shaking his head, "No!" But Catheryn insisted, "Lawrence, I mean it! I want to be sure he is okay." Now looking frightened while glancing nervously over at the empty box, Lawrence said, "What if someone sees us with the baby?" Catheryn placed the blankets in the box and the baby on the blankets and another blanket on the baby, instructing Lawrence, "I'll put the car in the garage, and you will bring the box to the car, place it in the backseat, afterward, I'll get in the back seat and take him out of the box." After Catheryn drove the car into the garage, Lawrence rushed out with the box, placed it in the back seat, and then went back to lock up but didn't have his house key. It was then Lawrence called out, "Catheryn!" His voice echoed as he realized that Catheryn and the whole neighborhood could hear. Apologizing, "I know, that was loud, but my keys are on the key chain, so I couldn't lock the door." After locking the front door, Catheryn gets into the back seat and carefully takes the baby out of the box. Once in the emergency room, the nurse who assisted them immediately noticed their nervousness and asked, "New parents?"

Ultimately shaking her head up and down, Catheryn nervously asked, "You can tell just by looking at us?" Smiling, the nurse said, "No, not by looking at you, but at your baby." At that moment, Catheryn felt the hair on her arms stood up as tears filled her eyes. "Don't worry," said the nurse. "What seems to be the problem?" Now wiping her eyes, Catheryn said, "I'm probably being overly concerned." Shortly after that, the nurse took some more information, and without looking up, she asked the baby's name. Lawrence quickly answered, "David, David Jameson." "Okay, come with me, David. Mr. and Mrs. Jameson, you can come, too." After what seemed like hours, the doctor completed his examination. "We have never seen a healthier baby. Mother, it seems you are having what most new mothers experience, and that's postnatal fears which are very normal. I recommend you take David home, and both of you get some well-deserved rest. Also, he is in need of a diaper change. Follow the nurse, and she will show you the nearest changing location."

Samuel, Samuel

After finally getting organized on her first day of work and having to deal with Neal's insecurities, Sevella went home and straight to bed. Suddenly her eyes opened, frantically sat up and looked around before realizing she was not on the couch but in her bedroom. Now loudly scolding herself, "How can you break rank? It hasn't been a whole day since I placed Samuel on those steps, and I haven't seen any sign of my neighbor since then." Walking in the dark, touching the wall to guide her from the bedroom door, through the kitchen, still scolding herself, *Really, are you so soon to forget him just because you've been promoted?* A streak of light shining through the partially opened blinds in the living room revealed a lighted path as she meticulously walked past the glass coffee table, being careful not to bump it and knock over Neal's very expensive vase. As she positioned herself on the couch, she spoke in a whisper, "It is so strange that I haven't seen any signs of the couple since I left the box, and I need to know why."

Once seated on the couch, she turned to face the back of the couch, shielding her eyes from the beam of light. Without any effort, Sevella fell into a deep sleep and remained asleep until dawn. During that time, she began to dream that she was falling and was awakened by the quick jerking of her body. Raising up on her left elbow, she began to reposition herself, at the same time glancing out of the window and was amazed and surprised to see the street lights dimming. Suddenly, car lights appeared, and a car pulled into her neighbor's driveway and stopped. Immediately sitting straight up, asking herself out loud, "Where on earth can they be coming from this time of the morning?" Prior to getting home, both Lawrence and Catheryn breathed a sigh of relief from the doctor's report. Just as Lawrence parked in the driveway, they both breathed a sigh of relief before getting out of the car. Catheryn got out of the back seat and walked around to the driver's side, holding what looked like a white sheet as Lawrence leaned into the back seat. After a while, Catheryn stepped back as Lawrence stood, appearing to be holding something close to his chest.

Meanwhile, Sevella was standing up on the couch, pressing her face up against the windowpane to get a better look. Now they removed the baby from the car; even though they were in plain view of their neighbors, it never crossed their minds that someone could be watching. "SAMUEL, SAMUEL!" Sevella yelled and quickly clasped both hands over her mouth as she strained to get a better look. Her heart was racing as she placed the other hand over her chest, saying, "Until now, the couple was parking in their garage, but now they are in the driveway, and without a doubt, they have Samuel!" exclaimed Sevella. Still covering her mouth and now in plain sight, she's resisting the urge to run out the door, rush across the street and take Samuel into her arms. "I can't do that, I can't do that," she repeated. "That would be a terrible, terrible mistake." As she watched the two walking closely, both were holding and touching whatever the man was carrying. "And that whatever has to be Samuel, I know now that they have him, and he's safe," whispered Sevella, now smiling with joy.

Fostering: Could It Be Possible?

Occasionally sitting and staring at the phone before checking for any missed calls, Lawrence pretended to check his messages from work. As the week progressed, Mr. Helm finally called and explained, "Good news and bad. First of all, I've been made aware of the center's volunteer program, where you both have done countless hours of volunteering; that's the good news. I am also associated with the center's interest in the fostering and adoption awareness program. According to what I've heard, you may have earned enough credited hours to become foster parents. The bad news, while investigations are underway, again, I repeat, 'may have earned.' I haven't all the details, but if the baby is taken from your home, it will only be until the case comes before the judge. However, I will have to get with the director of the center, and Attorney Miller, to get more information on the hours needed to qualify and recommend you for fostering." Before hanging up, he promised to discuss the matter on their behalf with Child Protective Services. After the conversation with Mr. Helm, both repeated the words of the attorney, "Foster parents. Could it be possible?"

At that very moment, both are looking down at David. Lawrence whispered, "The bad news is we could lose David." As Catheryn sat staring at the baby, Lawrence continued, "By the way, Charles Miller is an attorney but also a friend! Mr. Helm is actually going to discuss the case with CPS that sounds like bad news!" Two days seemed like two years, and the anticipation mixed with fear of rejection was overwhelming. Finally, a CPS representative did call the couple and explained the process, at the same time suggesting a visit within the hour. Following the Representative's visit, and as expected, David was placed into Service. Lawrence and Catheryn were informed by the representative that their friend Charles Miller and Mrs. Kennie, the Director of the Community Center, were both recommending them for fostering and had sent documentation almost a year earlier to CPS regarding Mrs. Kennie's recommendation, placing their names as interested parents in obtaining Fostering Certification.

Right after the phone call, Catheryn is now holding her face in both hands in total disbelief. "Honey, can you believe it? Mrs. Kenny secretly placed our names on the list for certification. Why, how… when, what I mean to say, how could she have known?" Lawrence is now sitting with his head hung down and secretly praying that their certification would qualify them to foster David. Lawrence, now looking up at Catheryn, confessed, "In answer to your question, two words: Charles Miller. In spite of the "may have" comment of Mr. Helm, the Representative said, "Charles Miller suggested that we would complete the required hours of training at the Department of Child and Protected Services." Looking up in shock, Catheryn almost yelled, "When?" Now lowering her voice as the baby moved, Lawrence whispered, "Honey, remember the other suggestion Charles discussed with me? Well, his suggestion was fostering. So, you see, honey, everything is working in our favor to secure our position as certified foster parents, good or bad news!"

As the week passed by quickly, the CPS representative called and informed them of the child's removal date from their home. After arriving, the representative admitted, "I should have taken the baby on my first visit, but he was sleeping so peacefully I couldn't bring myself to disturb him." Shortly after placing David's belongings in the box. The CPS representative and David was gone. Catheryn stood and walked over to the empty makeshift baby bed, looking down, but talking to Lawrence, "Did you say anything to Charles about our unfortunate circumstance?" Lawrence gasped, "Honey, I couldn't talk to you; how much more Charles Miller. Anyway, he's been a longtime friend, and I think he just knew." Later on, Lawrence walked over next to her, whispering, "I never let one day pass that I wasn't thinking of those Certificates and other documents relating to foster and adoption that covered Mrs. Kennie's wall or seeing my friend Mr. Miller's picture framed next to those Certificates. On several occasions, I had planned on asking Charles about his association with the Center but never got around to it."

As if to agree, Catheryn was vigorously shaking her head up and down, speaking with enthusiasm, "Except on one particular weekend when Charles mentioned the program called RESPIT, you know, temporary relief to foster parents. I remember questioning Charles; because I heard a co-worker discussing babysitting options for her foster child, and Charles' name came up." Lawrence was now preoccupied with his own thoughts of their childless marriage; therefore, being deep in thought, he subconsciously tuned Catheryn out, not realizing Catheryn was now staring at him in silence.

Call 911

Following a very hectic first week in the office, eventually, Sevella had everything down to routine. Until late one afternoon when Neal literally ran into her office, closed the door behind him, looking as if he had seen a ghost. "Neal, what is the matter? What is wrong with you?" Neal just stood there in silence before walking slowly over to a chair, absentmindedly rubbing his hands nervously together, slowly sitting and wiping sweat off his brow while speaking almost in a whisper, "I just received a call from a friend of Naomi, and they have not heard from her since Florida." Sevella quickly pushed her chair back from her desk and jumped up, demanding, "What on earth are you talking about? Are you telling me that all this time you have not heard a word from her: are you telling me you have not once inquired of her absence or called 911?" Sevella's hands shook as she placed one hand over her heart and the other over her mouth. Right after that alarming news, Sevella nervously paced back and forth, asking herself, "How could this have happened right under Neal's nose? Was he intoxicated, or was he too wrapped up in closing the next deal and less concerned about Naomi's safety?"

Since that horrible night in Florida, the reoccurring nightmares were a constant reminder of her attacker, at times leaving her frightened and unable to sleep. Staring intently at Neal, but she spoke to herself, *Now my gut feeling tells me that the same horrible thing has happened to Naomi.* Sevella quickly got up, left her office without a word, and rushed into the restroom: soon after closing the stall's door, she began to sob uncontrollably, feeling as though she was going to throw up. "My worst fear is that Naomi's attacker wasn't intoxicated, and he knew exactly what he was doing." As she exited the stall, she walked over to the sink and washed her face in an attempt to wipe away the unstoppable tears. Now staring blindly into the mirror until her gaze fell on her bare face. "Oh, no! I've washed off my makeup!" Again she began to feel nauseated, a very familiar feeling that first serviced when she discovered the definition of *orphaned*, the second time the night of her attack, the third time when she experienced morning sickness, and finally, when she imagined someone else had taken Samuel from her neighbor's steps.

"At last, living in fear for my life and in constant danger these past twelve months is no longer my nightmare. Oh my, poor Naomi!" Again she washed her face, but the tears refused to stop, "Alright already, just cry it out!" scolding herself as she splashed cold water over and over on her face hoping to wash away the reality of the tragic news about Naomi. After Sevella left the restroom, she rushed to the break room, hoping that the fear she felt wasn't as obvious as her shaking hands. The moment she walked into the break room and the door closed behind her, she broke into an uncontrollable sob, whispering, "What could have possibly happened to Naomi?" As she recalled those late-night investors meetings and the shady looks and busy hands of some of those investors. "Even worse, many of them thought I was Ellor's escort and expected the same service. Well, now I wonder why they would think such a thing."

I'm Living This Nightmare

After a long time of trying to compress her sobs, Sevella covered her mouth to filter her voice as she screamed into her hands, "I'm living this nightmare all over again!" As she grabbed one tissue after the other, she was convinced Naomi's disappearance was Neal's fault. "Otherwise," speaking as she attempted to get control of her emotions, "usually, I can fake a happy face, and I'm good at hiding my emotions, but not now." Sevella was unable to compose herself, sitting down at the table near the corner of the room, shielded by the vending machines; she then laid her arms and head on the table and cried as her body shook and trembled. Speaking silently, "First me, now Naomi." After several minutes had passed, she quickly walked over to the sink, took a paper towel, wet it, and washed her face several times, hoping that the wetness from the water would give her an excuse for the red eyes. She slowly walked back to her office with Neal's water and the wet paper towel still in her hand. As she opened the door, Neal was sitting with both hands covering his face. As she walked into her office, Neal stood and met her, taking the wet paper towel and the bottle of water, mumbling, "I can't stop sweating."

During that time, he was still wiping his forehead, insisting, "You must have read my mind; I feel as though someone has turned on the heat in this place." Therefore, both sat in silence as Neal opened the bottle of water, looking up at Sevella, noticing the redness of her eyes; he could tell she had been crying. He quickly drank the bottle of water. Standing, he walked toward Sevella, trying to bring some humor into the conversation, asking, "Sevella, who named you, and what nationality did that name originate?" Sevella was in shock; she began to experience shortness of breath as she tried to compose herself. Oddly, she stared down at her hands while cuffing them tightly together, "I don't know. My mother never told me." Neal seems to have forgotten that he asked the questions, mumbling, "I promise you that everything is going to be alright," as he patted her hands, attempting to comfort, and console her, "I contacted Ellor and shared my suspicion. And to my surprise, and contrary to his character, he sounded very concerned." It was then his voice trailed off as he tugged on his tie, "You know, Ellor promised to get his people involved in finding out what could have happened to Naomi and report back to me. The next thing I know, he's questioning me as if I was responsible for her disappearance."

Child Abandonment

Consequently, Catheryn and Lawrence are actively taking Mrs. Kennie and Charles's advice by signing up for foster and adoption classes through the Department of Child and Protective Services. Subsequently, and most importantly, along with this recommendation came the good news; that the court's decision was to return David back into their care as soon as their certification classes were completed. The couple was amazed and overwhelmed with joy and embarrassment as tears revealed their true feelings. They smiled shyly at one another after reading their copy of CPS caseworker's letter to Attorney Helm, Mrs. Kennie, and Charles Miller informing them that the couple's documents requesting fostering were up before the judge. Plus, the training they received as volunteers was being applied to their credit, which earned them qualifying hours to be eligible for foster parenting. Late one evening, after returning home from work and classes, they received a call from the Caseworker, sounding very excited, "I hope you are sitting down! Guess what? The hours you are now completing will also qualify you for adoption!"

After hearing this news from the caseworker, they couldn't believe it. They would have never shared their deepest thoughts about adoption to one another, not to mention Charles Miller. It was a forbidden subject. Now, after four years of waiting, not only has it become a reality, but an opportunity and a great and wonderful possibility. Momentarily in shock, Lawrence was now sitting quietly, thinking, *Fostering, I once believed that adoption was just plain giving up!* At the same time, Catheryn was thinking, *Now, with the help of Charles, Mr. Helm, Mrs. Kennie, and the Foster and Parenting Program, we have earned hours to foster and soon adopt, and our childless lives will be replaced by David.* "Not only....." Before long, Lawrence hesitated, now looking intently into Catheryn eyes, Lawrence admits, "Not only would I have not discussed this very sensitive subject with Charles, but I never ever would have discussed adoption with you," at the same time taking Catheryn into his arms, "but it was always on my mind." At that moment, they both burst into tears.

Eventually, Catheryn smiled, saying, "Lawrence, in the past, for fear of discouraging you, I secretly read everything I could get my hands on regarding adoption." After walking aimlessly back and forth, smiling, attempting to pull it together, Lawrence turned, walking toward the window and staring blindly into the night. At that point, the sound of movement behind him caused him to turn, only to see Catheryn rushing into the kitchen, hoping to shield her endless tears from Lawrence. His first impulse was to follow her, but he knew she needed her space as he needed his; therefore, he stood still and enjoyed the excitement that David would be placed back into their care. However, later that evening, Stan Helm called, informing the couple, "I need to be clear to inform you that there will also be an extensive search to locate one or both parents. Also, the possibility that one or both parents could be charged with child abandonment. Therefore, there will also be a search for relatives who would be willing to take custody of the child." In the meantime, the couple continued classes, even taking on extra classes just to be more informed and prepared to care for the baby.

Ask, and You Shall Receive

Once again, said Catheryn silently. *We must prepare our hearts; just in case, after going through the process of getting qualified and certified, we are not able to keep the baby.* On the other hand, Lawrence was thinking, *If, by any chance, they have to take the baby, I'm pretty sure it is going to feel very much like going back to the doctor and receiving a negative pregnancy report, only ten times worse.* Their thoughts were unbearable. Therefore, Lawrence spoke out loud, "For now, we at least have an opportunity the get David, even if it is for a short while. Right now, we'll just enjoy the moment; at this very moment, we are David's parents, no matter how temporary." One evening, after a very hectic work week, of rescheduling classes, Catheryn and Lawrence both flopped down on the couch, feeling completely exhausted. "I'm much too tired to climb those stairs," said Lawrence as he laid his head on the back of the couch, at the same time placing his feet on the coffee table. In the opposite direction, Catheryn folded her legs onto the couch as she laid her head on Lawrence's shoulder.

After a long period of silence, Catheryn couldn't hold back her emotions, so she slowly turned her face toward the kitchen as tears ran down her cheeks. Lawrence held his forearm over his eyes as he attempted to shield his emotions. Finally, Catheryn noticed Lawrence and thought he had fallen asleep. She slowly leaned forward for a tissue. Lawrence removed his arm and raised his head to look at Catheryn; now, looking into Lawrence's eyes,

Catheryn could no longer hide her tears. Lawrence admitted, "We are both very, very tired and a mess of emotions. Furthermore, once this process of documentation and investigation is over, we will get David back. That's been confirmed!" Between blowing her nose and building up her nerves to confess what she has held hidden for years, Catheryn takes a deep breath before responding, "While still hoping for natural birth, we never have, and could ever really discuss adoption openly without discouraging the other, it was too much like giving up. We insisted on believing with everything in our hearts that we would get pregnant."

Periodically interrupting, Catheryn said, "I agree," finally, he raised his left hand in defense, whispering, "I know we both believe the Scripture, 'You haven't done this before. Ask, using my name, and you will receive, and you will have abundant joy' (John 16:24, NLT). Well, guess what, Catheryn? I believe our prayers have been answered. Don't you?" Now laughing through her tears, Catheryn was now pointing toward the stairs, admitting, "Yes, I agree! I also believe we better get to bed if we're going to get enough rest and get up on time." The following week started with classes and training, as they laughed a little and cried. Lawrence and Catheryn rushed vigorously from work to classes and finally home. On this particular day, Catheryn asked Lawrence, "When we were at the hospital with the baby, how did you come up so quickly with the name David? Choosing a name was the last thing on my mind." Shaking his head up and down, Lawrence promptly responded, "You see while waiting for the pregnancy test results during our first doctor's visit, I remember choosing four names for our baby, two boy names and two girls. I found myself trying to remember those names, but I couldn't remember not one of them. Before Dr. Griffin, and as the nurse was asking for the baby's name, that's when the name David came to me."

Unsuccessfully Working at Being Happy

Now turning and looking wide-eyed at Lawrence, Catheryn joyfully responded, "All things considered, David has conquered the giant in our lives, that giant called Childlessness." Lawrence echoed questionably, "Childlessness, is that a real word?" Again Lawrence opened his mouth to speak, but at that moment, Catheryn held up her hand, interrupting him, "There was a time when I would get very upset with you, yes! That silent giant that has secretly affected our marriage: I know, and I'm the first to admit it; on several occasions, I wanted to talk to you about adoption, but I couldn't." Lawrence now insisted, "Wait a minute! Of course…" However, Catheryn interrupted, saying, "Listen, please, I know what you are going to say, but hiding our disappointments only caused silent suffering, which created a lack of communication, and you know what they say about no communication, no association.' From then on, we only pretended to be happy. We created suffering that caused both of us deep pain and regret. That pain and regret prevented us from being open and honest, and that's why I can truly say; we were unsuccessfully working at being happy."

What about Naomi?

On several occasions, Neal would glance over at Sevella, noticing her hands shaking, unlike anything he had ever seen. Neal stood up quickly and walked toward Sevella, taking both her hands, but was speechless as he tried to think of something to say to calm her down. "I… ah, ah… I, I mean, what I mean is, it's nothing wrong with her jumping on the opportunity to go with another investor or any of the other companies. Although I really don't believe that is the case for Naomi, especially since I had to supervise her work before handing it over to Ellor." At that moment, Neal repeated a statement made by Ellor, "Also, I remember Ellor commenting that he didn't think many of the attendees were legit." Neal then realized Sevella was calling his name. Looking at Sevella, Neal continued, "I just remembered, since the investors' meeting was my idea, Ellor made a couple of suggestions. First, he insisted that it was my responsibility to sift out the phonies from the real investors. Next, he suggested that I set up a screening system that would help us to eliminate our clients from the phonies."

Occasionally pausing, Sevella had an opportunity to comment. Instead, she sat staring blankly into space. Neal continued his attempt to convince her. "Most importantly, I really wished that you would have been there instead of Naomi. Even before I promoted you, I recognized your ability to meet the challenges, no matter how difficult." A moment later, after hearing the word "promote,"

Sevella was now looking at her hands covered by Neal's at the same time. She asked, "What… what about Naomi!" She pulled back from Neal's grip, picked up the receiver, and dialed Florida's Police Department. "Hello, please, I need to report a missing person!" Neal, again speechless, watched wide-eyed Sevella's shaking hands as she spoke on the phone. Her stomach knotted up as she imagined the worst for Naomi, shaking as she reflected on her own horrible experience that went unreported, but she was determined to be there for Naomi and do for Naomi what she was unable to do for herself.

Once again, the nauseating feeling returned, but Sevella fought the urge, eager to get to the bottom of Naomi's disappearance. As she answered one question after the other, finally, she paused and indicated to Neal to take the receiver. Neal whispered, "Ellor is handling it! Remember?" Without hesitating, Sevella quickly passed the phone to Neal, whispering, "Do you know anything about the people you are involved with in Florida? I can't answer these questions; here, you talk to her!" Neal stood up and walked around the desk, motioning for Sevella to get up as he took a seat; he covered the receiver as he motioned for her to bring him some water. As she walked out of the office, tears began to run down her cheeks; she angrily wiped away one tear after the other as she noticed how badly her hands were shaking. After that incident, Sevella found herself waiting impatiently to hear from the Florida authorities while keeping busy but always reflecting back on her attacker. Occasionally, she became busy enough to focus on getting back into the habit of working and keeping focus.

No, I Will Not

"From this point on, I will keep busy and stay focused until we know for sure, just in case Naomi took another position with a competitor." It was then Samuel became her primary focus; first of all, she was getting home at the same time every evening, next to positioning herself on the couch to watch for Samuel (now called David). Thankful she has now seen what appeared to be a small bundle of joy; however, she now wondered, "I've seen the couple on several occasions without Samuel. Maybe they have turned him over to the authorities, and they were now investigating every possible suspect and soon to be knocking on my door." Now a different kind of fear gripped her heart. Different from the orphanage and foster homes. This fear took her breath away, a fear of being found out as the woman who abandoned her child. She then cried out, "NO! I will not make myself a criminal! I have done nothing wrong; because I am the innocent party, and that man who assaulted me is the one who needs to be arrested or, better still, dead!" At last, falling across her bed, engulfed in tears, only to cry herself to sleep.

The following day, before leaving for work, she glanced across the street, but this time she stopped for a brief moment staring at the neighbor's empty driveway, then back to their front door. After getting to work, the call they had been expecting finally came, and the authorities in Florida were requesting Neal's return for more questioning. Neal was absolutely out of character, speechless, as he packed and gave orders for running the office. Now turning and looking at Sevella, Neal motioned for her to close his door; he took a tissue and wiped the sweat forming on his bald head, saying, "You asked me if I really knew the people in Florida. Why would you ask me that?" Sevella just stared at Neal in total silence. Once again, Neal seemed to have forgotten the question as he continued, "Once I get back from this trip, we can plan your travel to Florida on your first official executive trip." In turn, Sevella is now thinking, "I hope during that time I don't hear back from the doctor accusing me of lying to him, and most importantly, I desperately hope he believed my story that I miscarried and there will be no more questions."

Meanwhile, Neal continued with another rhetorical question, "Should I practice my answers to the questions asked by the authorities in Florida?" A moment later, Sevella watched as Neal paced back and forth, as she thought silently, "I've never seen Neal so nervous. Could he be hiding something?" Neal continued to pace, staring at the floor as if searching for the right answer and hoping to find it before being interrogated by Florida's authorities. Following that horrible day of bad news, and after arriving home, Sevella looked out of the window toward her neighbor's home, still wondering if they were just being careful after finding Samuel, and their strategy was to stay out of sight in order to hide the truth. Now speaking aloud, "That's right, that's it! First, they park their car out of sight, now coming home at the most ridiculous hours just in case the person comes back for the baby. That's it! They are probably watching to see if the person will come back. Oh, no!" Sevella exclaimed as a figure appeared in the window across the street.

My Neighbor Is Like Hannah

Moments later, she was off the couch and hid in her bedroom while whispering, "What if they are now watching me and can see me watching them?" She slowly moves toward her bedroom window, worried that her obsession with watching her neighbors has finally caught up with her. Apprehensive at being discovered as a peeping tom, Sevella was worried that the police would be called to investigate her weird behavior, only to discover that she was the abandoned child's mother. As she slowly peeped through the opened blind, the first thing that caught her attention was the *For Sale* sign hanging on her outer gate. Vigorously shaking as she moved slowly away from her bedroom window, she walked through the dark room to her bed, "I don't care, I don't care!" she cried out as she stood in the dark room, looking at her darkened image in the mirror. "Furthermore, deep down inside, I remember the two dreams of the couple with a child! And no matter what, I know they now have Samuel; most importantly, I believe that is where he should be."

As time passed, watching for Samuel every morning and evening was exactly what Sevella would do. As she positioned herself on the couch, she felt a sense of fulfillment because she was now convinced that the change in her neighbor's schedule and suspicious behavior was a definite indication that they were shielding Samuel. Late one evening, as she watched and waited, feeling very tired, she positioned herself on the couch and slowly dozed off to sleep. With a jolt, she woke up, breathing hard and, at the same time, frantically fighting the air. Now a little over a year since her attack and only weeks after they reported Naomi's disappearance, she was again having reoccurring nightmares about the man that sexually assaulted her. Sevella sat up, whispering, "Since his interrogation and Naomi's disappearance, Neal postponed my trip to Florida, and no doubt he's having second thoughts." She began to reposition herself as she lay back on the couch, staring at the ceiling, watching the sparkling colors created by the beam from the street lights shining onto the overhead Chrystal lamb, creating a complementary pattern of colors, watching until she eventually fell into a deep sleep.

One week later, as Sevella waited for news on the disappearance of Naomi, she sat on the couch just in time to see her neighbor's door close behind them, "What, how did I miss them? Their schedule is totally off?" Instead of feeling alarmed, she recalled the dream of the couple walking to their car and holding a child's hand. *Of course, I had that dream before Samuel was born and again after he was born,* speaking to herself as she made the comparison between her prayer and the dream of her neighbors. "I remember the story and the title of the book that spoke of Samuel," she then picked up the book from the coffee table and turned to the page. She read how Hannah, the lady without children, had cried and prayed for a baby. After Samuel was born, Hannah made a vow to give the baby away (1 Samuel 1:28, NLT). With that thought in mind, she said, "That's it! Without a doubt, the woman across the street is like Hannah!" Finally, Sevella was feeling some relief; she got up from the couch and walked toward the bedroom, hoping a new day would bring good news about Naomi's whereabouts.

You Are Responsible

Beginning with the following evening, after arriving home from work, Sevella quickly opens the book to reread the story about Hannah; she knelled down beside her bed and began to pray, "Hello, here I am again. I know I can't pray like Hannah or Miss Timothy, but I am going to give it a try. You let me know that the baby's life was important to you and you wanted him to live; I also believe you led me to the couple across the street. Now I don't really know how to take care of anyone but myself, and I believe through the dream, you let me know who to give Samuel to. Please, let me know that he is safe, and help me to forget the bad dreams, the bad man, and move forward with my life." Now recalling her six-week examination and the news about Naomi, Sevella whispered, "Also, help Naomi, and I know I lied to the doctor about a miscarriage, but please let Naomi be alive." Momentarily wiping away tears, Sevella continued, "Unlike his father, who doesn't deserve to live, please let Samuel be well and alive. I don't really want to bother you with all of this, but I need you to help me, and thank you! Goodbye for now."

After a long wait to hear from the investigators, and because of the intense interrogation, Neal's plan to visit Ellor was canceled. Therefore, his trip to Florida was short and unproductive. Nevertheless, he remained excited for Sevella to step into her role as his executive. Also, Sevella knew that in order to avoid another episode like her first trip to Florida, she was going to take charge of her own safety. Therefore, she arranged a meeting with Neal with prepared instructions, "Consequently, I will go back to Florida and accept the position; but first, I would like to make it known that I would have never left Naomi on her own or left Florida without her. For this reason, you must agree to never send me or any of your female staff all alone on any business trip as someone's assistant or escort. You must agree, first, to secure our stay as well as our travel. Secondly, whether or not you believe this, it doesn't really matter to me, but you are responsible for Naomi's disappearance." Understandably angered by Sevella's accusation, Neal jumped to his feet, but she only waved him off, refusing to be interrupted. Sevella continued, "During business trips, you are legally responsible for the safety of your employees; you will no longer put us in harm's way."

Despite Sevella's demands, Neal attempted to ignore her by refusing to be silenced, being very persistent, more so than ever, "Is there something you are not telling me, Sevella? Did something happen in Florida that you kept secret?" Startled at his perception of the incident, mostly based on her stern demands; therefore, Sevella became nervous about sharing too much information but was determined to get her demands met. "Although I didn't complain, I was so afraid and nervous, especially after Ellor passed the check back to you, all I could think was, sold to the highest bidder." In his defense, Neal interrupted again, "What!" Neal exclaimed, "What do you mean selling you to the highest bidder, and what do you mean I put you in harm's way?" Now feeling very angry at Neal's insensitivity to the whole matter, Sevella said sternly, "Just don't send us to the wolves, okay?" As she stood, she turned to walk out of the door, but not before looking back toward Neal and demanding, "Understand?"

Put It in Writing

As a result of that conversation, Sevella remembered her last foster parents' instructions, saying, "Sevella, every agreement should be in writing and proofed for efficiency. Child, one day, you will need to know how to put an agreement in writing." With those instructions came a long night of proofing, retyping, and rereading legal court documents and placing files in alphabetical order for her foster mom. Sevella began to speak out loud, "It gave me a sense of accomplishment and belonging. Therefore, I didn't mind going to bed late and getting up early the next morning for school!" Recalling that moment, then smiling, Sevella turned back toward Neal's office, knocked, and entered before he could answer, speaking boldly, "That time is now!" Neal turned at the sound of her voice, "Excuse me." Sevella continued, "Neal, please put my new position as executive in writing. This contract will detail each scheduled trip my assistant and I will take. Whoever you choose, just make sure it appears in our agreement."

In that moment, the feeling of confidence gave her the strength she needed to focus, and she began her new position. She then turned and walked out while Neal sat speechless, which was a miracle in itself. Sevella stopped short as she turned the corner toward her new office to peep inside, but before she reached the knob to open the door, all of a sudden, her thoughts immediately went back to Sam, "After giving Samuel away, I have totally avoided my best friend." Sevella also knew that Sam would ask many questions about Samuel. Now holding her face in the palm of her hands, she attempted to fight back the tears that wet her hands, "That will be the hardest thing to explain since I haven't seen the couple or Samuel since that early morning." Now she turned to walk toward her old office after slowly closing the door behind her while speaking to herself, *That is why I cannot get back in contact with my best friend, and I really, really miss and desperately need to talk to her. Neal will think I'm in the restroom; I'll just hide in here until I get my emotion under control.*

Although Sevella believed she was justified in speaking to Neal in such an authoritative tone, however, she understood the importance of respect and honor; furthermore, she didn't want to start her new position as a hostile employee, "In spite of Neal's faults, and goodness knows they are many, I need to apologize to him for my rudeness," speaking silently as she stood, putting her strong-will aside hoping to put an end to the controversy between them. After passing the conference room, she noticed the light was on; slightly opening the door, she peeped in to see Neal sitting alone and very preoccupied with a pile of scattered documents. "Can I help?" whispered Sevella, at the same time stepping inside the opened door. Only glancing up momentarily, Neal nodded his head but kept his focus on the documents. Presently hoping to change the tense atmosphere, she decided to speak a little louder but in a more cheerful tone, "Did you call a meeting without first informing your Executive?" Neal again nodded but kept his focus on the documents. Notably upset with her, Neal continued to ignore her; apart from the silent treatment, his body spoke volumes.

Something Horrible Has Happened

Now very determined to clear the air between them, Sevella sat in the chair at the opposite end of the conference table as she continued her attempt to break the ice. "Matter of fact, the last time we were in this conference room, you sent me away without formal notice and with people I hardly knew." Neal quickly glanced up, startled, looking in Sevella's direction as though in a trance; Neal stared in silence at Sevella for several minutes before responding, "Earlier, so much was going on when I brought up that subject, but I don't recall your answer. I guess I was too focused on my own problems." Now staring at his hands before rubbing his palms together, afterward, he picked up a document while absentmindedly speaking to himself, *There you are. I've looked everywhere for you.* Purposely moving her chair to get Neal's attention, Sevella knew exactly what to say to Neal, thinking to herself, *So he wants to apologize, but he needs my help.* In order to move past her earlier display of disrespect, Sevella began by reasoning, "Certainly, Neal, you have a right to be upset with me, and I understand that. However, I must ask,"

Apparently thinking of getting another tongue-latching, Neal was looking so intently in Sevella's direction that she wanted to run from the conference room like a frightened little puppy. Meanwhile, Sevella was thinking, *I must be nicer.* Therefore, she asked, "I was just wondering if the meeting this afternoon is a repeat of the first meeting." Neal, now looking very embarrassed and uncomfortable, tried to explain, "You were right to speak out on Naomi's behalf, and I wasn't thinking that anything bad had happened to her, but now I know it is a possibility that something horrible has happened while she was in my employment. By the way, the authorities also stressed that same point; however, this meeting is altogether different." Sevella quickly interrupted Neal by holding her hands up, signaling for Neal to stop. "Look, first of all, I need to apologize for my rudeness this morning because… I don't want to start my new position as a hostile employee. Secondly, I believe something horrible has happened to Naomi. At this point, I can't go into details, but mark my words, something horrible has happened to her."

Before speaking, Neal was now rubbing his hand over the top of his bald head and nervously loosening his tie, "Sevella, I hope and pray that you are wrong, and the worst-case scenario is just what I've always believed, and let's just leave it at that." Periodically wiping sweat from his forehead and then his baldhead before speaking in a more assuring tone, "From now on; as your boss, and founder of New Business Ventures, LLC, it is my responsibility to make sure my employees are safe when traveling, working in or out of the home office. Also, I would like to hire a male assistant to act as your office manager and travel companion." Following that statement, Sevella jumped up, speaking in a tone unfamiliar to Neal, "What now, I've been demoted?" Neal motioned for her to sit, but the ringing of the phone interrupted their conversation.

With one swift move of his chair, he was at the credenza and engulfed in the caller's conversation. "I will not sit," said Sevella under her breath, "or will I accept being demoted without first experiencing the benefits of my new position!" For several minutes she rehearsed her speech, practicing what she would say.

High Fashions

"After a few…. that's right." The sound of Neal hanging up the phone startled Sevella, jumping, then turned to look in Neal's direction just as he continued to explain, "By the way, his job description would be to attend investors' meetings and get the job done on your behalf. In other words, he would be totally responsible for keeping an eye on you as your stand-in. As for you, my executive, you can give him whatever title you, please. Agree?" Sevella didn't answer; therefore, Neil continued, "I believe this plan will initiate safety for you and other female staff as you travel on behalf of the company. By the way, the meeting this evening is to introduce you to our new client and a new concept of New Ventures, the world of fashion. Sevella… high fashion is on the rise, and I want new business ventures to take part in its rise to fame." Shortly after that unexpected announcement, Sevella was apprehensive since neither she nor Neal knew anything about the fashion industry. Therefore, she disagreed, "In the first place…" but before she could continue, Neil spoke up, reinforcing his argument.

Rarely did Sevella challenge Neal's idea regarding his company, but today she felt that her life and job were on the line, but Neal insisted, "Although we may not know anything about that particular industry, that's okay, we just need to figure out what items would be appropriate, such as business apparel. Better still, how about LLC apparel?" Now carefully choosing her words, she leaned forward, persisting, "To begin," while holding both hands in front of her, signaling for Neal to stop, before asking, "What…why on earth would you venture into an industry you have no former training, education or experience? Risking everything!" Neal shook his head from left to right while holding up his right palm facing Sevella, continuing his argument, "In the same way you learned this business; you can learn the ins and outs of the modeling industry, which means we will employ aspiring models to model new venture line of clothing. By the way, as it happens, and regarding your suggestion of a contract is absolutely perfect for what we are getting ready to do; you see, as my new executive and overseer of new business ventures, I need you to have some knowledge of legal agreements."

Ordinarily, Sevella knew what Neal was going to say, but today she was blindsided by his insisting on her overseeing this new venture, especially without any prior training. Nervously shifting in her chair, she absent-mindedly picked up her bottle of water, but instead of opening it, she just held the bottle between both hands. "In the first place…" regardless of this great opportunity, Sevella wasn't convinced. Looking down at the bottle of water, she asked, "I think your idea for my assistant is excellent: but why modeling?" Smiling shyly, Neal explained, "The first day you applied for the receptionist position, I noticed how poised you were. Although you dressed like you needed a consultant to pick your clothes, it didn't matter because you were so confident in the professional way you carried yourself convinced me that you were moonlighting. So… I figured you were an aspiring model going through tough times and looking for something part-time. You know, just to keep food in your mouth and pay rent, you know what I mean, at least until your career took off."

Undercover Strategy

Now feeling very relaxed, smiling inside at the compliment because all she ever heard was, "tall, skinny, and ugly old foster girl," lovingly called by her foster sibling and some of her classmates. Sevella was now wondering, *He's a charmer. Should I believe a word he was saying?* Then asked, "So, who is this male assistance?" Meanwhile, Neal was, sensing the tension subsiding and feeling less pressure, shriveled from one side to the other in his chair while pointing and instructing Sevella to bring him the documents from the credenza. Occasionally looking from one document to the other, Neal continued, "In addition to your new position, you will also have your very own assistant to help you navigate through the office as you train to do your job. Furthermore, I'll have to hire two more employees. On the other hand, I'd better give your male assistant the title as your boss, only when you are traveling!" Neal noticed Sevella's very familiar disagreeable facial expression, then quickly explained, "That way, he will always know where you are and what you are doing, just for safety measures. Would you agree?"

Before addressing Neal's suggestion, Sevella slowly placed her bottle of water on the table, agreeing, "All things considered, I was just about to disagree, you know, my assistant being my boss, but as a safety measure, I especially appreciate the undercover boss strategy." Right after receiving the documents, Neal was completely engulfed in one particular document but quickly realized he was predisposed and began to finger through the stack of documents while looking up at Sevella; he continued, "In the meantime, you will be traveling with a female assistant, just until I hire the male assistant; until then you will be known by everyone involved as the boss. Especially now that I know that you are well able to handle whatever assignment I entrust you with. Sevella, you have proven to be just the person I needed to help run this business." Afterward, Neal candidly announced, "On the other hand, I need to replace Naomi." As he arranged the papers in front of him, he was silent; carefully considering his heartless words hoping Sevella wasn't disturbed by his apathy.

Now attempting to do his best to change the subject, "Equally important, hiring an office manager will be your responsibility. You may choose to keep the Temps to help with the running of the office while you are traveling." Following the meeting, Neal directed Sevella to step into his office, pointing toward the chair in front of his desk, and motioning for her to sit, before saying, "Next week, we will be meeting with Ellor's Public Relations representative, and I want everything running smoothly, so I need for you to go through each of these power points and get them organized." Later that afternoon, they are both engulfed in arranging PowerPoint presentations for both meetings. Neal began to explain, "This is your first project as Executive, plus this project is number one on your priority list; next, we will go over the client's schedules, especially transportation to the office." As a result of Neal's instructions, Sevella was now nervously looking through the PowerPoint presentation as Neal continued, "For now, let's just focus on organization."

Unprepared

After returning to her office, Sevella began to feel the pressure of her new position. Once she located Neal's preferred Temp service, she immediately glanced over her to-do list, nervously saying, "What have I gotten myself into?" As a result of the pressure, the sound of the ringing phone startled her, and she quickly picked up the receiver, but instead of answering the call, she continued to question herself, "I wonder if this meeting is going to be anything like the first?" Suddenly Sevella became aware of someone's voice, "I'm sorry, but I don't really understand your question, responded Dorothy." Now feeling very foolish, Sevella responded, "I was thinking out loud, my apology." Dorothy continued, "Mr. Nest instructed me to send this call to you." Then transferring the call to Sevella, "Yes, this is Mr. Kingsley, and we will not arrive as scheduled but will have to reschedule. Please inform Mr. Nest of these last-minute changes. My receptionist will call tomorrow with update." Sevella moved the phone away from her face; glanced down the list, asking herself, "What on earth is the new client's first name? How can we move forward without knowing the first name?"

Despite the constant interruptions, Sevella made one last attempt to talk to Neal, only to be placed on hold. Now switching the line, Sevella murmured, "I'll get it myself." Then she heard, "Talking to me?" She shook her head left to right but remained silent, hoping that Dorothy would not think her a crazy lady going out of her mind. At six o'clock, the day drew to a close, but Sevella's to-do list only grew longer. Following a hectic week of long hours, she would position herself on the couch in front of the window, attempting to get a glance at Samuel, but would always fall asleep, eventually deciding to go straight to bed. As she settled down, her exhaustion made falling asleep effortless. As she dozed off, she whispered, "I hope after this very important meeting, I can go back to my regular schedule of watching for Samuel." The following morning before work, Sevella was determined to get up early enough to watch for Samuel but woke up just in time to get dressed before heading for work.

After arriving at work, the first thing she noticed was Neal's distraction. Twice she attempted to ask the first name and discuss the new arrival time of their client, but each time Neal was either on the phone or making a call. Once again, she rushed into his office, hoping to get the client's information. As she knocked and peeped inside, Neal was on the phone but motioning for her to come and have a seat, but she motioned back, saying, "I'll be back," and rushed to the front desk to ask Dorothy if she had the itinerary of their new client, but instead, she was greeted by their guest standing in the lobby. Once Neal was informed, he Instructed Sevella to show him to the conference room and offer him some croissants and coffee. Obviously shocked, after greeting the client and offering him coffee, Sevella then rushed to the break room to make preparation; in that moment, Sevella decided to have Kathy call Neal's office for instructions and get the client's name. As she rushed from the break room to the conference room, at the same time mentally arranging the PowerPoint, set up the projector, and placing folders on the conference table, thinking, *We are so unprepared.*

Florida Detectives

All of a sudden, Sevella stopped, then quickly turned toward Neal's office, retrieving the other documents; rushed back to the break room, took croissants out of their box, placed them on the serving tray; next filling two pitchers, one with water the other with orange juice. Finally, placing everything on the cart, she grabbed napkins, cups, and saucers while placing coffee in the peculator. She momentarily stopped to lean against the wall to catch her breath before dialing for Kathy, instructing her to show their guest to the conference room. Before hanging up, Kathy informed Sevella of the call from Florida's Detective earlier that day. Again, the ringing of the phone interrupted their conversation. Sevella slowly hung up as she backed into the cart, almost knocking it over. "Get a grip!" she said out loud. "Just focus, and the other things will work themselves out." In that moment, Neal was hanging up the phone as he sat up, pressing his back against his chair, straightened his tie, slowly took a Kleenex, and wiped the sweat from his forehead.

At this point, his hands were trembling, and he was unable to think straight. The call was about Naomi, and it wasn't good news. "How am I going to tell Sevella? I'll just tell her that the Authorities did call but couldn't go into details over the phone." Suddenly Neal remembered the detective saying, "Until we get this case solved, we will be getting back with you for more questions." Knock, knock, knock, Neal jumped from the unexpected knocking on the door. "Yes," Sevella peeped in and then slowly walked in, asking, "What did the detective say; is it bad news, or was Naomi found, and is she okay?" Before speaking, Neal slowly stood and walked passed Sevella, hoping when he spoke, he would sound convincing. "Well… apparently, they have some information, but they couldn't go into details over the phone. Why did they bother to call if they couldn't talk to me? Oh, by the way, did the receptionist get with you?" Sevella turned quickly to catch up with Neal, breathlessly responding, "No, she didn't."

Suddenly, Neal stopped, causing Sevella to bump into him; Neal strumbled forward, Sevella grabbed the back of his arm to steady him; at the same time, Neal was taking Sevella by the arm and pulling her back into the office. "What did you say? I told her to get with you immediately! Now you are telling me nothing has been prepared!" As Sevella pulled her arm from Neal's grip, she motioned toward the lobby, saying, "Your client was in the Lobby, but Kathy has shown him into the conference room. You go ahead while I get the coffee. By the way, I had to rush, but everything has been prepared." Neal suddenly went from looking very disturbed to very pleased as he rushed toward the conference room. As Sevella poured the coffee into its container, she couldn't help but wonder, "Why was Neal looking so disturbed, and what on earth did he mean by 'they couldn't go into details over the phone?' Well, I guess I'll find out soon enough." Sevella then rushed into the conference room, only to discover that no one was there. Apparently, Neal invited their guest into his office. She then poured herself a cup of coffee and breathed a sigh of relief while taking a quick sip before taking her seat.

Great Minds Think Alike

"Moreover," Neal continued while directing their client toward the Conference room, "I have an efficient and very professional executive that will be working alongside you; oh, here she is, Sevella Thorn, my Executive Assistant Edward Kingsley, our new client." Standing to shake his hand, speaking silently, "So, the new client's first name is Edward." The meeting is underway, and Neal has the floor. Before the presentation was over, another person walked into the conference room and sat next to Mr. Kingsley. During Neal's presentation, Sevella was giving Mr. Kingsley the once over, thinking to herself, *Mr. Kingsley appeared to be engulfed with the documents during Neal's presentation, a clear indication he was interested in details and wanted to be well informed of this new venture. Unlike Ellor, he was looking to impress or put on a show while actually deceiving his potential investors. I think this Mr. Kingsley is serious and a man of real integrity, a business owner looking to implement change and growth into his new business.* In that moment, Neal instructed Mr. Kingsley to take over the meeting.

"Equally important," stated Mr. Kingsley while turning to introduce his assistant, "Mr. Nest and Miss Thorn, this is Miss Leia Allen. She is our director of Human Resources, and I think she has a keen sense of judgment." Afterward, he began to explain his company's expectations, "During all of my interviews, I make it a point to discuss with future clients and employees the importance of I.H.E.E—Integrity, Honesty, Experience, and Expertise, which are cornerstones beneath our youthful company. In addition to," now standing, but before Mr. Kingsley could continue his sentence, Neal being true to his nature, impatient and impolite, stood announcing his own goals and aspirations, "What do you know, Miss Thorn and I had a similar discussion before your arrival. Also, I have just promoted her to my executive administrative assistant; what do you know? As the old saying goes, 'Great minds do think alike.' I suggest, in the interest of both companies, that Miss Thorn assist Miss Allen in the infrastructure and planning of Future Investors, Inc." Mr. Kingsley graciously agreed to Neal's suggestion, and immediately all focus was on the PowerPoint.

At the completion of the meeting, and just before signing the documents, Neal took liberty to introduce to Mr. Kingsley the prospect of a modeling agency as an avenue to bring more revenue into both businesses. He went on to say, "Investors are the infrastructure and gut of both businesses, but let's just think outside the box: what if, other than our investors, a new source of revenue was possible, a very lucrative source? In other words…" Sevella quickly intervened, asking, "Will this idea of modeling, or a new source of revenue, have the same impact as the long and short-term goals, vision, and mission as New Ventures, LLC., and Future Investors Incorporation; or will both businesses have to reinvent themselves in order to conform to this new modeling venture?" Neal completely ignored Sevella's question, turning to Mr. Kingsley and insisting he responded. Before responding, Mr.

Kingsley turned, looking intensely toward Sevella, "Excellent question, Miss Thorn, and I would also like to know how the idea of a modeling industry could possibly become a much more lucrative source."

An Unexpected Reminder

Meanwhile, Mr. Kingsley and Miss Allen had their heads together as Neal prepared to respond to Mr. Kingsley's question, but at that moment, Mr. Kingsley whispered to Miss Allen as she began to take notes. Neal nervously began to loosen his tie, picked up his coffee cup, and took a sip before starting his speech. On several occasions, Miss Allen looks in Neal's direction, only to resume her note-taking. In the meantime, Neal raised his coffee cup momentarily and paused in mid-air; after observing Mr. Kingsley and Miss Allen's demander, Neal finally took a quick sip of his coffee. At the same time, Sevella was once again distracted, reflecting on the first meeting in that conference room, "Sold to the Highest Bidder," the words sounded like a trumpet in her mind, so much so that Sevella suddenly jumped forward in her seat; with that sudden movement, every eye is now on her. Thinking fast, she raised her hand, saying apologetically, "Please excuse my reaction, but, Neal, you never responded or answered my question regarding the connection between a modeling agency, New Business Ventures, and Future Investors Incorporation's vision."

Due to that direct question, Miss Allen and Mr. Kingsley turned from Sevella and looked questionably in Neal's direction. Now thinking to herself, *Oh my, that night in Florida! What an embarrassing and unexpected reminder!* In addition to Sevella's unexpected response, she hoped that she didn't appear too ridiculous to their very distinguished clients. While all eyes were on Neal, her nerves subsided; therefore, she took a deep breath while seriously hoping this trip to Florida would not be a repeat of the first. As her thoughts slowly gravitated to that incident, she was again distracted. Sevella silently scolded herself in order to focus, thinking, *I need to focus, just in case Neal needs me to answer questions, or better still, rebuke me for putting him on the spot.* Next, an unexpected feeling of excitement replaced her obvious nervousness as she began to focus on the meeting, silently rehearsing the words, "I will soon be the boss."

Understandably apprehensive at the sheer thought of returning to Florida under any circumstance, she was determined to keep her focus on Neal, although it wasn't easy. Meanwhile, Neal has made several attempts to convince himself, as well as Mr. Kingsley, of the Modeling Venture. In the meantime, a nagging feeling of fear arose as Sevella became completely distracted, thinking, *Is this another one of Neal's games, and I'm once again a pawn on the game board? Apparently, Mr. Kingsley was not just any businessman, and Neal wouldn't dare risk offending such a distinguished business partner as Mr. Kingsley.* Occasionally pulling on his tie, Neal's tone slightly changes from firm to a humorous pitch as he attempts to explain his modeling theory. "This plan, I assure everyone, will be very beneficial for New Business Venture and New Investors Incorporation. Let me further share that; the first time I laid eyes on Sevella, I wondered why she was answering my advertisement. I actually thought she was an aspiring model looking to moonlight for extra money."

Another Florida Investor

Not only did Neal appear uneasy but he was also lost for words. Quickly taking a sip of coffee before continuing, "However, from that day to this, I've been brainstorming and researching the modeling industry, and I know a good business opportunity when I see one, and I believe the modeling industry is a good business opportunity." In that moment, Sevella is feeling very confident after receiving such an indirect compliment, and again, in deep thought, *I have never received so many compliments ever!* Neal continued, "After working with her these last nine years, I've discovered her efficiency as a turnkey employee. My original idea; you see, I plan on making her overseer of my modeling agency." Caught totally off guard, Sevella responded, "What?" Neal ignored her response, "Most importantly," Neal continued, now sounding very confident, "Even though I haven't officially discussed this idea with her, at the time I came up with this idea, I was implementing this concept to bring more money into the company in order to increase her wages." Now turning to Sevella, "All the times you hinted at a raise, I was thinking of ways to make it possible."

Shortly after that surprising display of goodwill, Neal directed his attention to Mr. Kingsley. "I did my homework and ran a background check on her; not only was she clean, but she was the right person to entrust with running the office. Speaking of investors. Our first client, Ellor Charmen, after working with Sevella and observing her office skills, gave her his approval.

Furthermore, he suggested that Sevella helps with their startup for his new office in France. Of course, I didn't agree right away, only later agreeing to let her help them get through the first two weeks. Mr. Charmen immediately made a very generous offer that I could not resist. So, you see, this is not Sevella's first business assignment, and may I add, the first was in Florida with this same investor and, of course, turned out very, very successful." Momentarily taking a sip of his cold coffee before continuing, "On the other hand, I think Sevella has her own success story regarding her first trip. Isn't that right, Sevella?" Distracted by her own thoughts, Sevella was hearing all of this for the first time and wondered why Neal never discussed any of these planes with her, especially on another solo trip to Florida.

"In addition," Neal was going non-stop, "I just recently learned of Sevella's legal knowledge, so I'm convinced that no matter what we throw her way, she can handle it." Sevella knew he was referring to the earlier conversation regarding their agreement in writing and was surprised that he brought it up in the meeting. Neal continued, "I believed with all the hard work and the hosting of many investors' meetings; she has proven to be the excellent executive assistant I know her to be, just like I know this idea for a modeling agency will be just as successful, and beneficial to everyone in this meeting." Immediately, Neal turns to Sevella, "From this point on, and as my new executive assistant, when you travel to Florida to assist Mr. Kingsley or out of the country, you will have an assistant assigned to help you." Panic-stricken, she was suddenly frightened, speaking silently, "No, not another

Florida investor! Is Neal determined to put me in danger a second time? Do I have to spell out every sordid detail for him and say that it's all his fault?"

Robbed of My Innocence

As quickly as the thought came, she dismissed it, saying to herself, *No way! I can never tell him or anyone else involved in this company. Surely, as soon as I do, there will be a domino effect until everything is uncovered!* Once Neal completed his speech, Mr. Kingsley signaled to Miss Allen, and she opened the briefcase and took out the contract, gave it to Mr. Kingsley, and he carefully turned one page after the other, signing his signature before passing it down to Neal. Sevella silently sighed, thinking, *Here we go again.* After the meeting, Neal insisted that Sevella take a taxi home and charge it to the company's account. As Sevella reflected on Neal's unexpected compliments, she couldn't recall ever receiving so many from anyone. *But again*, she thought to herself, *Neal is a charmer and very good at getting his way.* As she settled into the back seat of the taxi, she decided to dismiss the troubling thoughts and welcomed the idea of being an Executive as she considered silently, *No longer will I have to sneak around like a thief when coming from those late investors' meeting or parties. Or will I?*

Now considering the For Sale sign that hung on her front gate, "Oh, no! I still need to keep a low profile to avoid being found out, even more so since abandoning Samuel. Being discovered as the mother who abandons her child would ruin everything; therefore, I must make sure no one will ever tie me to Samuel." Sevella sat up, looking at the taxi driver, realizing that he wasn't her regular driver, and she had given him her address. Thinking fast, at the last minute, she instructed him to drop her off at the address a block from her home. At the same time, sighing a sigh of relief, thinking, *That was close.* She then remembered her lifestyle before the attack and how living in the shadows was to prevent her neighbors from seeing her on a regular basis, especially late at night after an investors' meeting. She began to make comparison, "Before the attack, I lived a double life, hoping to avoid appearing scandalous; while slipping out later in the evening to catch a taxi or arriving in the early morning hours after an extended meeting. The only difference is that I was innocent then, but not now. Especially since that horrible, horrible man robbed me of my innocence, now everything is scandalous. Still, it is not what it appears to be. He could easily accuse me of being a liar or, even worse, paint me shady and completely ruin my life."

After a while, Sevella became aware of the taxi as he drove down the quiet neighborhood streets. She also realized that it had been almost three weeks since she last saw Samuel. In an instant, she sat up in her seat, whispering, "Oh my, what could have happened to him? One minute he is with them, and the next, he is not!" Furthermore, as she settled back into her seat, she realized that she still doubted Neal's work ethic as she remembered him saying, "I thought she was involved in modeling." Then she said audibly, "Really." Now turning slightly, the cab driver responded, "Excuse me." Now waving her hands, Sevella apologized for again thinking out loud. At that point, the taxi was pulling up to her stop; Sevella quickly and quietly walked behind the high shrubbery, her head down, counting every line on the sidewalk. Suddenly experiencing a relaxed but somewhat annoying feeling as she finally walked through her front gate; before unlocking her door, she looked over her shoulder at the house across the street.

Just a Hoax

Moreover, with the new position and all the praises coming from Neal, even then, Sevella began to doubt his intention, "I expect to oversee, instead of hosting the meetings. Also, as executive, I will assign that position to my male assistant if necessary. As frustration replaced the calmness, Sevella whispered, "Something has to change! I know Neal, and I know for a fact this whole idea of a promotion is just a hoax." As she slowly turned to look behind her, she noticed the street light shining through the slightly opened blinds. Sevella sat on the couch, looking toward the home across the street as she looked from one dark window to another, wondering, *What has happened to Samuel?* The next morning was another long day of training and conference calls. Sevella was once again being careful to be dropped off a block from her home, and as usual, she would walk in the shadows to keep out of the light. Once inside her home, she was again so thankful for the shrubbery that hid her and kept her out of sight.

However, on this particular night, although exhausted, her growling stomach insisted on having her favorite food, a homemade hamburger. After her meal, she crawled into her bed; laid back on the pillow; as a habit, she would glance over to the wall where Samuel's crib once sat, except for that night. As the excitement filled her heart, she slowly closed her eyes, imagining what it would be like as "the boss," she whispered, finally dosing off to sleep. The following day, the office atmosphere was quite different. As the new Temp, Dorothy navigated calls, set appointments, arranged for meetings, and efficaciously navigated her way throughout the office. In spite of the change of atmosphere, Sevella sensed an eeriness that she could not shake. Startled by Dorothy's announcement, "Miss Thorn, you have a call on line four," Sevella slowly picked up the receiver just as Dorothy walked into her office with an arm full of files. Determined not to be overwhelmed, Sevella remembered all the proofing and typing her foster mom taught her and decided, "No matter what, I have to perform the duties of an executive secretary. I can't buckle under, not now."

Occasionally, with the new schedule, Sevella had little time for anything else, no room for a break, lunch, or otherwise. Except for filling in for Dorothy or Kathy, Sevella would grab a quick snack before tackling the next assignment. While sitting at the receptionist's desk, she questioned herself audibly, asking, "What has changed? Why haven't I seen Samuel in public since that early morning?" Before completing her sentence, the phone rang. She quickly answered, "Yes, New Ventures. How may I help you?" She didn't hear the response because she was thinking to herself, *I barely have time to watch for Samuel, and not only is Neal expecting me to be Executive but still serve both morning and evening meetings.* Suddenly she was made aware of the receiver in her hand and quickly answered, "Hello, are you there?" But there was no answer. "Man, I've got to get it together! Samuel is fine, but I am not; plus, I have to remember to remain focused, and I can't let anything distract me from exceeding Neal's expectation of me and this new position."

Unpleasant Advances

Once again filling in for Kathy, Sevella listened as the phone lines lit up, ringing in the distance, and then Dorothy's voice, "Hello, New Ventures! How may I help you?" First, the background noise and finally a click. "Hello, is anyone there?" Dorothy then calls into Kathy's office. "Yes, Dorothy," responded Sevella. "I think there may be a problem because someone continues to call but never answers." Noticing the itinerary on Kathy's financial report, Sevella was now focused on a possible trip out of the State; "Great, Neal once again failed to discuss with me these travel plans." Still waiting for a response from Sevella, Dorothy Continued, "Miss Thorn, did you hear me?" Picking up the financial report, noticing the consistency of her travel schedule almost every other month. Sevella suddenly realized Dorothy was speaking to her. "No problem, Dorothy, it happens all the time," she said while thinking, *Again, I should have negotiated my raise instead of settling for what Neal offered.* Suddenly she was becoming breathless; she began to speak jokingly in order to calm herself, "Neal mentioned a raise but conveniently forgot to mention how much. Besides that, I should now be a partner in the firm."

Now, fighting back tears, gazing at her reflection from the glass desktop, she reflected, *I've helped Neal build this company from the ground up, not to mention putting up with all the unpleasant advances during those investors' meetings.* Shortly afterward, she remembered the missed call while sitting at Dorothy's desk, now feeling worried. "What did that person hear? I was talking about Samuel. I wasn't speaking audibly. Or was I?" Sevella became tensed as she considered the outcome of those mysterious phone calls, first to her, then to Dorothy. In addition to that, Sevella decided that her safety would be first priority, and Neal's company was second to that. She began to speak audibly, saying, "First, I'll start by asking lots of questions, getting names of all clients, and being very aggressive when responding to any sexual advances. From now on, I have to be aware of my surrounding at all times." As a result of her background in foster care, she learned the hard way to look out for her own safety.

In that moment, she turned and looked toward the large office window, noticing the lateness of the day. Again, speaking to her image on the desktop, "Since the first trip to Florida, I am more aware of what can take place during and after those investors' meetings. I must protect myself at any cost." Now attempting to focus but failing miserably, she continued, "Furthermore, if anyone ever finds out about Samuel, my name will be mud." Now feeling very confident, "If it ever comes to that, I will defend my honor and eventually get that rapist placed behind bars." Surprisingly, the thought pleased her as she smiled, staring at her reflection, whispering, "If I am found out, he will not go unpunished." Finally, the urgent ringing startled Sevella as Dorothy announced, "Miss Thorn, you have a call on line two." Quickly answering, only to hear Neal asking, "What's going on?" sounding very excited. "It seems as though, ever since I got off the plane, my phone has not stopped ringing, one client after the other calling, and all good news! Anyway, I'll be returning tomorrow. I'll see you then."

One Night of Horror

At the end of her conversation with Neal, Sevella slowly put down the receiver, still looking at her image on the desktop, smiling as she spoke, "Now I realized that it was not someone hanging up, but Neal. Still, I was speaking when sitting at Dorothy's desk. I wish I could remember what I said." After making it home, Sevella sat on the couch staring at the house across the street, hoping that Samuel was in the home, safe and loved. She continued watching as she thought bitterly of that one night of horror. That one night changed the entire course of her life. Now feeling too tired to be angry, she quickly fell into a deep sleep. The next morning, Sevella was feeling very relaxed but cramped after falling asleep on the couch. She sat up, stretched as she spoke aloud, "Finally, for the first time in my life, I feel as though I really belong! From the time I left Samuel on my neighbor's steps up until the agreement with Neal, I have lived in a trance, surrounded by a very dark cloud, but now I have a real smile on my face, and it feels very, very natural. My home, oh my, those words sound unreal, my home. Will Neal really keep his word and sell me this house? I must be positive and believe this is my home, thanks to Neal applying a portion of my wages toward its purchase."

Now feeling very safe and happy, she jumped up from the couch and slowly walked through the home as if seeing it for the first time. She walked from room to room, experiencing delight and pleasure that she never knew existed. Moreover, for the first time in her life, she felt more secure than ever before; as she prepared for work, her level of confidence was at an all-time high. At that moment, Sevella felt she had finally arrived at a place of security and happiness that no one could take away. She slowly went through her closet, looking for the outfit that had boss written all over it, glancing from outfit to outfit, occasionally turning and glancing at the wall clock, at the same time keeping in mind her new hours and new position. It was then she remembered the handbag she had recently purchased. After looking from top to bottom in her closet, she couldn't find it. All of a sudden, she remembered her storage. Rushing out of the backdoor to the storage, she flung open the door and continued to look for the new handbag, thinking, *A future of success and growth, and I know a secure and brighter future is ahead! No matter what my past has been, my life will never again be filled with uncertainty and regret.*

Nevertheless, her moment of joy was short-lived as anger filled her heart, and the memory of that night in Florida began to invade her happy thoughts. Now, the feeling of fear began to surface, and the first thing that fell on the floor was a handbag. Only it was not the new bag, but the bag that was stolen in Florida. Ignoring the bag, she continued to search for the new bag. Between the previous thoughts of that night and the bag that was stolen, without thinking twice, she grabbed the handbag from the floor and threw it into the garbage; her voice could be heard from next door as she threw the bag, saying, "The past should stay in the past!" After slamming down the lid and closing the garbage, she decided to take the garbage to the alley. She wondered if she was throwing away something of value. *No way*, she thought, *There is nothing in that bag that I want or even desire to keep. The bag and everything in it belong in the garbage. I will no longer hold on to the past. I must move forward!*

Love One, Hate the Other

Momentarily staring at the covered garbage can, eventually swiping her hands together as if wiping off dirt, she turned slowly, still staring at the garbage can. She suddenly remembered storing a large box of newly bought items to make room for Samuel's crib. Quickly she went back to the storage, removed the box that held the new bag, opened the lid, and was pleasantly surprised to see her new handbag and the new briefcase. She had completely forgotten about the new briefcase, now speaking in a more cheerful tone, "In the midst of all the chaos, something as simple as a new handbag and briefcase gives me comfort. How can something so insignificant bring so much joy? I once thought buying this briefcase was a waste of money, but at the same time, I hoped that I would someday have use it on a very special day and a day that would call for a celebration. Hello, now, as it happens, it appears to me that the money I spent on this case turned out to be a wise investment because that day of celebration is today!" As Sevella prepared to close the storage door, she noticed a box with something written on it. She looked at the box's covering and noticed the words "Trash, trash, trash." Curious, she opened the box only to see the dress that was torn off her the night of the attack.

Strangely, at that time, she didn't want to throw it away for fear of someone tracing it back to her. Meanwhile, she became deep in thought, so much so that chills caused the hair to stand on her arms. After arriving home from that first trip and unpacking her suitcase, the first piece of clothing was the dress. Therefore, she decided to keep it for evidence. She began to cry, speaking silently, "here is all the evidence I need, as she opened the box to examine the contents, which included the accessories she wore to the investors' meeting. She angrily grabbed the box and literally yelled at herself, saying, "Forget the evidence! Why on earth didn't you just trash it!?" She quickly closed the box and carried it out to the garbage. Afterward, she walked slowly back to the storage to get the box holding the bag and briefcase. Despite the nagging fear and the impulse to run away and hide, Sevella stood for several minutes in a trance, slowly placing the box on the floor. It was then she realized that she was standing near the place of Samuel's crib.

It was then, Sevella's anger turned into confusion. As her heart ached and tears began to fill her eyes, suddenly, she longed to hold Samuel. At the same time, her hatred for her attacker intensified; at that moment, all she really wanted was to hunt her attacker down and inflict pain upon him. "How ironic, love one and hate the other. How can I have these feelings? A desperate love for Samuel, on one hand, desperately hating that man on the other." She then remembered running across the street, placing Samuel on her neighbor's doorstep, then running away like a thief looking for a hiding place. Not realizing, from that day forward, Samuel would become her primary focus. Now vigorously shaking, "I am determined to move past the second most horrible day in my life! Get a grip; giving up Samuel was the right thing to do."

Hiding in the Shadows

Contrary to her belief, Sevella was stuck in her present situation. "As confusing as it may be, I have a right to hate that wicked, evil man who changed my life for the worst. I hate him, I hate him, and I hate Neal for not caring enough to protect me! Thanks to Neal, I will never be the same since that horrible night." Sevella cried out as she flung herself on the bed, sobbing uncontrollably. After scolding herself for being such a baby, she stood, turning and speaking to her image in the mirror, "Now It's time for you to move forward; I know Samuel is loved and safe, and I am starting a new life, a new position. Furthermore, I will soon assist Mr. Kingsley in his new company; I will no longer be a pawn, trophy, or just an employee; from now on, I am the boss! How I would love to share this news with Sam. That's it; that's exactly what I'll do! I'll contact her, take her out, and we can celebrate." As soon as Sevella spoke those words, she then became very sad because she had ignored every call from Sam and hadn't made any attempt to contact her. Now speaking to her image, "It is still too soon; I'll give it more time because my life is chaotic enough without me having to explain Samuel's disappearance."

In spite of her fears, Sevella agreed to accept her travel arrangements and future trips to Florida, even if it meant hiding in the shadows as much as possible. "I must reinforce our verbal agreement in regards to my new position and make sure Neal incorporates my demands by putting everything we agreed upon in writing." It was at that moment that she could see in the mirror the space where Samuel's crib once occupied. Suddenly her thoughts went back to Sam as she recalled the day Samuel was born and how Sam helped her with everything. "Of all people to be avoiding, Sam should not be one of them," still staring at her image in the mirror. She also knew that Sam would have questions about Samuel. "I cannot truthfully answer her questions," Sevella whispered as she looked away from the mirror toward the empty space and again to her image as she questioned herself, *So you believe that avoiding Sam is the only way to avoid answering those questions? Yes, I do, and I'm right, but I still miss Sam, and I really need to talk to her and see how she is doing.*

As it would happen almost two weeks later, while waiting for Neal to call, Sevella carefully looked over her to-do list for Kathy and Dorothy when her cell phone rang. Without checking the caller ID, she quickly answered, "Yes, Neal." There was silence on the other end and then a very familiar voice, "Sevella!" Shocked, and much to her surprise, it was Sam. Speechless, her brain was frozen, but Sam ignored the silence. "HELLO!" Sam shouted again as if talking to Jack. In that moment, Sevella began to smile and was glad to hear Sam's voice; it was as though they had never stopped talking. Therefore, she responded, sounding just as excited, "Oh, Sam, how are you?" A moment of silence seemed like an eternity. In the meantime, Sevella prepared herself for the worst. "Hello… Sevella," said Sam hesitantly; this time, Sevella could sense the uncertainty in Sam's voice, "I have been trying and trying to get back in touch with you; boy, you are hard to keep up with. Sevella, the reason I called is to find out if you would go out and celebrate with me?"

Saved by the Excitement

After a long pause, Sevella tried to think ahead, but fear left her speechless. Sam ignored the silence and continued, "I've been promoted to Assistant Manager, and I couldn't think of anyone other than you to help me celebrate this great day! Are you available?" Unable to think of an excuse, Sevella finally answered, "Sure, I would love to celebrate your success!" In that moment, the chatter and laughter started as they proceeded to make plans to meet while reminiscing over old times, eventually setting the date, selecting the place, and time to meet. Afterward, Sevella held her breath; she knew what was next. Still feeling apprehensive, assuming Sam was waiting to get the planning out of the way before asking about Samuel, Sevella literally held her breath. Finally, they were saying goodbye, but before hanging up, Sevella excitedly congratulated Sam for her accomplishment as the diner's new manager and breathed a sigh of relief that there was no mention, nothing about Samuel.

In the past, her accomplishments would have been celebrated alone side Sam's, but Sevella purposely avoided discussing her own promotion just to avoid bringing any attention to herself. Unconsciously standing when answering the call, Sevella is now falling back into her chair, speaking to herself, *I was literally holding my breath, literally, thank goodness I was spared. Thank goodness I was saved by Sam's excitement. Oh, my, I couldn't wait to hang up that phone. I wondered if I appeared too anxious or too hasty when saying goodbye. Never mind that I've escaped her questions for now, and I know what I have to do to be prepared for the celebration.* After a moment of silence, Sevella looks down at her phone, saying, "I can't believe my luck! In her excitement, Sam must have forgotten about the baby." Just as she placed the phone on her desk, Dorothy called in, announcing, "Mr. Nest is on line one." Jumping, Sevella quickly answered and listened intently as Neal went down his list of instructions. Once she received his approval on Kathy and Dorothy's new schedule for the evening, Neal abruptly hung up.

Agitated, she whispered, "So rude!" Again, her focus was on Sam. "I know Sam, and she is probably thinking I'll bring the baby with me." Once again, fear struck her heart as she spoke out loud, "I have the opportunity to share this very special day with my very special friend, but I don't want to chance 20 questions; that's the very reason I have avoided contacting her. Suddenly she thought, *I know, I can cancel by explaining to her that my boss has also promoted me.* With a slap on her thigh, and very frustrated with herself for accepting the invitation. Therefore, she decided to keep the appointment but somehow explained that her work causes her to travel extensively, and a very dear friend of the family is keeping Samuel until the new schedule is more manageable. One evening after a very hectic week, once home, Sevella settled on the couch in preparation to see Samuel; she opened the curtains and then the blinds to wait but quickly fell asleep. Sevella dreamed of her first meeting with Ellor the night before her first trip. Sevella remembered the conversation ended with Ellor's signature on the contract and finalized with a check.

First Meeting

In turn, Ellor began, but Sevella was deft to his words, and all she could think about was Neal leaving the meeting. Meanwhile, Ellor continued while winking at her before announcing, "Sevella, this moment is what we've worked so hard for." As Sevella watched in shock, confused and overwhelmed, she was unable to concentrate on Ellor or what he was saying. Suddenly interrupting Ellor, asking, "Where is he going?" In that same moment, Neal stuck his head in the door and announced happily, "Business is booming; this is our ticket to success!" "On the contrary," said Sevella, thinking to herself, *I am the one with the ticket to Florida.* Furious at his lack of concern for her safety, she turned to face Ellor and his assistant, thinking, *Not to mention his lack of business etiquette, walking out on his VIP in the middle of a very important meeting. More so, failing to inform me of the people I would be working and traveling with.* Feeling very angry, she had to fight to hold back the tears, determined to hold it together. At the same time, she pretended to be excited by putting on a brave face before attempting to make her speech.

The first thing she noticed was a very wide grin on Ellor's face. *I wonder*, she thought, *have I been sold to the highest bidder?* As her own words gripped her heart, she noticed an uncertain look on Ellor's face. Now speaking excitedly, "Yes, business is booming!" She repeated those words even though she had no idea what they meant. At that moment, the door to the conference room opened, and Neal was once again peeping in, agreeing with her remarks, which he overheard before opening the door. Neal then smiled, saying, "Hey, who would have thought ten years ago asking you to assist me as a receptionist would land us a successful investment business? For example," now stepping inside the conference room, he continued, "it didn't matter whether or not you could type; it was your commitment to learning, that's why I kept you on. In fact, and it may surprise you to hear me say this, I was still looking for someone with executive qualifications to replace you. Strange as it may seem, it was your executive skills that paved the way to our success!" Shortly afterward, Naomi was now announcing an incoming call for Neal, and quickly he was gone.

Silently crying within, Sevella watched the door close again; this time, it appeared everything was moving in slow motion, even Ellor's mouth. Her inner voice screamed, *He never really treated me as his employee; anything but a proficient, capable employee! Now more than ever, I believe that he is aware of his so-called client's sexual advances toward me. I never complained I did nothing, and I said nothing because I feared losing my job!* Sitting quietly while speaking to herself as she stared at Ellor's mouth, but listening to her own thoughts, "Neal really doesn't know that I can actually type sixty words a minute." Moreover, her thoughts went back to a certain time in foster care, "Thanks to my foster mother; she would always have me assist her with proofing, correcting, and later typing her legal documents. Afterward, my foster mom would go to bed, leaving me to finish up. Sometimes it would take me all night, even though I had to get up early the next morning for school. I remember her saying to me, 'My boss expects nothing but excellency; therefore, Sevella, I expect no less from you.'"

Waking Up to Reality

At that moment, Ellor was speaking to her, but she was still not listening; it was then that Sevella suddenly felt a wave of panic as she sat frozen in her seat, "Am I losing my mind?" Ellor noticed that Sevella was looking at him but wasn't speaking. "Is everything alright? Are you okay, Miss Thorn?" Now looking down at her notes, saying, "Yes, yes, I'm so sorry. I guess I was expecting Neal to peep in again, plus all of this is happening so fast." Momentarily studying Sevella's facial expression, Ellor then repeated himself, "I hope you will enjoy working with me as much as you have with Neal." Sevella was shocked at the words "work with." Now looking from Ellor to her note pad she searched for a calm way to ask, "What on earth do you mean 'work with,' have I been fired?" Again the words "sold to the highest bidder" took over her thoughts. Once again, she fought back the tears, along with the impulse to run from the room. Regaining her composure, she looked at Ellor, nodding and motioning for him to continue. Ellor, smiling reassuringly, nodded back before explaining, "No, my dear, you are not fired, but this is your opportunity for an advancement."

"To begin with," stated Sevella, but stopped abruptly as Ellor interrupted, saying, "Now listen carefully. I will be leaving tonight for a very important meeting, but everything has been taken care of. Neal has received your payment in advance." In that instance, Sevella silently began to angrily scream at Ellor, "So, you've paid in advance for me?" Once again, Sevella was completely ignoring Ellor as he was saying, "Also, you will receive a salary for your time spent in Florida, or should I say, paid handsomely for this trip. Are you ready to fly the friendly skies?" Hearing the word "friendly" caused Sevella to focus as she repeated, "Flying the friendly skies?" as she repeated those words, the sound of her voice awakened her; heart racing, Sevella slowly sat up, holding her face in the palm of her hands; shaking her head from left to right, seriously hoping it was a dream. Slowly and carefully, she placed one leg at a time from the couch to the floor while awkwardly staring at the floor. Afterward, slowly she stood and whispered, "If I don't get enough sleep, I'm going to have bags underneath my eyes, and Neal will certainly notice."

Right after regaining her composure, she sat staring at her shaking hands. Finally, she was able to get dressed for bed, realizing that she had been dreaming but waking up to the reality of what had happened in Florida. Now feeling emotionally tired, she laid her head on the pillow, eventually drifting off to sleep, only to dream again of that horrible night in Florida. Following another late investors' meeting, Sevella sitting alone in her hotel room speaking to her image in the mirror, saying, "Ellor and Neal are so much alike when it comes to money, both would have me host the meeting and serve their weird guest; although I must admit not all are like that, the few there are should be escorted out by security, ASAP!" In addition to the reoccurring dream, Sevella was waking up every fifteen minutes but didn't realize it. Each time she closed her eyes, the dream would reoccur. As she sat on the plane, looking out of the window, she noticed the runway getting smaller and smaller as the plane climbed higher and higher into the sky. Finally, gliding upward, higher and higher, until they were surrounded by clouds that seemed to cover the wings.

From Florida to Boston

Meanwhile, Sevella was tossing and turning in her sleep as she began to scold herself, *Look at me. I'm not the same person. My old life wasn't appreciated, and now I have only uncertainty to look forward to.* As she slowly opened her eyes, she sat up, but out of sheer exhaustion, she began to slowly drift off to sleep, now hearing the flight attendants announcing their arrival to Boston. Sevella then looked out over the very tall buildings that adorned Boston's crowded city, and it was then that she realized from that moment on her life would be a living nightmare. While exiting the plane, she slowly took in the view of the airport, noticing all the people rushing and moving quickly through the airport, but she appeared to be moving in slow motion. Momentarily glancing behind her, and again from side to side, wondering if that man, her attacker was somewhere in the crowd, even worse, on the same plane also traveling from Florida to Boston.

Now parked in front of her home, the neighborhood seemed so very strange and unfamiliar. The joy that once filled her heart was now replaced with regret. Walking from the taxi up her steps, her place appeared so very small compared to the lavish hotel. She looked over her shoulders toward the home across the street, something she promised herself she would never do again. Ring, ring, ring!!! Startled at the sound of her alarm clock Sevella sat straight up in her bed, glancing quickly from side to side only to see her reflection in the mirror, clasping her hands over her chest as a wave of relief filled her heart. "Oh my goodness! I was dreaming again, having that same awful nightmare of leaving Florida after the attack." At that moment, Sevella had to look around her home and make sure she wasn't still on the plane or, worse off, still in Florida. "That dream was so real," said Sevella, still unsure of her surroundings as she carefully looked around her bedroom. Finally, she took a deep breath; sat up slowly on the bed, feeling groggy as if she had drunk the mixture her attacker forced her to drink.

Eventually, she frantically gazed around her bedroom, convincing herself that she was safe in her home but still unable to make sense of it all. Sevella began speaking in a very low tone as if she could be heard by outsiders, "I wonder if these reoccurring, very vivid dreams of that horrible night are a result of the meeting and my trip back to Florida?" Now feeling very tired, she quickly glanced at the clock, thinking she must surely have overslept, but the time was only 3 a.m. At that moment, Sevella realized the reality of the dream had shaken her to the depth of her soul. Now she asked, "Why did I have to relive that first trip, strange as it was, I only dreamed of going and returning, but not of the horrible attack on my life?" She then placed both feet on the floor, again sitting on the side of the bed while speaking to her image in the mirror, "I wonder, will I ever be able to get past that horrible night?" Deep down inside, she knew that whether awake or asleep, her thoughts would always be on that night.

First Trip as Executive

Equally excited to take her first trip as Executive, by the same token, it was terrifying because she was once again alone on her second trip to Florida. Briefly taking in her surroundings, she settled in her seat, but this time with their new client, Mr. Edward Kingsley. Upon their arrival to Florida, Sevella was given an office as Mr. Kingsley's second assistant, assisted by Peggy Pleasant, her assistant secretary. Speaking silently, *Just as Neal had promised, but now that I think of it, this is probably Mr. Kingsley's idea. In* spite of her uneasiness, the first week in the office was hectic but not overwhelming. During the second week, after setting up the projector and arranging the PowerPoint, Sevella whispered to herself, "Unlike the first trip with Ellor, and much to my surprise, this trip with Mr. Kingsley is all business." As Sevella surveyed the conference room, she spoke cheerfully and audibly, "I am actually engaged with the running of this company! I'm completely amazed that Neal hasn't called to check up on me. On the other hand, he's probably directing all calls to Mr. Kingsley."

Momentarily distracted by her PowerPoint Presentation before reflecting back on Neal's arrangement with Ellor, "All the while I assisted Ellor, Neal communicated more with Ellor than me. No doubt, it's Mr. Kingsley whose running things, and I have no doubt he will keep me informed of his transactions with Neal. Mr. Kingsley has treated me as an executive on every occasion. He escorts me to the evening investors' meetings, just in case he needs documents. Also, my assistant and I are seated next to him at every meeting. Instead of being handled by clients, expecting more than copies. On the contrary, Mr. Kingsley orders dinner after the meeting while my assistant and I look over signed contracts," said Sevella as her lips shaped into a smile. She secretly hoped Mr. Kingsley could be her permanent employer. Meanwhile, days turned into weeks, and now it was time to close out the last meeting before heading back to Boston.

After she completed her packing, Sevella realized that she did not at all feel tired or disappointed, "I'm looking forward to the next business day because I am too excited to sleep," she said as she lay awake, imagining what it would be like to work for Mr. Kingsley as his Executive and living in Florida. Soon after saying the word "Florida," her imagination was once again on her attacker as she spoke audibly and angrily, "Never again, I can't let my guard down no matter what. I must stay alert!" Therefore, raising up one arm, she glanced toward the hotel's window as her joy quickly turned into regret realizing that Samuel was living proof of her attacker and that horrible night. Soon after, she slowly laid back on her pillow, but she knew that sleep at this point wasn't going to happen. Therefore, she decided to get up and go over notes, hoping she could get some sleep on the plane; instead, while proofing the document, she soon began to nod, finally laying her head on both arms before falling into a deep sleep. Next, she was awakened by her phone ringing. "Hello, yes, Ms. Pleasant, no problem. I was just sitting and going over notes. Yes, and thank you for the reminder. I'll see you in the morning."

Laughed Out Loud

The following day was hectic as she prepared to head back to Boston, but before leaving, Mr. Kingsley called for a meeting with Peggy and Sevella giving both a basket of fruits and chocolates. Finally, Sevella was on the plane and headed home; after arriving at Boston airport and getting into the taxi, Sevella repeated, "The boss!" Over and over until her thoughts were interrupted by the taxi pulling up in front of her home. She climbed out of the taxi only to notice a baby stroller inside the front gate of her neighbor's house. Now angrily scolding herself, "How could I not remember to give the address a block away; now I am in plain view of my neighbor's searching eyes? Needless to say, my regular driver was too busy, so I got stuck with a different driver and thrown off of my regular routine. So excited that I forgot!" After telling the cab driver to sit the luggage on her steps, she quickly ran up the steps through the gate and immediately into the house. However, before the taxi could drive off, she parted the curtains, and that's when she remembered her luggage. Glancing from left to right and again at her neighbor's house across the street, she quickly ran outside, fearing being seen a second time, grabbing her luggage as she rushed inside to open blinds.

Eventually, settling into her comfortable spot on her couch, instantly, Sevella's thoughts were on the dream on the plane and how real it felt. Fear crept into her heart as she then looked around her home and back to the window as she waited for the couple to walk out. Time passed quickly as she lay awake, waiting until she fell asleep. She was awakened by a sharp pain in her back; slowly sat up, bending her body from one angle to another, but could not bear the pain. As she sat up and glanced out of the window just in time to see her neighbor's door open, and out walked the couple, the man was carrying in his hands what appeared to be a large box. Sevella was shocked when she realized it was the same box she had placed Samuel and his belongings. Frightened, she wondered if they were going to the police and if the box was evidence. Then she noticed Samuel being held by the woman, and she could see his face and what he was wearing. Sevella soon forgot about the fear and began to ache for Samuel. He is now six months, but he is still being shielded by his parents. "His parents," she whispered, "What a wonderful, wonderful thought."

Occasionally, the woman would quickly kiss Samuel's pudgy cheeks as he giggled while reaching up for the woman's earring. When Sevella heard Samuel's mother giggle, she laughed out loud. The sound of her laughter echoed throughout the house. Sevella ducked to hide in case they glanced in her direction. Clasping both hands over her mouth while scolding herself, "I said that I would stop spying on them!" As it happened, the thought of being reported petrified her as she trembled, only to have the pain in her back worsen. Now holding her back, she walked away from the window over to the front door, picked up her luggage, and headed for the bedroom. The following day, after getting to work, Sevella busied herself knowing her work would keep her too busy to think about the laughing incident the day before. During the winter months, her neighbors traveled or kept pretty much to themselves. "Except for yesterday," she grumbled.

I Resented the Baby

Not long after Neal bought the property, and before allowing her to housesit, during the remodeling process, he sent Sevella over to oversee and manage the progress of the contractors. She notices all the beautiful homes and especially the *For Sale* sign on the front gate of the house across the street. After several visits to the property, she hoped to meet some of the neighbors. Apparently, they were either very busy or not very social. Therefore, the quiet and private atmosphere of the neighborhood worked well with her hectic schedule. Because of her schedule, she had to keep a very low profile when arriving home after the late investors' meeting. Especially when walking from the cab to her home; once the Model home was completed, featuring a curved walkway creating a distance between the gate and the house, mostly concealing the front entrance. Therefore, her front entrance was less visible to her neighbors. Two weeks later, after arriving home, waiting for the right moment to get on the couch, just in time to see Samuel and his new mother going into the house. Samuel was now looking over his mother's shoulder in her direction, right where she was sitting on the couch.

Shortly after that, Sevella signed, "His mother," as tears ran down her cheeks, remembering wanting so badly to say those words to her foster mom. Slowly she pulled the curtain closed stands up, still looking toward the window as she walked backward until she reached her bedroom door. "From now on, I must take every precaution, being very careful not to be seen a second, third, or fourth time, whatever." After a while, she crawled into her bed, hoping to get a good night's rest, "Otherwise, I will be a bundle of nerve, and Neal will want to know why. Doesn't matter, I'll just say, another disturbing dream of that horrible nightmare of Florida. You know, remember the time you sold me to the highest bidder? Only if I could tell him, only if I could." After relaxing, she was able to think clearly, momentarily covering her head, speaking to herself, *I hated and resented the pregnancy; resented the baby and hated the attacker. The hatred was so intense that I began the resent Neal, my job, and, worst of all, my very own life.*

Right after falling asleep, Sevella began to dream of her first visit to the clinic. However, the clinic resembled her office, and the doctor was Neal. She immediately ran out of the clinic and noticed across the street was the breakfast diner. As she ran across the street and into the Diner, stunned at the appearance of the diner, it was similar to her bedroom. Overwhelmed by the confusion, at the same time, bitterness submerged as she looked around her bedroom and noticed a dark image in her mirror, but the image wasn't her. Walking slowly toward the image that never moved, suddenly, her vision became very clear, and the image was of a man wearing an overcoat. With all her might, she attempted to scream, but there was no sound. Then she cried out, "Sam, Sam! Where are you? Help me. Please help me!" She then ran from her bedroom into the kitchen, but immediately she was back in her bedroom. Gradually the scene changed again, and she could see herself sitting on her bed reading the book about Samuel.

I Must Be Dreaming

At that very moment, her image went from reading to kneeling down beside her bed and beginning to pray for help while deciding not to get the abortion, instead taking a job at the diner. She then whispered, "I must be dreaming because I can see myself and hear myself thinking." Right after speaking those words, the scene changed again as the sound of her voice awakened her. She quickly sat up as the pain in her back reminded her of sleeping on the couch. Holding her back, she whispered, "Not again. What is really going on? I need my rest before tomorrow's meeting." Sevella stood up and stumbled through the dark from the bedroom to the couch. After opening the blinds, she placed herself in a different position, with her face on the back of the couch facing the window. At last, tiredness caused her to fall into a deep sleep, this time dreaming it was the next morning and she had overslept. She jumped up and looked at the clock, and it was already 8 a.m. She rose to dress, but most of her outfits were too tight. She reached for her phone, forgetting Neal's phone number. After searching her memory, Sevella quickly went through her closet for her large bag and pulled out her phone book, but much to her surprise, the number she dialed wasn't a working number.

She dressed and decided to visit the breakfast diner. After arriving at the breakfast diner, excitement began to creep into her heart at the idea of seeing Sam and Jack. She rushes to pay for the taxi. Before closing the taxi door, she glanced to her right, looking through the Diner's large picture windows at each booth. Finally, she closed the taxi's door, and slowly walked toward the diner, hoping to surprise everyone. Once inside, Sevella noticed Sam waiting at a nearby table; out of habit, Sam would greet the incoming customer without taking her eyes off the customers she was serving. Looking up and then taking a second look, Sam couldn't believe what she was seeing. She then squealed, "Sevella, Sevella, where have you been?" Sam is now running toward Sevella, arms stretched out in front of her, ready to give Sevella a big hug. Caught off guard and feeling embarrassed at the same time, she was delighted and speechless.

In the meantime, she thought, *I have never in my life felt such happiness!* Eventually, Sam realized her customers were waiting, so she directed Sevella to their favorite booth. Shortly after she completed her customer's order, Sam quickly took her seat across from Sevella. Unable to look Sam in the eyes, Sevella glanced down at her trembling hands, cuffing them while thanking Sam for helping her bring Samuel home from the hospital. Sevella and Sam both stood at the same time as they hugged and cried, then the question, "His name is Samuel? What do you know? He has part of my name!" By this time, all eyes were on them. Therefore, they quickly sat down, hoping to hide from the stares of everyone in the Breakfast Diner. Although sitting in a somewhat secluded high back corner booth, the attention was so overwhelming that Sevella began to toss and turn in her sleep, attempting to shield herself from the gazing stares. All of a sudden, Jack calls, and Sam hurries over to Jack, exclaiming, "She's back. Look who is back!"

Not Wanted

After Sam had completed the orders, she rushed back to Sevella with a list of questions about Samuel. As fear and sadness crept into Sevella's heart, she knew that there was no easy way to avoid the truth. Now thinking, *I have to tell her that I gave him away.* Worst of all, those unforgettable words began to scream from within, "NOT WANTED!" as Sevella sat paralyzed with fear, speechless, desperately searching for the right words to say. Words that would not paint her a thoughtless, uncaring monster. "How do I tell Sam about Samuel? Now I wished I had never made this trip." As Sevella nervously waited, Sam's smile turned into a frown and from a frown to a look of fear as she studied Sevella's facial expression. Nervously, while carefully choosing her words, Sevella began to explain, "I gave him up for adoption!" Sam gasped as she quickly placed both hands over her heart. Sam's voice was trembling, "If I had known, I would have taken him!" Now crying, "Why didn't you tell me and give me a chance to adopt Samuel; you know I would have, don't you?" In that moment, Sevella wanted to comfort Sam but could not find the words.

Periodically whipping tears from her eyes, still clasping her trembling hands, Sevella explained, "It was done so quickly." Without a word of warning, Sevella changed the subject, "In addition to that, I really need a job? Can I come back? Will I get my job back, and is it still available?" Before long, Sam's expression went from shocked to surprised as she once again extended her arms to hug Sevella. Because of the sudden movement of her arms, Sevella was then awakened as she opened her eyes to see her arms raised and stretched out in front of her. Soon after waking up, Sevella whispered, "I now realize that my busy schedule has kept me so preoccupied that I've barely thought about my dear friends, Sam and Jack. Wow!" Sevella grumbled, "I am so very selfish, but after I explain to Sam, I'm sure she will accept my apology!" In that moment, she recalled living from one foster home to another, always wanting to fit in but never being allowed to. She was forced to have imaginary friends as her only source of companionship. Therefore, she spent many days having no one but herself to talk to.

Afterward, determined to never again be labeled "Not wanted," Sevella remembered the two promises she made to herself; first, to be a better person than those who treated her as an outcast. Secondly, "When I grow up, I will get an office job just like my foster mom, and I will make all new friends." In that moment, the tears began to fill her eyes and ran down her cheeks onto her pillow. Other than the pounding of her heart Sevella hears the tick-tock of the wall clock, turning to look at the illuminated hands only to see a very small stream of light from the street lamps shining past her couch onto Neal's crystal vase, now realizing that she is on the couch Sevella sat up; looked out of the window, that's when she saw the light in the upstairs bedroom across the street. In that instance, Sevella was totally unaware of her image seen from the outside, cast by the stream of light coming through her window. She then gets up without closing the blinds while glancing at the time; "8:30 p.m., hum, it feels more like 3 o'clock a.m." Due to the early hour, Sevella decided to remain on the couch.

An Acute Hangover

Turning again as she sits to position herself to face the back of the couch, making it easier to sit up, at the same time looking out of the window. Noticing her shadow, she sat up with her back to the window, staring at the floor, studying how the light formed her shadow on the floor. For several minutes she sat very still, observing her shadow before repositioning herself, then laying back, covering her eyes with her forearm, whispering, "Thank goodness for my new hours; I still have enough time to get a good night's rest." Again, without much effort, Sevella quickly fell asleep as she imagined her new working hours as executive. "Yes, that's right! I have an assistant, and I'll train her to open the office and prepare documents, and I'll just focus on getting some rest." After getting up the next morning and getting dressed for work, Sevella enjoyed the freedom of her new position and hours by taking advantage of the extra time and making breakfast before heading off to work. Once at work for most of the day, Sevella moved about her duties in somewhat of a trance. Neal had to ask several times, "Sevella, are you okay?" He even accused her of having a hangover saying, "Sevella, if I didn't know you, better I would say that you are suffering from an acute hangover."

Occasionally holding on to her chair, Sevella mustered up a smile, explaining, "Not a hangover, just excitement, and too excited to sleep." Unable to shake the uneasiness brought on by the dream, she couldn't wait to get home and get some rest. Once home, she went straight to bed but was unable to fall asleep. Instead, she focused on the empty wall. At that very moment, she reflected on her pregnancy and the days prior to starting work for Jack and meeting Sam. She smiled as she slowly dozed off to sleep; at the same time, hearing her voice, "The diner doesn't pay much, but I would rather have a pay deduction and the time to see Samuel than all the money in the world, some money is better than none." The sound of her voice woke her as she began to reason with herself, saying, *Money? What money?* That's when she remembered her pay from Ellor was placed in an account, "An account that has not been mentioned since the Florida trip!" Sevella began to reason, just to give Neal the benefit of the doubt, "Maybe it's the account for the down payment on this home, and he's been too busy to discuss the matter."

Occasionally looking around the room, making sure she wasn't still dreaming, she sat up, rubbing her eyes, reminding herself, "NO! Not Neal. He may forget many things, but never money. I'll wait for the appropriate time, and then I'll bring the account to his attention," Sevella murmured as she glanced at the clock before turning over and immediately falling asleep. RING, RING, RING! She was sitting straight up before reaching for the ringing alarm and mumbled, "Wow, I actually slept through the night." Feeling very relaxed after breakfast, she called her taxi, and as she walked out of her front door, unaware of her neighbor's watchful eye, she spoke to herself as she headed down the street to catch her cab, *The wages I received from Ellor was my bonus, and Neal knows it! Neal conveniently failed to mention or initiate a conversation as to when I would receive that bonus.* Even though she slept through the night, Sevella felt very tired as she walked swiftly to the next block. *I know it's just lack of rest, no problem, but I must do better at resting.*

A Figure in the Window

After a long day of phone calls and rescheduling, Sevella was headed home. Just before going to bed, Sevella made a pot of hot tea, remembering Miss Timothy's whistling tea kettle, *Yes, and the many nights of sitting and watching her silently sipping her tea and reading her Bible. She would say, "A nightcap to calm the spirit." Again I'm talking to myself. This is becoming a very bad habit. I'm going to lose my mind if I don't tell somebody what happen to me in Florida. I just know it!* Tears were now running down her face, the voice was trembling, "Since the attack, my sleep and rest are interrupted by that reoccurring nightmare, but now my dreams are about me seeing Sam." Sevella didn't quite understand the reason behind those dreams, but she knew more dreams like the last one would be the very things that would drive her over the edge. "That's right, forcing me to tell Sam the whole truth about Samuel. Maybe, it is because I have hidden Samuel's whereabouts from Sam, and that's why I've had this succession of recurring dreams!" The following day, for the most part, her schedule was manageable. After three weeks of processing and familiarizing herself with the new responsibilities, Sevella finally had the routine down to a science.

However, one afternoon, three months later, as Sevella sat on the couch still looking out of her window and calculating Samuel's age since birth, "Oh, my, he is now nine months," she tried to imagine his new parent's joy. On the other hand, her neighbors now called him David; for the most part, he was attempting to sit up on his own only to fall backward. Nonetheless, and not to be defeated, David would continue to sit up until he succeeded without falling backward. Lawrence would grab him up and sneak into the kitchen while mom was getting ready for bed; Lawrence would get the cookie jar, then the milk out of the refrigerator as he and David would go into the den, hide to secretly eat their cookie, and drink their milk. Afterward, Lawrence would take David upstairs and sit down by the window near David's baby bed and watch the planes take off and fly overhead until David was finally asleep. On this particular night, as Lawrence was standing and positioning David on his shoulder, he glanced toward the home across the street, and for a brief moment, he thought he saw an image in the window.

After placing David comfortably into bed, Lawrence turned off the lamp with only the night light visible, went back, and stared out of David's window toward the house across the street, but there was no one there. Shortly after that, he tipped toed toward the door, whispering, "No way! The house is vacant and for sale." Quietly opening the door, with a last glance at the crib and David's motionless body, leaving the door ajar, Lawrence slipped out of the room. Only nine months old, David shocked his parents by standing and holding on to the coffee table. Both jumped up as David fell backward, startled by his parent's reaction. Crying from the fright, Catheryn quickly picked him up and began to make funny faces while saying, "Daddy and Mommy better stop scaring that baby," as she pretended to spank her hand and then

Lawrence's hand, as David began to laugh through his tears. After putting him to bed, Lawrence remembered the night he thought he saw the image in the window, so he asked, "Honey, is the house across the street occupied?"

Cut Off All Contact

Momentarily preoccupied with tipping out of the room, Catheryn beckoned for Lawrence to lower his voice before waking David. Undoubtedly curious, Catheryn thought for a moment, asking, "Why do you ask about the house for sale?" As he glanced over his shoulder to check on David, Lawrence shrugged his shoulder, saying, "Never mind, just my overactive imagination." The following day, after getting dressed for work, Sevella was met by the bright light from the sun shining through her living room window. She quickly rushed over to close the blinds and curtains; as she closed the curtains, she noticed her hands trembling. Speaking audibly, "This is the second time I've left that window open. Oh my, have I been seen? Besides that, I should have stopped weeks ago, but that's easier said than done. I don't care; I have to know how Samuel is doing!" She remembered when Samuel and his mother laughed so that she laughed out loud. Now wondering, *Did they hear me?* Apart from the disappointing news, now fear and regret welcomed her as she started her day.

As much as she wanted to share her secret with Sam, she feared losing her only friend. She also knew it would be the right thing to do, even though it would make her appear heartless and selfish. The next day Sevella carefully walked the block to catch the taxi while instructing herself, "It must remain a secret, and to keep it a secret, I must cut off all contact with Sam; before I do that, I'll contact her, and cancel our celebration meeting, explaining an unplanned business trip." After a while, Sevella takes out her phone, slowly dialing the number while taking a deep breath. After a few rings, an unfamiliar voice answered the phone. Hesitantly, Sevella asked to speak to Sam. Sevella heard Sam's voice, "Hello." Greeted Sam enthusiastically. Sevella held her breath, "Hello, this is Samantha Douglass," Sam repeated cautiously. Sevella's heart rate increased as she struggled to answer. "Hello! Hello, my friend. It is so good to hear your voice. However, I have some news." Afterward, again and again, she apologized to Sam for having to postpone their celebration.

Once the conversation ended, after hanging up, Sevella felt a sharp pain in her chest, "Wow, what is this all about?" Sevella stroked her chest near her heart until the pain subsided. Eventually, turning her attention to the first business trip to France and meeting their new business associates and owners of Brauy Modeling Agency. Occasionally, the pain would come and go. Finally, she began to feel some relief and was able to relax. Speaking silently, "Just think, I will be traveling to France, and instead of being frightened, I am very excited and very happy. I once thought Florida would be my Disneyland, but no! I believe now it must be France. Wow! I am going to France, and I am going as the boss! Furthermore, I owe my foster mom an apology for thinking she was mean when she made me stay up late typing and proofing her documents. Plus, in the past, that was a very difficult time in my life. By the way, I wonder if she would be proud of me if she knew her training had landed me an executive position in my company as the boss."

Caught Off Guard

As a result of that reflection, another memory submerges the one that forced her to leave that particular home, "Just like that horrible night in Florida, another time in my life that haunted me forever. Never mind that, if she knew she would be proud of me. After two years of long hours and little sleep, I've finally achieved my dream job and dream life." Resting her head on the taxi's headrest while momentarily dozing off. Once arriving at the office, she met Neal, as usual, smiling as if he knew a secret. Not wanting to be ruffled by his discretion, she smiled back and said, very happily, "Good morning!" Neal responded, "You must be a little apprehensive about this trip to France. After all, you will be in training, and you will be over there for a while. Also, you've never been out of the country before. Quickly, she responded, "You will succeed in discouraging me if that's your goal. However, I am aware of my training for at least six weeks. Now calculating Samuel's age, she whispered, "My next trip home, Samuel will be almost ten months old." Neal interrupted, "Tentatively six weeks, but it could be longer."

Immediately Sevella's heart skips a beat because Neal heard her say "ten months," therefore she quickly spoke up, saying, "And it is a long way from home, and no, I've never been out of the country before, but I am very excited about going to France and working with Mr. Kingsley!" Right after that statement, Neal was amazed at Sevella's confidence. Laughing jokingly, he said,

"Sevella, you don't have to pretend for me, I know you, and it is okay to be afraid." Focused on her itinerary before placing it into her new briefcase, she purposely ignored Neal and missed her opportunity to bring up Ellor's bonus money; instead, she began to explain, "And you know if I didn't know you, I would say that you are trying to discourage me from going. I was just thinking of the time you shipped me off to Florida, without any warning, without any formal notice, and you sent me away all alone with complete strangers. No, believe me, Neal, when you sent me to Florida without warning, that experience was a crash course in fear management."

Apparently, Neal was curious to know about the crash course, stating, "Incidentally," Sevella was now waving her right hand, interrupting Neal. Sevella continued, "I know we haven't discussed my bonus money for Florida, but we will." Confused, Neal again began to speak but considered the reason he hadn't mentioned her bonus. Neal is now waving his hand, responding with uncertainty, "By the way," but Sevella again interrupted him, "So please don't worry about me; I will be just fine. After all, I learned survival from the first trip. Also, I'll be with Mr. Kingsley, and I'm sure he will take very good care of me." Neal responded, "What do you mean, crash course and survival? Did something happen in Florida?" Caught off guard by Neal's question, Sevella laughed nervously and said, "What, what do you mean, what could have happened? Now, if you don't mind, I need to go to my office and make some calls and get in touch with Mr. Kingsley before I leave for the airport." Now distracted by his phone ringing, Neal responded, whispering, "Excuse me? Hello!"

A Listening Ear

At that very moment, Sevella felt a feeling of relief at the chance to tell Neal off without losing her job. She sighed, "Whew, good call!" She quickly waved to Neal as he headed to his office. Still not convinced that she would have been sharp enough to avoid Neal's gazing stare after questioning her careless statements. Therefore, she quickly followed Neal's instructions as he covered the receiver, directing her to get some documents from an executive's office. Once she opened Delmecia's office door, Sevella stood motionless and surprised. Without warning, tears swelled up in her eyes. She had no idea what she was walking into. "Is this my new office?" As quickly as the tears started, they stopped. The office had an additional piece of decoration that Delmecia, his former executive, didn't have; a very large and beautiful bouquet. Temporarily frozen in her steps as she stared at the colorful flowers in a vase similar to the one in her living room. She stepped closer and suddenly stopped, looking from the painting and back to the matching vase beneath the painting.

Moreover, still teary-eyed, the door opened. Startled, Sevella turned quickly, looking toward the door. Neal, also startled at Sevella's reaction, responded, "What's wrong? What is the matter?" Then looking in the direction of the arrangement and back at Sevella, he began to nod his head up and down, speaking sympathetically, "I come to see if you are okay, but no doubt the arrangement has left you teary-eyed." Up until that time, she felt very much in control of her emotions, but the incident with Sam left her feeling overly emotional. Soon after, Sevella was thankful that the arrangement camouflaged the real reason for her tears and hoped desperately that Neal would forget about her earlier remarks. She knew that all she really needed was a sympathetic and listening ear, and everything about Samuel and that horrible man would pour out like water without restraint. "I don't need Neal's prying into my personal life, so I must be careful not to volunteer any more information." Slowly rubbing her chest, but managed a smile, feeling relieved that she could use the arrangement to cover up the real reasons for her tears,

Occasionally wiping the tears as they ran down her cheeks, "I hope they're for me; otherwise, I going to be very embarrassed," whispered Sevella as Neal turned, rushing to his office. Gradually turning her attention to her desk and the itinerary, Sevella gathered the prepared documents and placed them into her new briefcase while instructing Dorothy to have Chuck help get her suitcase to the taxi. Suddenly, a knock on the door and a young lady walked in and introduced herself, "Hello, Ms. Thorn. My name is Emilia Cu'Dull, and I will be traveling with you to France. I have been appointed by Mr. Brauy to work with you as your assistant." "Wow!" exclaimed Sevella. Emilia asked, "Is something wrong?" Sevella spoke hesitantly, "No, no, I'm sorry. Please have a seat. I just remembered I have one more very important document to get from Neal, and I'll be right back. I just want to make sure we are all on the same page." Apart from the earlier close encounter, Sevella was now the one asking questions; but she wanted to be tactful, not rude. Rehearsing her questions, speaking silently, "When did Emilia get hired, or when were you going to tell me? I hate being the last to know anything."

What Just Happened?

Still focused on her questions, Sevella walked into Neal's office without knocking; he looked at her but remained on the phone. She stopped quickly while slowly closing the door behind her, but not before she noticed Neal's body movement after uninvitingly entering his office. While still standing near the door, she waited for Neal to finish his conversation. "That's right, that's right, no problem, I'll handle it. Thanks, goodbye. What's wrong? What's the matter?" Neal asked, somewhat annoyed. Sevella murmured, "Oh, sorry for interrupting you, but there is a young lady in my office, Emilia Cu'Dull; Mr. Brauy sent her to assist me as my assistant. Do I have an assistant?" Neal hesitated, "Well, yes and no. What I mean is yes, but she can't start until tomorrow." Slowly moving forward while holding her hands in front of her, "What is this tomorrow?" Neal began to explain, "Please, please calm down. It is okay, she is already in France. Her name is Ms. Tramishia Rams. She is a friend of Ellor, and she lives there."

Almost breathless, Sevella repeated, "Ellor, Ellor will he be there, or I mean will his associates be there? No, I mean…" Neal was now standing and moving very quickly toward Sevella and hoping he would reach her before she fainted. He quickly grabbed hold of her outstretched arms and slowly guided her toward the chair closest to the door. Now sitting, Sevella stared blindly toward Neal's office window; although he was very close, she couldn't hear Neal's voice. As if in a trance, she turns slowly, looking in

Neal's direction, recognizing a look she was well acquainted with, a look of fear. Staring into Neal's eyes, she realized she had to think fast. Thinking quickly, she suddenly remembered the orphanage and her fainting spells when she felt really hungry. *That's it. I'll try that. Moments later, Sevella began coughing in order to distract Neal from her previous reaction. The last thing she needed was to give any indication of the terror because of what happened in Florida. Therefore, she placed her hands over her mouth, saying, "I'm sorry. I thought for a moment I was going to faint.*

Neal moved closer, asking, "What just happened?" Sevella was now smiling. "I thought skipping breakfast might just slow me down, but I skipped lunch as well. I'm so sorry, Neal. I didn't mean to frighten you, but I forgot all about eating." Neal was now attempting to sit in a chair that wasn't there, but Sevella quickly stepped behind him before his body hit the floor. Neal looked behind him to only see Sevella and realized that there was no chair. Feeling embarrassed, he explained, "I guess we are both a little off balance." Now appearing calmer, he said, "Really? You haven't eaten since yesterday?" Sevella laughed nervously and said, "Well, I'm just so excited. Like I said, I forgot all about eating." Meanwhile, Neal's mood also changed. Appearing to be annoyed, Neal was pulling up a chair as he took a seat, now focused on his pants as he pulled up one pant leg and then the other while showing off his black silk socks. Momentarily glancing up at Sevella and again at his pants, finally, he looked up at Sevella, explaining, "This trip is more for Mr. Brauy and his company's expansion than for New Ventures. I am only acting as a broker or middleman connecting investors in France."

Dreams, Visions, Dynasty

On the other hand, you will be representing New Ventures, LLC, being our eyes and ears by orchestrating, organizing, and keeping up with all the documents transmitted from our office to Mr. Brauy's. You are to make sure everything runs smoothly on our behalf. You see, in the long run, Mr. Brauy will help our company expand. Not just expand but help increase exposure for New Ventures, LLC on foreign and domestic soil. Although our new investors are more acquainted with Mr. Kingsley, I believe he will be our ticket to the top investors in the modeling industry. Shortly afterward, Sevella remembered to ask about Delmecia. First hesitating, Neal looked up, asking, "What is it?" Sevella waited before asking, "I was wondering why Delmecia left so quickly." At this point, Neal was looking down at his shoes before answering, "As you know, Delmecia has always wanted to go to Paris. By the way, she is one reason I promoted you; because when I first introduced the idea of modeling, I intended to place her on the project. While you were in Florida, she received several calls, but the caller never left his name. Finally, she left without giving notice."

Consequently, at that moment, Sevella was wondering why Delmecia never mentioned the modeling concept or her intentions of leaving the company. Therefore, she wasn't really listening but responded, "Oh, I see." Neal continued, "You being in France working closely with Tramishia Rams, who is over business operations and finances, will help us gain the business knowledge needed to run operations for our company. Now, do you understand? My goal is to turn this dream into a vision and the vision into a dynasty." Interrupted by the ringing phone, Neal rushed to answer the call while Sevella examined the documents scattered over his desk. Suddenly she remembered for almost twenty minutes, she had left Emilia Cu'Dull sitting in her office. She quickly rushes back to her office to find Emilia going over some notes while talking on the phone. "Sorry, Miss Thorn, but I was hoping to get this done before you returned." Sevella motioned with her hands for her to continue as she grabbed her purse; before walking out of the office, Sevella motioned to Emilia that she was heading down the hallway.

Previously, after hearing that Ellor recommended Emilia, Sevella's emotions were obvious. However, she was very grateful that Emilia Cu'Dull came along when she did. Otherwise, she believed Neal would have eventually figured out that her outbreak was tied to hearing Ellor's name. It was then Sevella felt the pain in her chest. Slowly walking down the hallway toward the lady's lounge, Sevella nervously rubbed her chest near her heart. Once in the bathroom, Sevella looked around, making sure she was alone; then, she began to watch her face over and over as the tears ran down her cheeks, mixing with the cold water until she felt some relief. As a result of that unexpected announcement, Sevella's hands were still shaking. She looked at her image in the mirror and realized that she had washed off all her makeup. Picking up her handbag and pouring the contents on the dressing table, speaking to her image, *This pain, it has to be stress. I heard that it is a silent killer. Nevertheless, before it kills me, I need to pull myself together. That name, Ellor, threw me into a panic attack releasing all kinds of emotions, emotions that I couldn't hide.*

Don't Worry

After reapplying her makeup, she realized that the makeover helped her look more relaxed. In the meantime, Sevella is unaware that she is rubbing her chest until she looks at her reflection in the mirror. Before heading back to the office, she decided to wait for the pain to subside, wondering, *Could I be having a heart attack?* Just as she walked out of the lady's lounge, there stood Neal in front of her office. He opened the door just as she approached him and noticed Emilia Cu'Dull looking intently at her phone but looked up as Sevella and Neal walked into the office. Prior to entering the office, Neal waves his hand to get Emilia's attention, then, speaking to Sevella, "I was thinking I might need to take this trip and leave Sevella to run the office. Your reaction to hunger worried me, but I could see that you just needed to get something to eat. Ms. Cu dull told me you were headed down the hall, and I knew then you were headed to the café. Now, ladies, since you have officially met, it's time to head to the airport. The cab just called up, and I came to let you know. With that being said, let's get busy."

After saying their goodbyes, Neal helped the ladies load up the cab and waved them off. After taking their seats on the plane, Sevella and Emilia Cu'Dull began to compare notes regarding the itinerary laid out by Ellor and Neal. There were some similarities that made them both laugh together and some differences that caused them to really wonder if these men were somehow related.

After spending several hours going over notes and schedules, both ladies fell asleep. "No! Please no! Please don't. Get away from me!" Jumping forward with such force that Sevella accidentally elbowed Emilia, she was awakened by the impact. "Don't worry," Emilia said sluggishly. "It's probably an air pocket." With that being said, Emilia fell quickly asleep. Sevella lay motionless. She couldn't remember what that frightening dream was all about, but it wasn't pleasant. Finally, she relaxed and eventually fell asleep. Finally awakened after hearing, "We will be landing at Charles De Gaulle Airport France in thirty minutes." Sevella looked out of the window. She was surprised to see the sun bright and beautiful, just as her new career in a beautiful new country with new acquaintances.

In light of the earlier incident, Emilia asked cheerfully, "Well, what does the weather look like out there?" Startled, Sevella jumped at the sound of Emilia's voice, sighing and shaking her head before responding, "My goodness, you scared me," said Sevella, still looking out of the window. "I thought there would be dark clouds and smog, but the sun is beautiful." Emilia laughed teasingly, "Are you still shaken up from that air pocket? Well, it may be sunshine, but the weather is in the forties and cold, but thankfully there is no rain." The flight attendant's voice interrupted their conversation, "Please, fasten your seatbelts." Finally, they arrived in France. Once inside the terminal, Sevella's heart skipped as her eyes took in all the different nationalities rushing to and fro throughout the airport. One particular woman passed Sevella wearing the most colorful and beautiful outfit. Sevella complimented her as she passed by, "I love your outfit," but the lady ignored her. Emilia interjected, "She doesn't speak English, and you will get a lot of that. Just remember to smile and nod. That will be greetings enough."

Love without Prejudice

Shortly after that conversation, and as they were walking through the terminal, Emilia suddenly noticed that there was a woman waving a sign reading, "Sella Tureth," quickly, Emilia pointed and said, "There, over there on the poster, I think she is our contact person!" Waving back, Emilia signaled the lady, saying, "Yes, here she is!" Sevella, now feeling overwhelmed with emotion, thought, *The last time my heart skipped a beat, I had chest pains, but now my heart skips a beat because of this wonderful, indescribable feeling!* Once joined by Emilia and Sevella, The lady with the sign introduced herself, "Hello, I'm Tramishia Rams." Now extending her right hand, first shaking Emilia's hand, then Sevella's, greeting them, *"Mademoiselle Sevella, bienvenue en France."* Emilia responded, *"Parlez-vous Anglais?"* Tramishia Rams smiled and said, *"Oui,* I mean yes. French is my first language, but I will be translating for you and Ms. Tureth." Following the introduction, the ladies were rushed off to the office, where they were introduced to the office staff and, right away, began work.

After a smooth morning transition, the three ladies sat down at lunch while Tramishia gave a quick overview of Sevella's duties as acting Executive. After several missed pronunciations of Sevella's name, Emilia quickly corrected the spelling of Sevella's name by taking the sign carried by Tramishia and crossing out the name Sella Tureth, and rewriting the correct spelling, Sevella Thorn, before handing the sign back to Tramishia as they all burst into laughter. Tramishia turned, facing Emilia and Sevella, explaining, "The work schedule involved weeks of appointments with very important clients." As it happens, the schedule was overly hectic; therefore, Sevella was struggling to keep up and was thankful for her foster mother's training. One evening after settling into the corporate apartment, momentarily, Sevella reflected back to the homeless shelter. Tears began to fill her eyes and roll down her cheeks; slowly, she closed her tear-filled eyes, attempting to blot out that very sad memory.

Not long after, Sevella sat down at her kitchen table near the window, admiring the endless beauty of the blue sky before falling asleep with her head on the table resting on her arm. After a few hours of napping, she turned her head, opened her eyes, and looked carefully around the small kitchen, "I'm not dreaming. This time, it's real." First, she stood and pushed her chair underneath the table, saying, "If I was living here in France and working for Mr. Brauy, maybe I would not have given Samuel away! No, no, that's not true; I have so much hatred and resentment for that evil man I don't think I could have loved Samuel without prejudice. But how is that? When all I think about is Samuel: maybe giving him up was the best thing for both of us." At the beginning of the following workday, Sevella had to make several calls to Neal. As time went by, Sevella was involved in several weeks of meetings, conference calls, leadership training, and different workshops on personality and diversity. Finally, it was time to head back to the States.

Our Night

Prior to leaving Boston, Neal sternly cautioned Sevella saying, "The last meeting with Mr. Brauy will be the most important. Therefore, pay close attention to every detail involving financing and infrastructure." Apart from the timely breaks, the last meeting was very long but successful. Not long after, she contacted Neal, going over every document and giving him an update on the meetings as instructed by Emilia. The calls to the State were to keep Neal current on details and changes from both sides but, most importantly, to ease Neal's nerves. It was obvious Naomi's disappearance weighed heavily on his mind. "I wonder if he thinks I'll abandon him for Mr. Brauy, whispered Sevella as she reflected on his nonchalant attitude after Naomi went missing." After weeks of endless conference calls, the business trip concluded with the office team properly welcoming Sevella and Emilia by giving an office party. The following day, Sevella boarded the plane alone for Boston.

Meanwhile, hiding in the den with David, Lawrence explained, "Son, this is our night for cookies and milk, and the den is one of our favorite spots to hide, and the next place to hide is in your bedroom. First, the den because here we can hide from Mommy before heading up stars to drink milk, eat our cookies, and talk about the planes that fly different places all over the world. Someday just maybe, you will travel and meet new people." Before going upstairs, Lawrence made a second trip to the kitchen. He picked up a small blue plastic pitcher and matching cup, saying, "David, tonight I'm teaching you how to one day pour milk from this pitcher into this cup. Also, there will always be two cookies, one for you and one for me. From this moment on, you are in charge of the pitcher and the cup. Listen carefully. The container will only hold two cookies, son. How many did I say?" David, now almost a year and walking since nine months, replied, "Two," while holding up three fingers. Together with David in his arms and milk in hand, Lawrence headed up the stairs while asking David, "Did you say two?" After hearing it again, Lawrence could no longer hold his laughter as he caught hold of the three fingers held up by David.

Now laughing very loudly then covering his mouth, he placed one finger over his lips, afterward placing the same finger over David's lips as they tiptoed into David's bedroom. Once inside, Lawrence sat down in a chair near David's window, which looked directly over the roof of the house across the street to watch the planes fly overhead. "Okay, son, on our next cookie and milk day, we have just enough milk in the pitcher for you to pour into your cup, and don't worry, it's spill-proof. Next, there are two cookies left in the container, one for you and one for me." Although David wasn't ready for such a task, Lawrence realized David's innate ability to grasp details; therefore, he continued to teach David in that capacity. As they sat waiting for the planes, just before the first plane appeared, David's head eventually rested on Lawrence's chest, "Off to bed for you, buddy." David quickly placed the small piece of cookie in his hand into his mouth while drinking the last of his milk. Shortly afterward, David spotted a plan and pointed while attempting to say the word plane, instead saying, "Pane." His father laughed at David's annunciation, and David laughed at Lawrence.

Can I Handle This?

In the meantime, Sevella is back in the States and has made her way back to her regular routine. Suddenly she became concerned with the seriousness of her new position; she began to feel uneasy as the reality of the promotion set in, asking herself, *Can I really handle this job? As a homeowner, I must learn the upkeep and responsibilities that come with homeownership.* Momentarily feeling thankful that her trip to Paris paid off, and her income almost doubled. Now looking at her bills, she was thinking, *I'm so thankful that Neal took care of these bills instead of pushing them off on me. He must have known I wasn't ready for such a huge financial responsibility. At first, I struggled financially, but now I am an executive, a homeowner, and overseer for New Ventures Modeling Agency.* In addition to her becoming the new owner of the investment property and the amazing experience in France, six months later, after settling into her new office and role as executive assistant, Neal surprised her with a week's paid vacation.

In that moment, Sevella remembered Tramishia and Emilia. She couldn't believe how life-altering her promotion had become. One day after a brief meeting with Dorothy and Sitting in for Kathy, Sevella noticed that Neal had made several calls to Florida. She wondered if he was trying to set up something with Ellor but quickly dismissed the thought. Her only concern was staying on top by getting everything ready for Emilia's return from Paris. Emilia had remained behind at the request of Ellor. Something about "tying up loose ends for Mr. Brauy." She also noted various documents assigned by Neal for Emilia to proof upon her return. Still feeling uneasy about the calls to Florida, Sevella couldn't help thinking to herself, *Why so many calls to Florida, and so soon?* Finally, putting her focus on her vacation, she dismissed the thought and started to make plans.

As the weeks passed, it was almost time to start her vacation. It was then that Sevella began to feel a sense of satisfaction as she headed for home. "My home," she said as she spoke to her silhouette reflection in the elevator's door. Although many changes have been made, her main objective was to keep one thing constant, and that was to keep a watchful eye on Samuel. "Yes, sitting at the window, parting the curtains to watch for Samuel, will be vacation enough for me." As the elevator doors opened and closed slowly, her reflection again appeared in the doors. Sevella began to talk to her image, *Finally, I now realize that the couple across the street represented all the things I have dreamed about but never dared to hope for.* Still very concerned about the time she laughed out loud while watching Samuel, Sevella was being very careful to watch and not be heard as she eagerly watched every morning and every evening for the couple and Samuel.

A Child in the Middle

On this particular day, the two walked out with Samuel in the middle as his mother and father each held a hand. Immediately, Sevella recalled the dream before Samuel was born of the couple walking with a child in the middle. "Wow! That's exactly what I saw in the dream. Oh my, could this be happening!" At that moment, Sevella realized that there had to be something to those prayers, "Maybe that is the reason Miss Timothy and the lady in the Bible always prayed because they knew that something would soon happen." Other than France, never before had Sevella experienced so much excitement. Now watching Samuel's shaky, little legs as his parent helped to support him each and every step. She threw both hands over her mouth to smother the sound of pure joy as tears ran down her face. In that instance, she realized that before, it was the couple she wanted to see, but now, it was Samuel and only Samuel. Whispering, "As amazing as the experience in Paris made me feel, it fades in comparison to watching Samuel take his first steps, and there is nowhere else in the world I would rather be."

On another particular day, Sevella watched long after the Couple and Samuel drove out of sight. She recalled the dream she had before Samuel was born and wondered about the prayer. She remembered the name "Samuel," and she opened the book again and began to read. She read how Hanna cried out to the Lord before Samuel was born and how she made a vow unto the Lord. Sevella closed the book and began to pray. "I know I am not praying about a vow like the lady in the book, but you let me know how much you loved Samuel and that you wanted him to live. You also let me know that you wanted him to be taken care of and the people you've chosen for the task. I believe the dream directed me to give him up; now, if you please, help me to let go and move on with my life! Thank you, and goodbye for now." She then crawled into bed, feeling a sense of fulfillment as she looked forward to going to work the following morning.

Weeks turned into a month, and for weeks on end, Sevella made several attempts to avoid the couch. Finally, Sevella gave in, promising herself, *I will only watch once a week and no more. In the meantime, my focus will be on my work.* In addition to her promise to stay focused, she busied herself with organizing PowerPoint for the next meeting, except on the day Kathy asked her to sit in for her. After getting her documents and getting comfortable at Kathy's desk, she accidentally opened a folder containing some documents and notes addressed to Emilia from Neal. After closing the folder, she whispered to herself, saying, "I realized that I have a right to examine these documents. Yet, still, I have not been informed of their contents. I could put the document back in place. No, I better not snoop." Eventually, her curiosity got the best of her just as the phone lines lit up simultaneously. Grabbing her notepad to assist Dorothy, answering the third line, "Hello, hello," but no answer. Then a call was directed to her. The caller asked, "Yes, I'm calling to find out if Neal will be picking me up at the airport?" Sevella informed the caller that Neal was out of the office but will call within the hour.

You Almost Had Me

As a rule of thumb, Sevella knew to get names and phone numbers, only to be distracted by the list of calls to Florida and forgetting all of her professional phone ethics, "First the endless calls to Florida, next, the notes for Emilia that Neal failed to share with me, now this. I made fun of Kathy, but her absent-mindedness pales in comparison to my mistakes." Suddenly, the word "airport" rang out in her mind, *Airport, who's at the airport? Oh, now you asked, but you can't answer that question, can you?* The sound of the phone startled her. She quickly answered, thinking it was the call for Neal. "Hello, how can I help you?" She was waiting for an answer so she could correct her earlier mistake and get the gentleman's information, but to her surprise, it was Emilia. After a few moments of silence, Emilia spoke as if she was reading from a script. "I am preparing to pack and catch the next flight to the States." Surprised at Emilia's cold demeanor, Sevella excitedly greeted her, "Hello! What is the hold-up? Since I arrived a month ago, Neal had documents waiting for your expertise. By the way, I ah, accidentally opened the folder. Never mind that, ma'am, you were supposed to fly back a week after me?"

Once again, silence and an eerie feeling came over Sevella as she listened quietly. Also, realizing since their last conversation that something had changed. Sevella continued, but speaking more professionally, "You don't have to explain to me. I know all too well about the last-minute change involved in Ellor's scheduling. Emilia, how are you doing? Has your stay in Paris tempted you to stay just a little longer?" Emilia didn't respond. Instead, she laughed sarcastically before saying, "Don't act as though you don't know what's really going on, or maybe you don't know, and if that is the case, let's leave it at that. Just know that we are being played, and they are just using us as the pons." For the most part, everyone on their team knew that Emilia was the prankster of the group; therefore, Sevella decided to play alone, "I'll just add to the fun because I know she's trying to trick me." Now speaking in a more serious tone, Sevella insisted, "Oh, I really don't know. Please tell me." Unable to hold back the laughter, she could hardly get her words out for laughing so hard. No longer able to keep up the pretense, Sevella confessed, "Emilia, you almost had me."

Unquestionably weird, thought Sevella. Therefore, she asked, "Ms. Prankster. How are you handling things all alone in that beautiful country?" Now thinking, *She is acting so weird.* It was then in the background that Sevella heard a knock on Emilia's door and a voice that sounded very familiar, Emilia's whole attitude changed as she happily greeted her visitor, "Come in!" The person answered sternly, "Are your bags packed?" In that moment, Sevella felt chills went down her spine when she recognized that voice. "I must be losing it: it can't possibly be the same man that attacked me." It was then that Emilia directed her conversation to Sevella, speaking in a more cheerful tone, "Yes, I'm packed, ready to go, and I can't wait to get back to the States and get to work!" It was then she heard the sound of the door closing. Again silence on Emilia's end of the phone. Sevella's heart was beating so fast that she could hardly breathe. Mustering up the courage to speak without sounding too afraid, she asked in an upbeat tone, "Hey, was that Ellor?"

I Can't Do This

From time to time, Sevella could hear background noise, and other times it was dead silence. Too frightened to wait for Emilia's answer, Sevella nervously continued, "Ellor and Neal are so much alike when it comes to last minutes schedule changes. What time will you arrive in the States?" Emilia responded, sounding very angry, "I will arrive there at 6 p.m. Can you arrange for someone to pick me up?" It was something about Emilia's tone that created an atmosphere of alarm; Sevella knew right then and without a doubt that Emilia was in trouble. Sevella, still holding the receiver, spoke, "There is no doubt in my mind that voice is one and the same. I wasn't able to see my attacker, but I did hear his voice, and I know the man speaking to Emilia and my attacker are one and the same." The next sound Sevella heard was the dial tone. Sevella sat in fear and silence, desperately wanting to call the French authorities. Suddenly the ringing startled her. Sevella jumped, quickly answering the incoming call thinking it was Emilia calling back, but it was Neal giving her a list of things to do before Emilia's return. Afterward, quickly hung up.

After completing Neal's to-do list, Sevella sat and, for several minutes, stared at the list, especially the note instructing her to call Florida and get the name and itinerary for Ellor's public relations representative. Sevella was now frantically shaking her head from left to right, saying, "This can't be! No way is he sending me alone and back into that dangerous man's territory." Immediately, she began to recall a time in the orphanage, saying, "I had to fake a happy face or pretend the abuse didn't happen, but that experience pales in comparison to this ongoing panic at the thought of once again being confronted by my attacker. Especially since I heard his voice again, and I knew it was a possibility that he and I were in Paris at the same time, and I wasn't aware that danger was so close by. Oh, no! Could he possibly be traveling back to Boston with Emilia?" Overwhelmed by the idea that her attacker could be the client from Public Relations, all of a sudden, it was too much, and at this point, Sevella was at the breaking point. Her heart raced as her hands shook profusely. Unquestionably shaken and engulfed with fear, Sevella screamed, "I can't do this!"

Apart from the thought that Emilia was alone in Paris with that monster, Sevella shivered at the thought of Emilia's words, "Don't act like you don't know what's going on." "I was joking with Emilia, but she was not joking or laughing. Oh, my! Did something happen, and that's why she thought I was pretending not to know?" Sevella tried to dismiss that unwelcome feeling of uneasiness as she picked up the phone and forced herself to contact Ellor's office. After several rings, someone answered, "How may I help you?" answered Tramishia Rams. "I am so glad to hear your voice!" said Sevella as she waited for Tramishia's response. Suddenly, there was silence on Tramishia's end, so Sevella continued, "I am shocked to hear you answering Ellor's phone! What are you doing in Florida?" There were a few seconds of silence, and then Tramishia said in her French accent, "Hello, Sevella, how are you? How can I help you today?" Tramishia ignored Sevella's question, but Sevella pretended not to notice. "Tramishia, I am calling to get the itinerary for Ellor's PR person." It was at that moment that Sevella heard a click.

Something Strange Is Going On

Despite Tramishia's coy greeting, Sevella was now feeling very angry and annoyed at the mere thought of the danger Tramishia and Emilia were facing, and Ellor is either unaware or very much involved and responsible for endangering the women in his employment. Shortly afterward, Tramishia answered, "The itinerary will be emailed shortly. Thanks for calling, and have a nice day." As Tramishia hung up, Sevella whispered, "I'll be as guilty of harm as my attacker if I don't speak up." Her first response was to call Tramishia back and question her about the man working with Emilia but she changed her mind knowing the long-distance charges may just come out of her salary. "No, they want," speaking into the phone receiver. "No, this is a business call, and Neal would understand if we were somehow disconnected. How can I be thinking of charges when my friend's life could be in danger? Something strange is going on. Why has Neal Planned my vacation just when I needed to get familiar with my new responsibilities; why were Tramishia and Emilia acting so strangely, and who is that man working with Emilia?"

In spite of nothing making sense, the urge to call the French authorities was pressing on her, but she wanted to be sure; therefore, Sevella began to feel fearful and quickly decided, "When Neal returns, I'm going to get to the bottom of this. After all, Neal said that New Ventures, LLC was the middle man for these new companies; well, if that is the case, why shouldn't they have their leading people travel from one business to the other?" With that thought in mind, she instructed Dorothy to transfer all her calls to voicemail and quickly grabbed her handbag and headed down to the café. Once backed into her office, Sevella completed her to-do list before contacting Neal to inform him of Emilia's arrival and the email from Ellor's company detailing their Public Relations itinerary. Once again, that frightening thought overwhelmed her, and this time she was not able to dismiss it. Again she recalled the conversation with both Tramishia and Emilia and tried to read between the lines. Sevella also remembered before landing. She heard Emilia talking in her sleep and crying for help. Sevella recalled a similar experience and wondered if Emilia was ever an orphan.

Gradually leaning forward in hopes of easing the nauseating feeling, suddenly she remembered the man calling from the airport, "That's something," she said, realizing that an hour had passed since she had spoken to the man, and wondered why he hadn't called back. She then glanced at the clock and noticed that it was right at 2 p.m., over an hour since she last spoke to the caller. Instead of calling Neal, she decided to wait for the man to call back and then contact Neal. After thirty minutes passed, Sevella frantically reached for the receiver just as her phone ranged, "Miss Thorn, Mr. Nest is on line one." Quickly answering, almost in a whisper, "Hello," Neal sounded angrier than she had ever known him to be. Now shouting from the other end of the line, "Sevella, why on earth would you put off taking information from a client, especially our top client's VIP?" Obviously offended and on the defense, Sevella replied sternly, "I did receive a call from a gentleman, and he asked for you. Also, he called just when Dorothy was going to lunch, and he didn't give me any indication he was a client."

Take the Pressure Off of Me

Besides Neal treating her as if everything was her fault, now he was yelling and accusing her of stiffing a VIP. Obviously feeling very angry at herself for not bringing in a temp to replace Kathy's sick leave, Sevella began to feel the pressure of her new position. She began to reason with Neal, "Apparently, he was under the impression you were going to arrange transportation for him because he asked what time you would pick him up. Now, if he needed transportation from the airport, he should have informed me of that need!" Again silence on Neal's end except for his heavy breathing. Sevella, now speaking defensibly, "By the way, I'm looking on my to-do list, and I see no notes for arrival of any VIP needing to be transported from the airport, and you failed to mention it when you called. Otherwise, I would have sent a taxi. I understand you're upset, but apparently, if you are confronting me on the client's behalf, he must have called you directly. How is it he can call you to complain, but he couldn't call me?" Neal was now stumbling, trying to find the words to refute Sevella's rebuttal.

Almost breathless, Neal responded, "Well, first of all, he didn't call me. I called him. Secondly, I knew he was arriving today, but it slipped my mind to inform you." "By the way, I have so much on my mind; plus, that's why I have promoted you to the executive assistant, so you can take some of the pressure off of me!" Now silence before Sevella heard the dial tone. Sevella was outraged as she yelled directly into the receiver, "No, he didn't hang up on me! What is going on with everyone hanging up on me?" Together with the awkwardness of Tramishia, and Emilia's calls, Sevella placed the receiver on the phone and took a deep breath to calm herself, knowing that if she didn't calm down, there would be an argument as soon as Neal walked through the door. Now she turned to the list, hoping to find anything that would help in her defense when Neal returned. As she searched through her notes, she began to recall her conversation with Tramishia and Emilia. Each one treated her like a stranger. "I know that feeling too well. I have experienced that type of rejection since my childhood, and the only difference is the people I'm receiving that behavior from; not my foster siblings, but my new friends."

"In my opinion, they have turned against me, and so quickly?" whispered Sevella as she doubled checked her notes. Unable to find any indication of the client's itinerary, she decided to focus on her conversations with Tramishia; and Emilia, concluding, "It is no coincidence that both Tramishia and Emilia's behaviors are identical, even though they are cultures apart." She reasoned before continuing, "However, in Emilia's case, I understand why she could be disturbed since I recognize that very familiar voice. I know what he is capable of doing. On top of all that, to this day, Naomi remains a missing person." In the meantime, Neal is rushing to the airport to pick up the client. Once at the airport, the first thing he noticed was this young man holding up a sign reading "Mr. Neel Nest." At that moment, Neal began waving frantically and rushing in the young man's direction. "Hello, I'm Neal; N-e-a-l is the correct spelling." Now embarrassed, the young man slowly extended his left hand toward Neal, apologizing, "Hello, Neal, sorry about chopping up your name; I'm Mr. Clarkson Clark, but everyone calls me Edmond. Sir, I'm honored to finally meet you, and I hope I haven't been too much of a nuisance."

Behind the Curtains

Ultimately waiving his hands in response to Mr. Clark's apology, at the same time whistling for a taxi, before continuing, "No problem, Mr. Clarkson, I just forgot to inform my secretary of your arrival, not to mention I have been totally swamped since she arrived from Paris, things are looking up!" Neal thought for a moment before correcting himself, "I said my secretary, but that's not correct. Ms. Thorn is now my executive assistant." Once the young man reached his hotel, he followed Neal's instruction to contact Sevella and inform her to set up a meeting for the three of them the following morning. He also informed Sevella to schedule a second meeting for the following evening adding Emilia, but first, confirm her arrival time. *Great,* thought Sevella, *here we go again with these after-office investors' meetings, but wait, this client is not an investor. Hmm, maybe this time I'm wrong. I shouldn't be grumbling. On second thought, maybe after the meeting, I can ask Emilia to explain her strange behavior. What's even better, my vacation starts the day after the meeting!* Now focus on getting the conference room set up, and preparing all the documents, suddenly squealing with joy, "Things are finally looking up!"

Following several trips to the fridge, a year later, David was two years old, and Lawrence was teaching David how to use his spill-proof pitcher and cup. On this particular night, Lawrence allowed David to pour, but David bumped the cup, and it fell over on the table. David's large brown eyes stared at the spill while Lawrence encouraged David. "Now, son, let me show you the correct way to pour milk from your pitcher." Lawrence held the pitcher between both David's hands and, slightly above the cup, poured slowly. Now David is jumping up and down, clapping both hands together. Lawrence placed his finger over David's lips to quiet him as he handed the pitcher to David and said, "Don't worry, one day you will pour milk into this cup without your father's help. "As the two prepare to go upstairs, David's mother called, "Lawrence, are you giving him milk? I told you that cold milk keeps him up at night." Smiling to herself, knowing both David and his father are eating her homemade coconut cookies and drinking malt milk. Now the two of them rushed from the kitchen into the den and hid behind the curtains.

Not a moment too soon, they heard her coming down the stairs and quietly stepped down as if to disappear, even though their feet were in plain view of her searching eyes. After several minutes of playing hide and seek, Catheryn called out, "David, Lawrence!" But they both remain wide-eyed and silent, except for an occasional giggle from David. Catheryn pretends to give up. She turns for the stairs, saying in defeat, "I wonder where those two are hiding. Oh well, they could be hiding anywhere. I'll go upstairs and look." Only pretending to search, she called out, "Lawrence, David!" At the same time, climbing into bed, knowing she would fall asleep before they finished their game, she would make one last attempt by speaking loud enough for them to hear from downstairs, saying, "If they should come back into the kitchen for milk and cookies, then I'll catch them red-handed." With that being said, she left the door partially opened so her light could be seen from the dark hallway as she listened for their footsteps. Now free from being caught, they both rushed up the stairs into David's bedroom and sat in the chair to finish the rest of their milk and cookies.

That Man's Voice

Subsequently, the following morning Sevella woke up to the alarm going off and quickly jumped out of bed. "Wow!" she exclaimed. "I didn't even hit the snooze button. I must be really excited to get to work." Sevella spoke to her reflection while pulling open the closet door. Suddenly, her eyes fell on the vacation brochure advertising a trip to Disneyland. "The perfect vacation for me, just the place to forget all my troubles. Besides, Emilia could probably use some vacation time, too; plus, she is arriving today, and I need to focus more on the meeting and less on my vacation. Most of all, before briefing her on the meeting, I can question her about the phone call." Before leaving for work, Sevella remembered the strange way Emilia and Tramishia were acting, along with the uneasiness that gripped her heart after hearing that man's voice. And so, she began to repeat over and over the conversation with Emilia and Tramishia. Once again, her excitement turned into concern as she made every attempt to remain excited. Now focusing on her reflection in the mirror, asking, "Has something happened? If that is the case, what on earth could be so horrible that they can't tell me?"

At that moment, while still home, she decided to contact Tramishia while she was still alone. She picked up the phone, dialed the number but didn't have the courage to complete the call. Then, she called for a taxi. Taking one last look in the mirror prior to going over to the couch, parts the curtains, opens the blinds, and waits hopefully for a chance to see Samuel. Just as she was getting comfortable, her taxi turned onto her street and headed to the address a block away. Quickly closing the blinds and jumping to her feet, grabbing her handbag and keys, "Surely, the taxi is early, or it must be for someone else." As she rushed to lock the door, then ran down the street. "Wow," she said as she climbed into the taxi. "You sure did get here fast!" The driver explained, "I had just dropped off a tab at the breakfast diner and was headed to the corner store near here to buy the best egg/cheese sandwich ever made! By the way, did I get the address wrong?" Taking a deep breath before responding, Sevella replied, "No, oh, not at all." The driver continued, "With my schedule, I like the egg sandwich while it's hot. For lunch, I'll only have enough time between calls to grab a candy bar. This is one of my busiest days."

Although smiling and nodding as the driver continued on about his day, Sevella wasn't listening because her thoughts were on the breakfast diner and her days as a waitress. Suddenly something else occurred to her. "Wow! It just dawned on me; the client at the airport. Yes, I think I've heard that voice before, but I just can't recall where or when." At the same time, another idea came to mind, and Sevella was once again focused on Sam. She wanted so badly to call her and meet with her, or better still, go by the diner and have breakfast with her. "Ma'am, ma'am, are you okay?" The driver's voice broke her train of thought. Suddenly, Sevella laughed jokingly, saying, "I just remembered that I forgot to eat breakfast. By the way, did you say egg or cheese?" The driver laughed, saying, "Yes, the store sells them for breakfast. If

I had known, I would have brought you one." Sevella reminded the driver that he had asked her a question. "Oh," he said, "are you headed for the airport?" Sevella responded, "Oh, so sorry I didn't give you the address. Now I am headed to work."

Fear Grips Her Heart

Not only was that day considered VIP day, but also Sevella would meet face to face the voice of the client that called from the airport. It was then Sevella heard the driver laugh, saying, "What a coincidence, the lady at the diner was excited because she was taking her vacation starting tomorrow." By now, the taxi is pulling up in front of Sevella's office building. In that moment, Sevella quickly paid and tipped him while saying, "Goodbye until 5 p.m.," all the while fighting the desperate attempt to ask him about Sam. Unsuspecting tears crept into her eyes as she walked through the doors of the office building. She struggled to fight back the tears as one dropped on her arm just as the elevator doors opened but closed before anyone else could get on. Sevella quickly wiped away the tear and began to smile as the elevator doors reopened. Often during the morning hours, Neal's office door was usually left open except on this particular morning. As she entered the office, the first thing she noticed was an attached case next to Dorothy's desk, and Neal's door was closed. Now rushing to her office, she heard voices coming from her office. She peeped in, noticing two figures, before slowly walking in.

Once inside, she was looking at the back of their client's head while Neal reclined at her desk. "Good morning, Neal!" greeted Sevella, speaking with a tone of enthusiasm. "Are we having a meeting in my office? Good morning, sir. You must be the gentleman we abandoned at the airport?" Neal stood to introduce the both of them as the young man stood to his feet, turning to shake Sevella's hand; as she extended her hand, they both stopped with hands in midair and stared at one another. "Hey, do you know each other?" Neal asked, surprised at their reactions. "No," said Mr. Clark. Sevella also responded, "No, but we have met." By this time, Neal was asking all sorts of questions, "Tell me, when did you two meet, how did you meet, and where did you meet?" Fear was creeping up Sevella's spine as she remembered the night she met this man. It was the night of her attack, and this man was standing at her door, holding her key as she walked up. Apparently, the intruder entered her hotel room only to drop the hotel key on the floor in front of her hotel room.

Shortly after that, she was speaking to herself while nodding in agreement with Neal, *Yes, I remember his voice, but I never looked at his face. A night I wished I could forget.* Both with hands still in midair as Mr. Clark turned to Neal, explaining, "Well, it was not a pleasant meeting. Actually, your secretary, excuse me, executive, was very angry with me for finding her hotel key." Neal sits down slowly, turning to Sevella, before asking, "You mean to tell me you met Mr. Clark in Florida? When was this?" At that moment, Sevella felt as though her heart had stopped beating as she gasped for air, breathlessly attempting to speak but choosing her words carefully, "It wasn't a pleasant meeting…. I was returning from a late investors' meeting that night, and I was, well, I was very rude to Mr. Clark." At this point, Sevella was frantic, trying to think of something to say as fear gripped her heart, "In the first place," Sevella began but stopped briefly to rephrase, "By the way, I am so glad to finally meet you face to face. I don't know if you remember, but we haven't officially met. I never looked into your face, only at my hotel key you were holding in your hand."

What Is He Doing Here?

At that very moment, Sevella felt faint but somehow managed to continue her explanation, "However, I do remember your voice. Afterward, I felt terrible for speaking so rudely to you, especially after you were such a gentleman to return my hotel key. I must have acted like a mad woman." Sevella then held out her hand for Mr. Clark to shake as he took her hand. Sevella turned to Neal while Mr. Clark insisted, "No, no, I could have easily taken your key to the front desk and reported your room number, but I thought you dropped the key while entering your room. Therefore, I was about to knock on your door. Allow me to also apologize for my rudeness for snatching the key from you and then tossing it back." Neal was ready to interrupt, but Sevella spoke first, "No, really, I was totally out of line." In the meantime, Neal stood up, looking toward Sevella, then at Mr. Clark, waiting for his chance to intervene. Finally, the room was quiet, "Now that you two have been formally introduced, I suggest we get to work," scoffed Neal.

Following that very uncomfortable introduction, the three of them headed to the conference room; Neal then instructed Sevella to get the documents off his desk and prepare some copies for Mr. Clark. Sevella then remembered the documents for Emilia and purposely spoke audibly, "Emilia's meeting is later on, so I'll leave those documents on your desk." On the other hand, deep down inside, she was frantic; as she turned into Neal's office, and before entering, she quickly looked over her shoulders to make sure the two men had entered the conference room. She then ran to the chair farthest from the door and sat down to silence any unwarranted sound coming from her mouth by holding her hands over her lips. Her hands were shaking, her legs were like jelly, and her brain was scrambled. She couldn't think or speak without her voice trembling. "How could this be? Surely, Mr. Clark knows more than he's willing to admit!" Sevella whispered as she remembered the night she lost her purse, which led up to her attack.

Desperately trying to control herself as she reasoned, "Could Mr. Clark possibly be involved or know what happened? Could he and Ellor be in conspiracy with my attacker? Impossible! Well, if not, what is he doing here, and why was he at the hotel?" Suddenly Neal's buzzer sounded startled Sevella answered quickly, "Yes!" Neal, laughing out loud, said, "Hey, glad you haven't left the office; please look into my top file cabinet and bring me those tickets. They are a surprise. I thought I would spring them on you before you made any plans; for your vacation." Apart from the panic attack brought about by Mr. Clark's unexpected visit. Sevella was trying to decide whether to stay, leave for the day, or continue on and pretend that she was holding it together. After a while, Sevella slowly stood, hands still shaking, and opened the top file as she responded enthusiastically, "Got them. I'll be right there."After hearing the disconnection, she audibly asked herself, "Why are these tickets a surprise for me or our client?" As she examined the tickets, her attention was drawn to the flight's destination… Florida.

Surprise Trip to Florida

Clearly panic-stricken, she dropped the tickets back into the file drawer while holding on to the cabinet to support herself. Feeling faint, she scolded herself, "Get a grip! You have been promoted, and this guy is my camouflage from my attacker. The orphanage was my boot camp, and I can handle this, but I must pull it together. I need a reason to excuse myself from this meeting. I needed to strategize my next move if I was going to be one step ahead of my attacker. Apart from this, that man could be associated with Ellor and Mr. Clark. On the other hand, it is possible that this man is unaware of my attack. After all, he was the good guy, and whatever he's doing here, it is because Neal and Ellor have arranged it!" She quickly grabbed the tickets and rushed to make copies, and made a fresh pot of coffee to explain her long stay during the process of getting the documents. As she steps into the conference room, she smiles happily and jokes with Neal, "I just put on a fresh pot of coffee, and I was totally caught off guard that you would go through so much trouble to send me to Florida for my vacation. Thank you! Oh, let me get the coffee. I'll be right back!"

Meanwhile, Neal was questioning Mr. Clark, "Did you get an opportunity other than the mishap to see her in the office or the investors' meeting?" Before Mr. Clark could respond, Sevella returned; at the same time, Neal was tossing his hands into the air, praising Sevella for being so efficient; while jokingly scolding her for holding up the meeting. Finally, Sevella took the coffee and filled the cups, and placed fresh croissants on to saucers. "Yummy," said Mr. Clark as he reached for a croissant, "I have not eaten since last night, and I am actually starving. Thank you, Miss Thorn. Hey, Neal, you are right. She is very efficient!" Neal's lips gave way to a smile while reaching for a croissant. Finally, the men's attention was on the coffee and croissants as Sevella tried desperately to pull it together before thanking Neal once again for the tickets. As she poured coffee for Mr. Clark, he was preoccupied with the croissants and coffee. On the other hand, Neal was very observant and quickly responded, "Sevella, are you feeling okay? You looked as though you had seen a ghost. What's wrong?"

Obviously still shaken, Sevella cleared her throat, thinking fast as she remembered the conversation with the taxi driver. *Well, just like Mr., oh, I'm sorry I didn't get your last name.* Neal quickly spoke up, "Well, I guess you two have not been formally introduced, Mr. Clark. Please, this is my executive Miss Sevella Thorn, and Sevella—this is Mr. Clarkson Clark," Sevella, now feeling more relaxed, once again extends her hand to Mr. Clark. While shaking her hand, he responded with a question, "Really? Are you okay?" At the same time, Mr. Clark reflected back to the meeting at the airport, remembering the sign reading "Neel," laughing before explaining apologetically, "My sign at the airport bore the misspelling of Mr. Nest's first name, embarrassing, but he was gracious enough to correct me but obviously agitated. With that being said, my friends call me Edmond to avoid the confusion between Clark and Clarkson." Now, smiling in Neal's direction as he shook Sevella's hand, they greeted one another a third time. Neal chided in, "Now, can we please get on with business?"

Reliving the Attack

Subsequently, all the attention was on the documents. As Mr. Clark distracted Neal, Sevella continued, "I was already hungry while preparing all that food and hadn't eaten. Now I'm feeling faint." "What?" asked Neal. "As soon as this meeting is over, the two of you will be flying back to Florida for your vacation slash business trip. Oh, by the way, have you heard from Emilia? I was sure she would be here by now." Momentarily stunned, Sevella looked at Neal but did not see him. With a quick move of his hand, Mr. Clark got Sevella's attention. At that moment, Sevella sensed their penetrating gazes, so she first took a sip of coffee while carefully orchestrating her thoughts, starting by saying, "Truthfully, and strangely enough, earlier, I was questioning whether or not to bring her folder to this meeting, and now you are asking about her. However, I did speak to her yesterday, and she requested a taxi be waiting to bring her to the office." Neal interrupted her, "Is that all she said?" Sevella looked at Neal and then Mr. Clark, speaking almost in a whisper, "Well," then realizing she couldn't say too much without giving herself away as she raised the tone of her voice.

On the other hand, to say nothing of her shaking hands and now her forgetting to inform Neal of her conversation with Emilia, now quickly speaking up, "Well, Emilia is such a prankster I'm probably reading too much into it. I'll just say that there may have been some last-minute changes to her schedule." Neal was prepared to get to the bottom of Sevella's strange behavior but became totally distracted by Sevella's last comment. Neal sat down looking more relaxed, and instead of interrogating Sevella, he actually agreed with her saying, "Well, if anyone knows about Ellor's last-minute schedule changes, it's me. Until Emilia shows up, I'll just contact the Temp service and ask them to send over a couple of ladies to cover for you and Kathy. After all that has been said and done, I have another surprise." Now it was Sevella's turn to interrupt, asking, "Surprise? What now?" Meanwhile, Neal was standing as he leaned over, placing both hands on the conference table, facing Mr. Clark with an uncharacteristic joyful tone, "You will also be flying back to Paris to meet with Mr. Brauy."

Now standing, Sevella prepared to protest, but Neal quickly interjected, "You, Sevella, will assist his team with the furtherance of the infrastructure for New Ventures, LLC's modeling agency, and I am sending Mr. Clark as your co-executive to handle the investors' meetings while you work alongside him during office hours. You can enjoy your vacation while in Florida. Afterward, you both will take off for Paris to meet with Mr. Brauy." Momentarily tuning Neal out, Sevella was now reliving the night of her attack as a dark image reached out for her. While pulling back from her attacker's reach, Sevella thrust her right arm forward, but Neal was so involved with his discussion to notice Sevella's untimely movement, but continued his discussion, "Now, the way you arrange your vacation time in Florida is really up to your assistant, Mr. Clark, hence the boss. Get it?" Once she heard, "Mr. Clark, the boss," Sevella was unable to finish her train of thought but disagreed, became indignant as she planned her words carefully, thinking, *First, he sends me on a vacation to hell. Secondly, I'm the assistant, and Mr. Clark is the boss.*

A Look of Panic

Moreover, a moment seemed like an eternity as she gazed at Neal in total disbelief. Thinking, *First, he ignores my hint of feeling faint!* She was attempting to manage a smile before speaking, but Mr. Clark spoke up first, "Miss Thorn, I know we got off to a rough start in Florida, but I assure you, your vacation will not be interrupted. I can handle it. Also, I can tell by the look on your face that this idea is not as appealing as a vacation should be or a vacation you would have planned, but I promise to keep the work off of you, except for a few minor questions." Momentarily taking a breath, Mr. Clark is now studying Sevella's facial expression. In the meantime, Sevella was unaware that all the attention was on her. As Mr. Clark continued, "It's just that I've only worked with Ellor since Florida and not at all with Mr. Nest, so please don't feel frustrated with this plan. Ellor even suggested that you would be an asset to the infrastructure planning committee and a big help to me." The name broke her train of thought, "Ellor, again," she moaned under her breath. The name hit her like a ton of bricks; therefore, for a moment, she went tone deft, not hearing a word after that.

In the meantime, Mr. Clark continued. *Except for the look on your face,* she thought to herself, *Is it a look of panic? I can't seem to hide it, so I better think of something fast.* Again remembering the taxi's conversation, she blurted out, "I would really like to have an egg/cheese sandwich!" With that, Neal and Mr. Clark broke into laughter as both simultaneously pushed the croissants in her direction. As the three finished up their meeting, Mr. Clark and Neal excused themselves as they headed for Neal's office. Meanwhile, Sevella took advantage of the solitude and took a big bite of her croissant and immediately felt as though she was going to throw up. She quickly stood until the feeling subsided, then she busied herself arraigning documents and straightening the conference room. Along with nausea, the overwhelming feeling of apprehension caused her heartbeat to accelerate to an enormous rate as the thought of being in the same city as her attacker. Suddenly she remembered, "That's right, he's flying here with Emilia, and I'm flying out with Mr. Clark!"

Suddenly she ran into Neal's office without knocking, speaking loudly, "Gentleman can we keep my visit to Florida a secret? If Ellor suspects I'm in Florida, well, there goes my vacation." Both men burst into laughter, at the same time shaking their heads, indicating that they agreed. Following the meeting, Sevella knew that right away she needed to speak to someone in Florida as soon as possible, so she gave instructions to herself, "Yes, I'll get Dorothy to set up hotel and accommodation and contact the company's go to people in Florida and Paris. I need to know exactly who I'm dealing with. Also, I need them to think that I'm setting up everything for my new boss, Mr. Clark. I also know that it would be wishful thinking to have Emelia and Tramishia join Mr. Clark on this business venture." It was then she realized that it would be impossible to continue to work with Neal as long as he had any business dealings with Ellor's company.

What Could Have Happened

Once back in the conference room, Sevella poured herself a fresh cup of coffee, hoping to calm her nerves before facing Neal and Mr. Clark. As she glanced at her reflection on the glass-covered table, she noticed the redness in her eyes. But that wasn't her main concern. At this point, Sevella wasn't quite sure when or how, but she knew that she had to figure out a way to get out of going on that trip. "Undoubtedly, my attacker will point the finger, accusing me of being the perpetrator. Fortunately for me, I am aware of his association with Ellor, Mr. Clark, or both!" As she cleared the conference table, she remembered the statement made by Neal at the very first meeting after he introduced her to Ellor, almost bragging, "I thought she was a model looking for part-time work when she first applied for the receptionist position." At the same time, her thoughts are now on Tramishia and Emilia, remembering their weird behavior. Now speaking audibly, "How could that be, and what could have happened to cause them to act so distance?" As shivers went down her spine, causing her to tremble, she placed both hands over her face out of sheer confusion, hoping to stop the tears before anyone saw her.

A moment later, the sound of Neal's voice over the speakerphone frightened her, "Sevella!" Neal was almost yelling, now standing quickly and clumsily dropping documents on the floor. She quickly grabbed the documents from the floor as she dashed by the tray of croissants. She shoved one into her mouth, hoping nausea would not return, poured a third cup of coffee, and rushed into Neal's office. As she entered his office, both men burst into laughter. "Hey," said Neal. "You look like a little puppy who just stole a bone and ran to hide it away." Realizing she must look absolutely ridiculous with that croissant hanging out of her mouth, she quickly took a seat next to Mr. Clark, apologizing, "Please, if you would kindly go on with your meeting, I will quietly make this coffee and croissant disappear." "On the other hand," Neal explained as he turned to Sevella, "I think it's best if you handle all the documents, starting with packing and labeling each one before you leave for Florida. Once you have arrived in Florida, the only thing left for you is to enjoy your vacation, to quote Mr. Clark, 'until you leave for Paris.'"

Waves of thoughts are now rushing through her mind; Sevella could sense that all eyes were once again on her. Staring blindly toward Neal and Mr. Clark, but directing her question to Neal, "Neal, what hotel did you approve for our stay?" Now looking very annoyed, Neal snapped, "The same as before!" Immediately her thoughts were on the night of her attack. "Well, if you don't mind," attempting to speak without her voice trembling, Sevella continued, "Since I am on my vacation, I prefer to stay in a different hotel. I will pay. I don't mind." At this point, Mr. Clark chided in, "Are you sure you're not trying to distance yourself from me?" Neal stood up, pointing toward his office door and politely motioning with the other hand, "Now, I want you both out of my office! I don't care, Sevella, you choose; I will still pay the bill. Just make the arrangement for whatever hotel. It's on the company's account."

Working with Her Attacker

"Furthermore!" Neal yelled out as Mr. Clark was closing the door. Sevella turned as Neal continued, "First and foremost, I'm sending you away for a vacation; secondly, I want to be sure that Mr. Clark has your cooperation at all intervals." Slowly nodding, then turning away, whispering, "I'll be there for him," but her words were heard by Mr. Clark. The following evening as she lay awake, Sevella found herself struggling with whether or not to take the trip. Speaking to herself, *Even if this next trip to Florida is vacation, there is no way I can or will be able to enjoy myself. What if the client with the familiar voice travels to Boston with Emilia? He could easily return to Florida once he finds out that I'm there. Oh, that's right, no one will know that I've traveled unless Neal tells them I'm there. I must remind Neal to keep my stay in Florida a secret. Otherwise, I will refuse to go!* Sevella practically stayed awake all night tossing and turning, worrying about the outcome of her stay in Florida. The following morning, after packing, she couldn't shake the thought of working with, or worse, running into her attacker.

Despite putting on a brave face, she felt mortified, knowing that her attacker knew her and the fact that she had no idea who he was. Speaking in a whisper, "Even more frightening, I know the sound of his voice!" Sevella decided right then and there to cancel, "I will not go. I'm canceling my travel since Mr. Clark has been designated by Neal to represent New Ventures, LLC; I see no reason for me to give up my vacation and possibly risk my life."

The moment Sevella arrived at the office, she was convinced the trip for her wasn't going to happen. However, in order to announce Mr. Clark's new position as New Ventures, LLC's Executive, several phone calls had to be made, contacting one person after the other. Eventually, time ran out, and there was only enough time to give Neal her final instructions. As she sat watching the clock, she whispered, "What if I stay behind and my attacker shows up here?" While sitting alone in the conference room, feeling trapped, she buried her face in both hands, attempting to stop the tears.

Furthermore, Sevella was thinking very carefully about instructing Mr. Clark about her incognito vacation but changed her mind; instead, she wanted to know how much Mr. Clark knew about her first Florida trip. Now expecting Neal or Mr. Clark to walk into the conference room at any minute and finding her in tears, she began to encourage herself, "Fine, I'll go! In the past, I've never let fear control me, and it's not about to control me now." Eventually, Sevella and Mr. Clark said their goodbyes to Neal, and while the men went over final plans, Sevella double-checked the labels on all the boxes while placing instructions inside each box for Mr. Clark to follow. As they left the office for the taxi, Mr. Clark helped the driver load the boxes, but in that instance, before climbing into the taxi, Sevella looked at Mr. Clark, and likewise, he looked directly at her, saying, "Whatever it is, Ms. Thorn that you want me to do, just ask." Sevella responded with a smile, "I guess you are now a mind reader, and you know exactly what am I thinking?" Looking even more serious, he repeated, "Just ask."

Kicking and Screaming

After sliding into the cab next to Sevella, Mr. Clark continued, "No, I can't read your mind, but I'm very serious about you being open with me." Now considering her response, she was now thinking, *As for me, I need to carefully choose my words,* calming herself before speaking, "Mr. Clark…. I don't want anyone to know that I'm in Florida; if possible, therefore, when you make your business calls to me, please be sure you don't call my name. If necessary, you can make up a name and give the impression that you are working with someone from the home office. Believe me, when I tell you that Ellor will be elated at the prospect of having his PR person running things for Neal. Nothing else will really matter. By the way, I did give Neal the same instructions. Remember, just don't use my name. I tell you what. Before we get to Florida, I will think of a fake name, a name you will use when addressing me in the meetings and in the office." Mr. Clark appeared to be confused. Finally, he asked, "You…are going to use a fake name, but why?"

Momentarily, Sevella struggled, unable to come up with a sensible answer, "Well, you see, it's like this, If Ellor or any of his team finds out that I'm there, I know he will want me to attend the investors' meeting, and maybe even assist you in the office. After all, once we get to Florida, Ellor will become the boss." Now nodding, Mr. Clark responded, "You know, you are right! Of course, Neal conveniently left out that pertinent information."

Now holding both hands in front of him, while looking into his palms, spoke hesitantly, "I tell you what, I will not even use your name. I will just say my secretary and excuse myself to call the office. What do you think?" Now moving her head from left to right, Sevella said, "No, I don't think that will work. This was a very fast-paced business, and we needed to be consistent and professional on every occasion. Trust me, out of sight, out of mind. I know what I'm doing." Now raising both hands up in surrender, Mr. Clark agreed, "Okay, have it your way. Out of sight, out of mind."

Shortly after takeoff, Sevella adjusted her seat in the reclining position, relaxing to the sound of the rushing wind as the plane took off. With her body completely relaxed, she quickly falls asleep. Undoubtedly, still uncomfortable at the thought of going back to Florida, she began to dream and suddenly heard the sound of her hotel door being swung open; immediately, she jumped out of her bed. Her focus is now on the interior door adjacent to Ellor's room, desperately hoping he would hear her knock, and quickly unlocks the door. She ran as fast as she could to reach the door before her assailant caught up with her. Tangled in the sheet, she slipped and fell to the floor just as her assailant grabbed the sheet from the corner and pulled her in his direction. Kicking and screaming, she attempted to escape, but her scream had no sound. Suddenly, she was face to face with her attacker, but the darkness of the room prevented her from seeing his face. All of a sudden, the man's hands were around her throat; she quickly rolled under the bed to get away from his grip. At the same time, her left arm bumps the lady seated next to her on the plane. Waking up from the impact and looking around frantically, the lady answered sleepily, "What, what?"

What's Going On?

Before turning her head in the opposite direction and quickly falling back to sleep, "I'm sorry; I guess I was having a nightmare," Sevella whispered apologetically, slowly turning toward the lady seated next to her. Obviously feeling very embarrassed but thankful that the lady had quickly fallen asleep. Sevella glanced past the woman's head and noticed Mr. Clark seated next to the window across the aisle. Now speaking in a whisper as she turns to look out of her window, "Yes, and it's the same nightmare that has been recurring since the attack." Again she glanced in Mr. Clark's direction, realizing that if he had been seated next to her, she would have bumped and awakened him. At this point, she is very grateful for the seating arrangement because he would have insisted on hearing all about it. After arriving in Florida, Mr. Clark was true to his word, working independently of her and contacting the office in Ellor's presence, but being very discreet in using a fake name when speaking to Sevella. Just as Neal promised, her vacation time started immediately after landing in Florida. Most importantly, Ellor and his staff were none the wiser and unsuspecting of any deception.

Except for one particular night, a couple of days before they were to leave for Paris, Mr. Clark called to inform Sevella that a man was asking about Neal's secretary. He explained, "I pretended not to hear him, so he finally left but came back later and approached me again. This time, I made up a lie and told him the only person I knew in that firm was Neal." After a moment of silence, Mr. Clark continued, "I went to the trouble of telling him how I was stranded at the airport, waiting for a call from Neal's secretary that I never received. I continued to tell him that Neal had to pick me up from the airport and feed me croissants and coffee to keep me from starving. Which was all true; eventually, he walked off, laughing hysterically." As they boarded the plane for Paris, the pressure of the following week and trying to keep a low profile left Sevella feeling overstressed. After boarding the plane and settling in her seat, Sevella remembered Emilia's weird behavior and the man's voice. Being overly tired and exhausted, she quickly fell asleep and began to dream of her attacker.

Unlike the other dreams, this time, she wasn't able to get under the bed because her attacker tied her up. Finally, and after several attempts to pull her arms free from her attacker's grip, her right arm elbowed Mr. Clark's left arm. Waking as her arm made contact with Mr. Clark's arm, hesitatingly, she looked in his direction and apologized for her unwarranted attack on his arm. Eventually, both settled back and were able to fall asleep. As the darkness of night faded and the morning sun shone softly through Mr. Clark's window, a strange sound from across the aisle awakened them. The passenger seated across the aisle from Sevella pulled down his seat tray. "Good morning, Mr. Clark," greeted Sevella, but at the same time, hoping he was too sleepy to remember the bump to his arm. Barely awake, and drowsily looking in both directions, and seemly very confused, questioning Sevella, "What's going on?" His voice was muffled as he covered his face with both hands.

Quickly Sevella pretended that something was wrong with him, and she reached out to him, speaking in a comforting tone, "What on earth is wrong? Did you hurt yourself when you jumped like that?"

The Suspense Is Overbearing

Meanwhile, Mr. Clark was still covering his face, at the same time shaking his head from left to right, still mumbling through his fingers, "No, I'm not alright. My arm is throbbing, and earlier this morning, I thought my heart had leaped out of my chest. Now, tell me, do I look alright?" By this time, the flight attendant is standing in the aisle between Sevella and the passenger across from her, asking, "Sir, would you like something to drink?" Ignoring Mr. Clark's previous question, Sevella turned to Mr. Clark, asking, "What would you like to drink?" Mr. Clark answered dryly, "Coffee." Sevella then turned to the flight attendant, asking, "Excuse me, may we get two coffees, one black, and the other crème and sugar." Mr. Clark is now turning toward Sevella while rubbing his face, mumbling, "I apologize for my rudeness earlier." Sevella smiled, now feeling much more relaxed, and responded, "No apology necessary." Mr. Clark is looking confused as he rubs his left arm, looking at Sevella, then asking, "By the way, were you getting back at me for something? Is that why you elbowed me?" Before she could answer, the flight attendant was standing at the end of the aisle with their coffee.

Shortly after that, Sevella passed Mr. Clark's coffee to him, but moments later, Mr. Clark repeated his question, "Why did you elbow me?" Sevella played it off. "I didn't mean to. I was waking up when I heard the loud sound, and I guess I must have jumped without realizing it." Mr. Clark laughed jokingly and said, "I was just guessing. I really didn't know what happened except for my throbbing arm." Now agitated, Sevella purposely ignored Mr. Clark while pretending to be preoccupied with some documents until the flight attendant returned to take their breakfast order. While waiting for breakfast and still looking very serious, Mr. Clark cautiously turns toward Sevella. At the same time, Sevella silently screamed, "Oh, no!" Then turning quickly, she pretended to look for the attendant, saying silently, "Don't tell me he is going to drive this arm-throbbing thing into the ground." Mr. Clark didn't speak right away but hesitated as if examining the tray in front of him. Finally, he spoke up, "First of all, I need to apologize for keeping a secret from you; secondly, I believe once I've revealed this secret, you'll feel more comfortable working with me."

It was then that Sevella felt chills go down her spine. Therefore, she suddenly sat straight up, attempting to act calm; instead, she felt faint, wondering, *What on earth is he keeping from me?* Sweat filled her palms; the suspense was overbearing, and the thought of his revelation was unbearable as she imagined him saying, "Sevella, you've been reported as a troublemaker!" At that point, Mr. Clark realized that Sevella wasn't listening. He then waved his right hand in front of her eyes to get her attention. As a result of the unexpected movement of Mr. Clark's hand, Sevella turned to look in his direction; again, Mr. Clark cleared his throat but remained silent, then he said, "Sevella, that same guy that was asking about you approached me twice. The first time he approached me, I was calling to inform you of Neal's most recent request. The second time I was about to call, but before I could dial your number, this same guy passed by, asking jokingly, 'Are you having an argument with your wife?' His timing was perfect; otherwise, I would have made the call, and he would have easily listened in on my conversation without me knowing it."

A Secret Admirer

Despite the feeling of relief, Sevella was now experiencing deep concern about the man in question. Meanwhile, Mr. Clark continued, "Most importantly, since you never gave a fake name, I would have mentioned your name. Do you have any idea who he is? He seems to be very infatuated with you," now attempting to pull it together and not sound insane, Sevella jokingly said, "He's… probably just a secret admirer." Mr. Clark, laughing half-heartily, responded, "Well, if that be the case, I'll say no more. By the way, did you enjoy every day of your vacation, and was I successful in keeping the workload off of you? Oh, before you answer, are you aware that your vacation ends tomorrow night? So, by the time we get to Paris, Miss Thorn, you will be fully staffed and, sad to say, my boss." In the meantime, Sevella is searching for an excuse, one that would allow her to act as an assistant but work from her hotel room. At the same time, the flight attendant was announcing their arrival in France. Sevella turned and placed her right hand on Mr. Clark's left arm, almost pleading, "Look, I know my vacation is over, but I want to stay in hiding a little longer."

Shortly after that, Mr. Clark turned and stared at Sevella but didn't speak. Sevella spoke almost in a whisper, "Don't worry. I'll work as hard and as long as you want me to, but let it be said, your secretary is on vacation but working from her hotel room when needed." Frowns in his brow with many questions to ask, instead, Mr. Clark whispered back, "What name shall I use?" Smiling a very large grin and wanting to throw her arms around his neck in gratitude, she quickly responded, "You choose." As they approached the first work week in Pairs, Sevella and Mr. Clark avoided each other except for quick meetings over the phone to exchange information pertaining to an upcoming meeting. As it happens, there was an awkward moment when the staff threw a surprise party for a coworker, and everyone in the office had to hide. Ironically Mr. Clark ran into a vacant office space, and right after him, a man came in laughing as he tried to catch his breath and stood behind him. Mr. Clark remained very quiet. The office was dark, and finally, the man whispered, "Are you here for the after-hour party?" Afterward, Mr. Clark whispered, "What?..."

What's more, before he could finish his sentence, the man changed the subject, saying, "You know, this job is no joke." Now nervously laughing and trying to catch his breath. "It is truly a learning experience for me, too," whispered Mr. Clark. A knock on the door interrupted their conversation. "Hey, you can come out now!" yelled Mr. Brauy. "We are all assembled around the conference table and resuming the meeting." As they were walking back to the conference room, Mr. Clark turned to look at the man behind him, but he was headed toward the door, and Mr. Clark could only see the back of his head. After contacting Sevella with an update on the final notes from Mr. Brauy, Sevella asked, "Is there anything else you want to tell me?" Undoubtedly, Mr. Clark felt as though Sevella knew more than she was willing to admit, but Mr. Clark avoided her question, explaining, "There was a surprise party. The noise from everyone assembling at the conference table was too loud for me to even greet the person seated next to me. However, there was this strange conversation before the surprise when hiding."

Nightmare a Reality

During that time, Mr. Clark realized this information could prove to be valuable, and keeping it to himself would be more practical than sharing it. Without waiting on his response, she jokingly teased, "You talking to me?" Mr. Clark's silence was very disturbing, and Sevella suspected that he heard or saw something that he couldn't or wouldn't share with her—eventually ending their conversation with quick goodbyes. Now realizing the fear she experienced in Florida had followed her to France, the nightmares were now becoming a reality. Standing and staring out of her window, she admitted to herself, *I believe Mr. Clark has picked up on something. On the other hand, I wonder if Mr. Clark is the person I can truly confide in. No way, I barely know him, definitely not! Besides, he is still a complete stranger, and you don't confide in strangers.* For the first time since arriving in France, Sevella remembered Emilia and wondered if she would be in Boston when they arrived. After boarding the plane for their departure, Sevella wondered if this trip to Paris would be the last.

Soon after boarding the plane, Sevella was now feeling very exhausted from little sleep. She knew she didn't want to sit next to Mr. Clark, so she chose a seat other than her assigned seat, and without warning, the heaviness of her eyes gave way to deep sleep. She was now seated next to the window, expecting someone would want their seat, and she would be forced to sit in her assigned seat next to Mr. Clark. "But not before getting a good nap," murmured

Sevella. "Ma'am, ma'am, I think you are in the wrong seat. May I see your stub?" Rising slowly from her seat, Sevella attempted to move to her correct seat, but the flight attendant motioned for her to sit, saying, "No, the person who should be sitting here took your seat in first class. I was wondering if you wanted to exchange with him?" Now looking baffled, Sevella repeated the attendant's questions; "First class, did you say first class? What was Mr. Clark thinking to book first-class seats?" Moreover, Sevella understood that the attendant was not going anywhere until she received an answer.

Before long, the flight attendant placed her hand on Sevella's shoulder while saying, "Ma'am, are you okay? You can remain here if you wish, but you will have to pay for your meals. Do you want to remain in this seat?" Looking curiously at the flight attendant, Sevella asked, "Can I get reimbursed for the ticket?" The attendant smiled politely and said, "No, but it's up to you." Momentarily sitting deep in thought, Sevella hesitantly admitted, "I will go to first class but allow me to pay for the person's next meal since I took their seat," Nodding agreeably, the attendant escorts her to her seat, and much to her surprise the person whose seat she was sitting in turned out to be Mr. Clark's. "I don't believe it!" Why on earth would you place me in first class and you in coach? Do you not know that Neal is going to faint when he finds out?" Now holding up crossed fingers signaling the time out, Mr. Clark finally gets Sevella's attention, explaining, "Look, Miss Thorn, it was Neal's idea for you to ride back in first class! He said that your promotion placed you in a different financial bracket, and since this is a business trip, first-class it must be. Don't you agree?"

A New Year, a New Career

With that in mind, pretending not to be excited, Sevella slowly takes her seat in first class. After a successful trip to Paris, she headed for home after a short meeting with Neal and Mr. Clark. Resting comfortably on her couch while peering through her half-opened blinds, eventually, Sevella closed her eyes, reminiscing on the days at the diner with her friend Sam. Remembering a night of bowling while attempting to hold the bowling ball over her very protruding stomach. That joyful memory was so overwhelming that tears rolled down her cheeks onto her arms as she glanced down, noticing the teardrop shaped like a very tiny puddle, which appeared to have an invisible border that prevented it from rolling off her arm onto the couch. Suddenly, the painful thought of the attacker and her decision to abort forced her to turn from side to side as she wrestled to escape the painful memory. Being unable to shake the memory caused more sadness and more tears. Now crying uncontrollably, she wept bitterly.

Later on, "Ring, ring, ring!" Sevella, startled at the ringing of the phone, unaware that she had fallen asleep, now jumping to her feet, she ran to quickly answer, "Hello," only for the caller to hang up without saying a word. Still very sleepy, she determined that it must have been the wrong number and went straight to bed. The following morning, once again startled by the ringing, Sevella jumped up runs to the living room for her phone, only to realize that it was her alarm clock. As she gathered her thoughts, she immediately realized that she had slept all night without once being tormented by that horrible reoccurring nightmare. Flashing a smile at her image in the mirror, squealing, "What a wonderful feeling. I was so sad in my dream, but I woke up refreshed. I know it's because I have begun a new career in a new year." For the most part, her memory of the strange call appeared to be a dream. As she reflected back on that very moment, her heart began to beat faster and faster. "It wasn't a dream. Should I be concerned, who could it have been? I'm just being silly. I don't just hand out my cell number to just anyone."

Eventually, glancing at the clock, now she's rushing to dress for work. Once arriving at the office, she was met by Neal, wearing that ridiculous smile on his face, a smile she hadn't seen since the meeting with Ellor. "Good morning, Sevella. How does it feel to be the boss?" Now wondering, *What is he up to?* In a curious tone, she slowly responded, "Good morning, Neal. What's up?" As if on a remote device, her office door opens, and out steps Mr. Clark. "What are you doing in my office, and why is Neal acting so strange? What is going on?" At first sight, she realized that Mr. Clark was not smiling but managed to smile when Neal glanced in his direction. "Well, I have another surprise for you. I bet you can't guess what it is?" Still wondering about the expression on Mr. Clark's face, slowly she turned to Neal, saying, "No, and I don't want to guess." Now turning to Mr. Clark, but was distracted by Neal gesturing for both of them to come into his office. Anger replaced the joy she felt earlier as Sevella shuddered as she walked into Neal's office.

No! Not Again

Occasionally, she would glance from Neal and then back to Mr. Clark. However, neither noticed since both men were preoccupied with documents and taking notes as Neal continued, "In addition," then pausing momentarily, motioned for both of them to have a seat before continuing his speech, "I want you both to know that the trip to Paris was an absolute success, therefore, in one month you both will be returning to Florida! This trip will not be like any other." Now asking rhetorically, "Why not?" Then answering, "Guess what? Ellor is going to help us set up New Ventures Modeling Firm Corporate office in Florida!" Without thinking twice, Sevella grabbed the arms of her chair as if to stand, but Neal ignored her gesture and continued his speech, "Sevella, just as before, you will be Mr. Clark's assistant." Sevella springs from her chair while pushing it backward. In the meantime, Mr. Clark quickly stood and looked very concerned but said nothing. Neal continued, "Calm down, and just wait a minute before you fly off the hook. I am making Mr. Clark temporary boss because we will be using the same successful strategy."

Eventually, Sevella lost all control of her emotion; at that moment, her stomach began to ache as if she had eaten something very bitter. It was then she screamed, "No, not again, I will not go!" On the other hand, Mr. Clark tried to calm her down; Sevella recognized the calming tone of Mr. Clark's voice and began to regain her composure; at the same time, she was fighting back tears. Consequently, Neal was gesturing toward Mr. Clark, hoping to get an understanding of her outburst, but Mr. Clark only had his suspicion but wasn't ready to disclose his suspicion to Neal or Sevella. Meanwhile, Sevella lost all composure and began to cry uncontrollably while Neal helplessly stood by. Taking the initiative, Mr. Clark spoke up. "There is something going on, and I would really like to know what it is. First of all, I applied for the security position in Ellor's firm, but instead, Ellor hired me as his Public Relations Executive. Secondly, Ellor suggested a dual position with both companies and quickly sent me here to assist you, Neal. Furthermore, Sevella seemed to be the last to know anything about what goes on, which is ironic since she's your executive."

In addition to the shock of another planned trip to Florida, Sevella was ready to tell all, but Mr. Clark interrupted her, explaining, "Most importantly, Sevella appears to be very frightened at the concept of any return trip to Florida. I think that's rather strange for an employee whose job description includes travel, and despite the fact that I've only known her a short while, I have observed signs of trauma in her behavior, and I know she is very troubled." Due to Mr. Clark's observation of Sevella's behavior, and after hearing the words, "very frightened," Sevella had time to regains her composure, shaking her head while admitting, "Something did happen in Florida, but I'm not ready to talk about it." In that instance, she changed the subject, "Now I agree with Mr. Clark that I am the last to know about any and everything, and that shouldn't be, especially now that I am your administrative executive. Not to mention, before any promotion, I had to go at it alone, just like Naomi, and that was before Cu'Dull or Tramishia; at one time, they were equally my assistants." Suddenly, Sevella was quiet and deep in thought.

What Happened in Florida

At that moment, Mr. Clark again interrupted, speaking calmly to Sevella, "By the way, I didn't expect this to come out so soon, Sevella, but my background is in investigations; let me explain, I'm not state, county, or federal, but in-house security, I've worked for several prestigious companies. With that being said, can someone please tell me what's going on? Or, better still, Neal, can you explain what happened in Florida?" With that question on the table, Sevella quickly attempted to take the attention off of her; and began to think of something constructive to explain her behavior. Clearing her throat, "By the way, Neal, I don't want to go into details, but we've heard nothing in months about Naomi's situation." The phone rang, and Neal rushed to answer, hoping the interruption would silence Sevella to keep her from discussing Naomi's disappearance. "Hello!" Neal's annoyance was projected onto the caller. "Oh, Ellor, yes, hold on," Neal motioned for privacy as Sevella and Mr. Clark left his office. "What's that all about?" Mr. Clark asked jokingly, hoping to calm Sevella down by changing the subject.

Similar to his first introduction to New Ventures, Mr. Clark is once again directed to the conference room, only this time at Sevella's invitation. As they both walked toward the conference room, Sevella asked, "Coffee?" Mr. Clark nodded his head vigorously. That unexpected reaction from Mr. Clark caused Sevella to laugh. While waiting on the coffee, Sevella felt safe enough to respond without breaking down, "It was a total shock to me that I was being demoted so soon after my promotion. Now that you are here, I really believe that Neal would rather have a male assistant to handle that group in Florida." At this point, hoping to escape Mr. Clark's investigative mind while attempting to fight back the tears, speaking as reassuringly as possible, "Hearing that kind of news before breakfast caused me to react as I did." Then she said, "After all, I've worked hard all these years, and Neal never really appreciated me or what I've done for this company."

Eventually, taking a sip of her coffee while taking a deep breath, she stared silently out of the window, whispering, "As always, it has been what he wanted. Please, please don't misunderstand me. I am so very, very grateful for all he has done for me. I really am!" After a lengthy pause, while slowly taking another sip of his coffee, Mr. Clark continued with a slight smile, "Believe it or not, I do understand." Unlike the first meeting, Sevella was now well aware of the danger lurking around each investors' meeting. She stood, pointing toward the door, not to interrupt Mr. Clark as he sat quietly sipping his coffee. "Excuse me," she whispered as she exited the conference room. Once securely secluded inside her office, before sitting down at her desk, she looked up to see Neal rushing past her office toward the conference room, only to find Mr. Clark alone sipping his coffee. Neal rushed straight for the coffee pot, glancing over his left shoulder in Mr. Clark's direction as he poured his coffee. Afterward, he stood sipping his coffee, staring at the floor as he considered a way to start the conversation.

Unexpected Reactions

After sitting, Neal picked up the documents as if to glance through the stack, and without looking up, he asked, "Mr. Clark do you know what's going on with Sevella?" Completely caught off guard, Mr. Clark choked on his coffee as Neal rushed to his rescue with two hard hits on the back. Afterward, Neal took a seat next to Mr. Clark, who was now attempting to catch his breath while coughing and carefully taking one deep breath after another. "First of all," whispered Neal, "I want to apologize for involving you in such a confidential and personal situation. Secondly, forget I ever ask you that question." As if Neal could read his thoughts, but before responding, Mr. Clark took another sip of his coffee, now smiling as he placed his cup on the table, nervously responding, "I didn't see that coming, however, and I must admit, Sevella and I have a lot in common. She also admitted to me the why of her unexpected reaction; with all the last-minute changes, she no longer felt that her new position at New Ventures LLC was secure."

"Furthermore," he paused, taking another sip of his now warm coffee, Mr. Clark continues, "Matter of fact, Sevella just informed me that her position as executive wasn't two days old when I showed up to become her boss. Not to mention all the credit for Future Ventures, LLC's success in Florida, was given to me!" A moment later, Sevella walked into the conference room just in time to hear Mr. Clark's remarks on "all the credit." Equally important, what she heard gave her the confidence she needed to address Neal.

Not long after, as she took her seat, clearing her throat, "Neal, I actually thought the whole idea of Florida was something you and Mr. Clark had agreed upon without my knowledge, but after talking with Mr. Clark, I realized that he was just as clueless. Needless to say, I can't stop thinking about Naomi's situation." Neal nervously took one sip of coffee after another before voicing his famous one-liner, "Oh, really." Mr. Clark interrupted, hoping to avoid another scene. "I said too much," stated Mr. Clark apologetically.

At that moment, the awkwardness in the room was so obvious that Neal felt very uncomfortable but very thankful that Mr. Clark spoke up before Sevella continued her discussion on Naomi. Now feeling very relieved, Neal began to laugh; Sevella was thinking, *Totally out of character for Neal and a clear indication that he was very nervous about something. But what?* Sevella moved forward in her chair. All eyes are on her, feeling completely revived. She smiled and said, "Oh, that's right, for a moment, I did forget the game, you know, 'switch the boss.' The truth is, I wanted to enjoy my vacation, so I asked Mr. Clark to go at it alone, so please don't take this the wrong way. I reacted to the news because Florida was more work than you can imagine." Surprised at her honest confession, Mr. Clark turned in disbelief, but Sevella ignored his reactions. *On the contrary,* stated Sevella as she gathered her thoughts, *I had to manage to stay out of sight plus keep Mr. Clark on track. Therefore, it felt more like work than a vacation. It would have been more advantageous for me to start my new position, but again, as I explained earlier, I don't want to go into details.*

Not Convinced

Now smiling and looking very relieved, Neal glances back and forth from Mr. Clark to Sevella, carefully choosing his words, "Initially, the trip to Florida wasn't on my agenda, but Ellor insisted that I send you back to work with his office staff to help them further Future Venture's growth and expansion. Sevella, I hope you don't mind if things remain as you and Mr. Clark arranged previously, and I'm expecting this project to last only a couple of weeks. Still feeling very uneasy, Mr. Clark was now wondering, *Exactly what did happen in Florida, and why is Neal suddenly so calm?* Earlier, prior to Neal rushing into the conference room, Mr. Clark was still trying to piece together Sevella's reaction to the Florida trip. Now raising his hands to get Neal's attention, and after getting a nod, Mr. Clark made his request, "Neal, I really believe that you should recommend someone other than Sevella for this job. I can even go alone; I know what Ellor expects. As for Sevella, she can stay here and set up everything."

Meanwhile, Neal was moving his head from left to right, all the while Mr. Clark was speaking. Finally, interrupting Mr. Clark, "No! I mean, no, or what I mean is, Ellor is a new client to the business, and he has done extremely well as one of our top investors; surely, we can't disappoint him now. Sevella, you know all the ends and outs of both companies. As you shared earlier regarding the first out-of-state meeting, confessing that you went at it alone and did extremely well. Also, and may I add, it was

Ellor's idea to send Mr. Clark, but it was my idea to allow Mr. Clark to represent both of our companies in France. Consequently, Sevella, since you were semi-on vacation, I arranged it so that not one plan was executed without you being at the forefront of each decision, although you were undercover. That's how important you are to this company and this venture. Now, what do you say? Can we get on with business as usual?" Afterward, smiling with a nod, she excused herself to the lounge before walking out of the conference room.

Meanwhile, she returned to the conference room with donuts; Neal stood up from his chair and walked quickly toward the donuts, asking, "Now, tell me, what did happen in Florida?" Still feeling very confident, Sevella turned, facing Mr. Clark, and said, "You said something earlier, Mr. Clark; you said that only after a short while, you noticed something was wrong, and you were right. On the first visit to Florida, on one occasion, there was this drunken gentleman who mistakenly came to my door. It was frightening. But afterward, I realized that he was lost, I called the head desk, and they escorted him to his room." After Sevella's confession, Mr. Clark was now looking very confused, but he was not yet convinced as he recalled their first meeting. "Therefore," stated Mr. Clark, "you had two callers that night. Who was first, him or me?" Now speaking more seriously, he looked at Neal, insisting, "I still would like to go at it alone."

I Must Be Dreaming

"Furthermore," stated Neal, standing and purposely ignoring Mr. Clark's remarks, "Mr. Clark, by the end of the week, I want you to contact Ellor and make arrangements for you and Sevella's flight back to Florida." Obviously, after Neal's impolite and annoying response, Mr. Clark was very annoyed but politely agreed as he excused himself, afterward quickly standing and walking slowly toward the door. However, before making his exit, he looks behind him, suggesting, "I may be wrong, but Sevella still deserves a vacation." On the other hand, Neal stood and sat next to Sevella, whispering, "You know, I really think that you should be the one to go at it alone. I believe you can handle the whole thing without an assistant. This arrangement of Ellor's to bring Mr. Clark on board is very questionable." Fear gripping Sevella's heart, she struggles to maintain her relaxed demeanor. "Well, if we want to impress Ellor, I think we should leave things as they are." Now frantically nodding his head up and down, Neal agreed, "You are right! Let's just leave things the way they are. My only concern is… that it may take longer than a couple of weeks."

Shortly after that, Neal got up and walked toward the door but stood in silence before saying, "You know, Ellor is notorious for last-minute changes; the way he's talking, this job may take much longer than a couple of weeks." Neal began to pace back and forth. In the meantime, Sevella felt as if her heart had stopped beating. Right after that, Mr. Clark walked back into the conference room and stood next to Sevella. Neal glanced up as Mr. Clark walked into the room but didn't say anything; they both remained silent until it felt uncomfortable for Sevella, "Neal, If I may, Mr. Clark and I decided that we will take the trip on one condition; we prefer to wrap things up within that purposed week; however, I understand Ellor's persistent in adding to the schedule. Most likely, we will be in Florida for at least three, but I insist on no more than three weeks. You can make up whatever excuse you wish, but three weeks is the max. I need you to insist that this assignment is wrapped up in that amount of time. Will you do that for me, Neal?"

Soon after, Neal turned to Mr. Clark, asking, "Does that work for you?" Before answering, Mr. Clark looked at Sevella and then at Neal, starred at the floor in stark silence before making his request, "Yes, but on one condition," Neal now motioned for Mr. Clark to sit before asking, "What would that be?" Mr. Clark continued, "While in Florida, I noticed that there were some shady fellows hanging around after office hours, and even during the investors' meeting, I was privileged to indirectly meet one of them. Don't misunderstand me. I'm not saying there was something shady about him. He actually left before the meeting started. I'm not saying it was anything wrong with the way we met. I'm just suggesting that I think it would be wiser if Sevella and I have adjoining rooms, if that's okay with you, Sevella?" Obviously overjoyed at Mr. Clark's suggestion, she quickly nodded yes while turning to face Neal.

My Bodyguard

As soon as he had Neal's cooperation, Mr. Clark knew that he needed Neal to work with him and not against him. Therefore, he continued, "Just to keep an eye on things." Neal happily agreed, turning to Sevella, "Now that's all settled. Let's focus on the trip." Along with shaking knees, Sevella trembled at the very thought of going back to Florida, knowing if that voice was heard at any one of those meetings, she could have a nervous breakdown. In spite of her apprehension, she felt safer with Mr. Clark in the adjoining room. "And my bodyguard!" speaking silently. Still distracted by her thoughts, Sevella managed to focus long enough to agree with a halfhearted nod, thinking, *I know my fears, nervousness, and the trembling in my voice will eventually expose my torment.* After signaling with her nod, Neal motioned for Mr. Clark to take Emilia's office and get things started. At the same time, he gently grabbed Sevella by her left elbow and said, "Come and see my surprise." As they walked past the conference room and toward the executive bathrooms, stopping in front of one of the executive's offices, she couldn't believe it, whispering, "I must be dreaming."

Momentarily and uncharacteristically silent but looking like his old self, Neal smiled before saying, "Apart from all this confusion, I know that your vacation was not what you planned, but I needed you out of the office long enough to prepare my surprise. You know, moving my office to the third floor was a real challenge, whereas moving your office was a double challenge. I didn't realize until then that the majority of my files were in your office!" In complete amazement, Sevella slowly turned, looked at Neal, opened his office door, and leaned forward while peeking through the slightly opened door, whispering, "Are you telling me that you are giving me the executive office? I don't believe it. I must be dreaming." Next, within forty-eight hours, Mr. Clark and Sevella adjusted to being back on the plane and headed to Florida. Strangely enough, Mr. Clark remained quiet during the flight to prevent sharing his real reason for working for Ellor. Tentatively going over his assignment, Sevella pretended to enjoy the flight.

Before landing, the two of them discussed their planned schedule and their assignments. Sevella was to work from her room, and Mr. Clark was to attend all meetings exclusively as New Venture's Executive. As the days turned to weeks, Sevella considered Mr. Clark a trusted friend. The idea of having a friend helped her focus on her duties and less on the incident. Every morning Sevella excitedly looked forward to waking up without the alarm clock and, only if necessary, arranging a meeting with Mr. Clark as he explained his meetings with his Florida Assistant, Syrriah Noble. She couldn't believe how at ease she felt, knowing Mr. Clark's room was next door and Syrriah's was her replacement, who happened to have a room right across the hall. With the current setup, she could work with Mr. Clark and Syrriah and remain in hiding. Looking into her mirror, she admitted, "I no longer have to stand or sit in a corner at those horrible investors' meetings."

Not This Time

Momentarily reflecting on a time before the attack, a time similar to one of her placement sessions in a foster home. A time when she was forced to sit alone in a strange place among strangers. "Yes," she whispered, "very similar, although different occasion, but the same feeling. Just after hanging up with Mr. Clark, a sudden feeling of terror engulfed her. Fortunately, through past experience in foster homes, she learned to pay close attention to this self-imposed alarm: knowing it would somehow alert her when trouble was brewing. She then rested on her elbows, speaking to herself, *"I believe this signal is going off right now, just like the first trip, except I ignored it, thinking it was just fear of being alone with strangers. I just knew something wasn't right, but I couldn't put my finger on it, so to speak. I somehow convinced myself that it was going to be alright. Now that same alarm is going off, and I'm going to listen. I'm not going to ignore the signs, not this time!*

Gradually sitting up in bed, and realized, "Despite the setup and adjoining rooms, I sensed this same warning signal." she whispered as she slowly laid back on her pillow and drifted off to sleep, mumbling, "I have to admit I am grateful for Mr. Clark; he promised to stand in for me so I can have some post-vacation time, and he has kept his promise. In spite of my 'vacation,' the importance of staying on schedule is my responsibility; therefore, vacation or no vacation, we have no time to spare; we must complete our tasks before returning to Boston. Mr. Clark is now the boss, and I must help him be as convincible as possible." The following day Mr. Clark informed Sevella of an after-office party planned by one of Ellor's clients. "Guess what? I've been asked to invite Syrriah Noble as my guest, which I find very unconventional." Sevella had never seen this side of Mr. Clark, sort of jolly and agitated at the same time.

Meanwhile, Sevella fell asleep but continued the conversation in her dream, "As in-house security personnel, I would think that a suspicious nature would be part of his training as an investigator. Suspicion should be, I would think, an asset." At this point, Sevella was awakened after hearing the word "investigator." Over a period of time, as they worked with team Ellor, approaching their third week in Florida, Mr. Clark prepared for the after-hour party but decided to go alone. Around 2 a.m., Mr. Clark knocked on Sevella's door, apprehended at the outside knock and not a knock from the adjoining door. Sevella sat up but continued to listen. First tapping, then knocking louder more frequently. Sevella slowly sat up, wondering if she was dreaming until she heard the fourth knock. Grabbing her robe and tiptoeing, quietly looking through the peephole, recognizing Mr. Clark, she partially opened the door as Mr. Clark quickly slid in through the slight opening in the door.

Stranger in My Bed

Before long, as her eyes adjusted, Sevella could see only his image, alarmed, she asked, "What's wrong, and why are you using the front door?" Without answering nor waiting for an invitation, Mr. Clark rushed past Sevella, bumping her and knocking her off balance. As he reached out in the dark, he surprisingly caught her, at the same time turning to close the door behind him. He stood literally shaking and feeling as though he was going to pass out. Sevella could feel his hand shaking as he held on to her arm. After several minutes passed, Mr. Clark finally whispered, "When I woke up, there was this strange woman in my bed! I don't remember going back to my room with anyone, but there she was, sound asleep." Sevella rushed to turn on the bathroom light for visibility and motioned for him to sit as she ran to get him a bottle of water. All the while trying to calm him, "Oh, I wouldn't worry if I were you; she probably came into your room by mistake." Now pacing like a caged animal, Mr. Clark turned, speaking in a louder tone, "That may be the case! So, please, explain; how could she get inside my room without me remembering unless I let her in?"

Now experiencing the fear of her own night of horror, Sevella placed one hand over her lips, signaling to Mr. Clark to lower his voice, at the same time fighting back nausea. Thankful for the dimly lit room, now with shaking hands, Sevella handed Mr. Clark the bottle of water, then placed both hands over her mouth. As Mr. Clark took the bottle of water, Sevella continued, "Maybe when she wakes up, she will realize that it's the wrong room and hurry to get out of there." Meanwhile, Mr. Clark was slowly shaking his head from left to right, whispering, "That's the strange thing; you see, she was fully dressed, but the covers were pulled up over her shoulders. With that being said, Sevella walked closer to Mr. Clark to hear him better. "Yea," continued Mr. Clark, "you may be right, but I'll just hang out over here until the coast is clear. Would that be okay?" She nodded her head yes, thinking, *No, but do I have a choice?*

In the meantime, Sevella was contemplating her next words, so she jokingly suggested, "No problem, I'll just order enough breakfast for the both of us," as she turned toward the clock and noticed it was only 3:00 a.m.; now thinking to herself, *What kind of answer was that?* She glanced toward Mr. Clark and noticed that the bathroom light had shown on his face and chest. She could now see that he was completely dressed, thinking, *Except his shirt was unbuttoned but still tucked in his pants. It appears something happened at the time he was undressing, or someone was attempting to undress him, or at the time, someone was undressing him.* As if he could read her thoughts awkwardly, Mr. Clark began to button his shirt. Sevella waited until he straightened his tie before continuing, "Were you dressing when you rushed out of the room?" Not sure of what actually happened, Mr. Clark struggled with his answer, whispering, "The last I remember, I was talking with this guy who volunteered to refresh my drink and laughed when I said I was drinking a coke."

Now This

In that moment, he began to slowly shake his head from left to right, finally saying, "As far as I know," suddenly he stopped speaking, lowered his gaze to the floor, staring as though the sound of her voice was coming up from the carpet. Before continuing, "When I awoke, she was lying next to me, I jumped out of bed, knocking over a lamp, but she didn't move, and that's when I ran out of the room. Thankfully no one saw me, and strangely enough, I was fully dressed; otherwise, I would have run out baring all." Apart from wanting to laugh out loud, Sevella insisted, "it's all probably a big mistake." From that moment on, Mr. Clark began to relax, taking very small sips of water to start, eventually gulping down the rest. Now feeling more relaxed, he spoke in a more cheerful tone, "Yes, you are so right! I was going to call the front desk to report a break-in, but I began to wonder if she was there by my invitation. No, Sevella, you're right. She probably just lost her way." Although, deep down, he knew that wasn't the case, but did not want to alarm Sevella after her emotional breakdown.

Eventually, feeling less nervous but suddenly began to experience a feeling of nausea and queasiness; therefore, Mr. Clark slowly leaned forward and placed both hands over his face to counteract the desire to regurgitate. After several minutes of being in that position, the nausea subsided. Now he thought to himself, *To say too much would eventually lead me to confess the real reason I took the job in the first place; being on the inside would help me get to the bottom of my friend's disappearance. Lost or purposed, I wonder. Somehow and someway, someone spiked my drink! There is no way I should be hungover drinking soda. But why?* Speaking angrily and audibly, "Now this!" Sevella looked blindly in his direction; on the other hand, her thoughts were on her attacker and how Mr. Clark's situation was so similar to the night of her attack. Mr. Clark was now apologizing for his outburst, "Sorry about that." Sevella nodded but was still distracted by her unnerving thoughts of her attacker and wondering where he could be at that very moment. Meanwhile, Mr. Clark was noticing her silhouette from the beam of light shining through her window as she sat very still, staring straight ahead.

Not long after, Mr. Clark laid his head back on the chair as his eyes grew heavier. In like manner, Sevella placed both legs on the lounger before laying her head back and eventually surrendered to the demands of her sleepy and very tired body. A few hours later, the sun began to replace the night beams from the street lamps, shining brightly through the partially opened drapes directly into Sevella's face. At the same time, the phone rang. Mr. Clark quickly jumped up and ran into the bathroom while motioning for Sevella to answer the phone. "Good morning, Ms. James!" greeted the concierge, but of course, this was her fake name. As she recognized the voice, it was the attendant who helped with her luggage, remembering his huge smile after receiving a generous tip. Occasionally waiving to get Sevella's attention, Mr. Clark was peeping through the partially opened bathroom door. Meanwhile, the concierge continued, "Yesterday, after checking in, you informed me that you didn't want to be disturbed, so I'm calling to inform you that breakfast will be delivered starting at 9 a.m.; therefore, you may want to remove the 'Do not disturb' sign from your door."

Is She Even Alive?

Otherwise, distracted by Mr. Clark's beckoning hand, Sevella then instructed the attendant to hold on as she cautiously walked over to the bathroom door and whispered to Mr. Clark, "Why are you hiding?" Now feeling very foolish, Mr. Clark annoyingly responded, "Because, I mean, I don't know what I mean!" Mr. Clark came out of the bathroom, slumped into the chair, placed both elbows on each knee, and placed both palms over his face, admitting, "I have no explanation." Equally confused, Sevella turned her attention to the phone, "I will be ordering for two, I'm on a business assignment, and I'm expecting my employer. I don't want to share my breakfast; therefore, I'll have two orders of eggs..." Sevella's voice faded as Mr. Clark fell into a deep sleep. After hanging up, Sevella turned to Mr. Clark, asking, "Would you like a hot cup of coffee?" but he had already fallen asleep. "Never mind, I'll make the coffee anyway, just in case you wake up and I'm asleep." Now glancing at the clock, she asked, "What time is it?" Noticing it was half-past seven, she sat on the lounger, staring through the tiny opening in the drapes as her eyelids gave way, and she fell into a deep sleep.

Not long after, Sevella began to dream of having a conversation, but the image before her seemed to fade in and out as she explained, "For now, I could use a good night's rest before the croissant with cream cheese, cereal and milk, muffins, bacon, egg and hash brown potatoes arrive. Hmmm..." Suddenly, she could hear her voice, slowly opened her eyes and looked around the bright sunlit room, noticing Mr. Clark, arm folded across his chest, face turned toward the adjoining door, but he appeared to be asleep. However, at the same time, the sound also woke Mr. Clark as his thought returned to the lady in his bed; therefore, he turned to reposition his body in the very comfortable chair, thinking, *I wonder if it's like Sevella suggested, and the stranger in my bed stumble into my room by mistake or did I invite her, and I just don't remember.* Mr. Clark's thoughts became scrambled as he began to remember a man's familiar voice saying, "She could be dead?"

All of a sudden, Mr. Clark sat upright, but Sevella pretended to be asleep. As Mr. Clark smelled the fresh pot of coffee, he tiptoed over to the coffee and poured himself a cup while attempting to recall the voice and exactly when and who made that statement. Mr. Clark began to think out loud, "That's it, the guy hiding behind me in the office, that was his voice! But how and when did we meet up again? Something is just not right. I wonder if that girl is still in my room." Now pretending to wake up and rubbing her eyes, Sevella sits up, looking in Mr. Clark's direction. Sevella's heart rate was now beating uncontrollably as she struggled to pretend that she didn't hear him saying, "That was his voice!" Sevella began to tremble so abruptly that she literally raised her voice, asking, "Do you want me to knock on the door?" Mr. Clark jumped at the sound of Sevella's voice, apologizing, "Forgive me, I was just thinking out loud, too loud, and I didn't mean to startle you awake." Now quickly, he nodded his head and directed Sevella to go to his door while handing her his hotel key.

Not My Nightmare

Before going to the front door, Sevella turned, asking, "Should I use the adjoining door instead?" Mr. Clark shook his head, indicating a no answer. After a while, Sevella was having second thoughts. She finally got up and grabbed a hat and sunglasses to disguise herself before peeping across the hallway, at the same time informing Mr. Clark of her plan, "I'll knock softly at first, after that slightly harder, before unlocking the door and peeping in." She slowly opened the front door, at the same time wondering if the lady could hear them talking, "Not once had I even heard Mr. Clark moving around in his room or on the phone." As soon as she saw that the coast was clear, she quickly ran to Mr. Clark's hotel door and knocked softly several times while quietly calling, "Mr. Clark," she repeated it a little louder each time, saying, "Mr. Clark, are you awake?" after no answer she quietly unlocked the door, open it, peeped in, and the woman was still in his bed. She quickly closed the door, looking left and right in the hallway, as she backed away one step at a time, then turned and rushed back to her hotel room.

Once the door closed behind her, she walked over to the lounger, sat on the side, and whispered to Mr. Clark, "She's still there!" Shocked at the prospect that the strange woman was still in his bed, he whispered, "It's not a good idea to keep this to ourselves; besides, she never got out of the bed to answer the door." He asked again, "Is she even alive?" In that moment, the memory of Sevella's attacker resurfaced, leaving her feeling very helpless, but this time, it was Mr. Clark's nightmare and not hers. Vividly she remembered the night of her attacker, and after discovering the man in her room, rushed into Ellor's room only to awaken by his alarmed voice. She had fallen asleep on his lounger. It was then she recalled Ellor calling the front desk and reporting the incident. "I'm calling the front desk." Now thinking out loud, she said, "He tried to help me!" Startled at her response, Mr. Clark turned, almost yelling, "What, what did you say, and who is he that you are talking about?"

As soon as those words were spoken, Sevella turned, speaking without thinking, "This is not my nightmare." As soon as the words left her mouth, she thought fast, remembering a strategy used in the orphan, and said, "What you need to do is go to the stairway, making sure no one sees you. I think the concierge said that the continental breakfast is served from 6 a.m. to 10 a.m. You still have time to get to the stairs before people are headed back to their rooms and before regular breakfast is delivered. You are already dressed, and looking as if you've been up all night, so just lay there on the stairs, and pretend you had too much to drink." Not really agreeing, for a while, Mr. Clark sat in silence, ignoring Sevella. Finally, Sevella spoke more forcibly, "Look, it would appear that you couldn't get into your room; therefore, you somehow found yourself on the stairway. Hopefully, they will think that you mistook the stairway door for your hotel room and eventually passed out on the stairs. I'll call from my cell so the call can't be traced back to my room and report that I tried to contact my employer and received no answer."

That Mysterious Voice

"By the way, I was thinking how you've helped me; now it is my turn to help you," whispered Sevella. Occasionally, Sevella would remember some of the strategies in the orphanage; she learned as survival tactic whenever the other orphans would come after her. She knew what time it would happen, so she would hide under the bed but leave the bathroom light on so they would think she was in there. After waiting thirty minutes, the perpetrator would eventually leave after realizing she was on to him. In the meantime, Mr. Clark was looking as if he was in a trance and not aware of Sevella's presence. Thankful he hadn't noticed the forgone look in her eyes, she said enthusiastically, "That's it, that's the way you should look, and so when they find you, you'll look convincing!" At this point, Mr. Clark had no idea what she was talking about, and, at that moment, he was again fighting back nausea. "In the first place." Now slowly standing with his left hand on his stomach, Mr. Clark slowly walks toward the adjourning door. Suddenly, he remembered someone saying, "She is probably dead." *That's it. Someone else was in my room, or on second thought. I could have easily been dreaming.*

Sevella was now walking over to Mr. Clark but stared in amazement at the thought of that mysterious voice. Mr. Clark continued, "Secondly, I know the last person I spoke with was the gentleman who asked about you. We had just finished talking about New Ventures when Ellor excused himself. That's when the man sat down and ordered two cups of coffee. I excused myself and went to the restroom. Once I returned, he sipped on his coffee, and mostly my Coca-Cola, and I don't remember anything after that." About this time, Sevella's head was spinning, and the anger in her eyes could not be hidden. "What did the man look like?" she demanded. Stunned by her response, Mr. Clark was now looking at Sevella in total amazement. Realizing her reaction was questionable, she changed her tone again, asking, "Do you remember what he looked like? I mean, would you recognize him if you saw him again?" Now looking very angry, Mr. Clark responded, "Yes, I can, but there was another man, and his voice was similar to the voice that said, 'I think she's dead,' and I didn't see his face."

"From this point on," instructed Mr. Clark, "we have to stick together and, if possible, get out of here as soon as possible. Now, what was your plan?" Afterward, both peeped through the slightly opened front door, making sure no one was in the hallway. Mr. Clark rushed down the hallway toward the door marked "stairs." He opened the door running up and down the stairs several times, completely out of breath. He stopped halfway between the second and third floors and lay down. "I wonder if I've gained weight. In the past two years, I haven't been inside a gym much. There were times when I could do stairs all day and never get out of breath." However, after his friend became missing, his primary focus was on finding out what happened to her. Within minutes after lying down, the door to the second floor opened, and he heard footsteps on the stairway. He heard the man asking, "Hey?" But Mr. Clark lay very still, thinking. *Great, my eyewitness!* The man again spoke, but this time louder and sounding very nervous, "Sir, sir, are you okay?"

What Was Your Plan?

At first, Mr. Clark pretended not to hear and remained very still. Then the man walked quickly toward him while talking on his two-way, saying to the person on the other end, "There is a man lying on the stairway, and I don't know if he is dead or alive." Then he said, "I don't know, but I'll check to see." After checking to see if Mr. Clark was breathing, the man responded, "He's breathing!" Then moving close enough to touch Mr. Clark, the man hesitatingly reached out to shack Mr. Clark, then jumped back when Mr. Clark grumbled and moved as if to turn over. The man said to the person on the two-way, "He's alive, but I think he may have had too much to drink." After a moment of silence, the man said, "Okay, I will ask." Then shaking Mr. Clark again, he said, "Sir, what is your name?" Mr. Clark then said, "My name! What is my name? Who wants to know my name? My name is Mr. Clark; now, get out of my room and leave me alone and let me sleep."

At the same time, the man turned and walked toward the second floor so as not to be heard by Mr. Clark and said, "Okay, I will ask him." The man went back to where Mr. Clark was lying and said, "Sir, what is your first name" Turning and reaching for imaginary cover, Mr. Clark grumbled, "My name is Edmond, now get out of my room!" Then the man answered the person on the other end and said, "Yes, okay, I will get him to his room." Meanwhile, the desk clerk received a call from Sevella to report her difficulty in getting an answer from her boss, Mr. Clark. As the attendant was getting Mr. Clark up on his feet, he received a call from the front desk, "Hey, the guy's employee just called reporting difficulties in contacting Mr. Clark. Hurry and get him in his hotel room. After that, I will let the person know we've checked on Mr. Clark and he is alright." Then the Front desk clerk instructed the custodian, "Make sure not to cause any confusion, and after you've gotten him into his room, let me know so I can inform his employee that he is alright."

After a while, the custodian reached Mr. Clark's room, unlocked his door, and immediately saw the lady in the bed. He pulled Mr. Clark into the room, sat him on the lounger near the window, and ungently called the front desk, saying, "Hey, there is someone in his bed. What shall I do?" The head clerk said, "He probably lost his key and couldn't get into his room, and whoever is in his bed probably found his key and took advantage of the vacant room. I tell you what, take him on the next floor to the room right above his and lay him down on the bed, and don't try to undress him, just lay him there. By the way, who's in his bed?" The custodian quickly responded, "It's a woman." As the front desk clerk checked the guest list, he was hoping to see a guest signing in with Mr. Clark. Presently, the custodian was looking from Mr. Clark back to the woman in the bed. Finally, the clerk said, "No one else should be in that room. Once you've got him safely upstairs, I will call his employee and tell her that we found him in the wrong room, and we'll go from there."

Trespasser

In addition to trying to get Mr. Clark to the elevator without being noticed, the hotel custodian was struggling to get past the four hotel rooms on the way to the elevators and feeling thankful that he found Mr. Clark before the servers were in the hallway delivering breakfast. Mr. Clark sighed with relief, at the same time, realized that the custodian was almost dragging the polish off the tip of his new shoes, so he decided to give him a helping hand and pretended to pull away, staggering at the same time while placing his arm around the custodian's shoulder, purposely slurring his words, "Hey, where are you taking me, and why have you gotten me out of my bed?" The custodian then answered him, "Sir, you must have lost your way, and I am taking you back to your hotel room?" Mr. Clark pretended to stumble while saying, "Good, thank you. I need to get there so I can get ready for work." Smiling, the custodian remarked, "Maybe you should get just a little more sleep." Mr. Clark nodded, agreeing, while slurring his words, "Maybe you are right."

Finally reaching the spare hotel room, the custodian helped Mr. Clark to the bed. As soon as Mr. Clark laid his head on the pillow, he pretended to snore so the man would think that he had fallen right off to sleep. The man then picked up the phone and contacted the Front desk clerk saying, "Hello, is Keri there?" After waiting a few minutes, Keri was on the other end, asking, "Ray, how did it go?" Looking over his shoulder after the snoring stopped, Ray answered, "Yes, and the room is ready, and the guests have arrived." Now hanging up the phone, Ray took one last look at Mr. Clark and said, "As soon as we get your room clear of the trespasser, we will get you back inside." Feeling very sleepy, Mr. Clark realized he needed some rest, so while the man was making his second call, Mr. Clark fell right off to sleep, and this time his snoring was no pretense. At this point, Ray pulled his two-way out as he headed for the door, calling Keri; shortly afterward, Keri answered, "What about the trespasser, and what's next?"

Once Ray finished talking to Keri, he hurried back to Mr. Clark's room, slowly unlocked the door, and cautiously walked over to the bed, at the same time wondering to himself, *I hope she is alive.* Slowly reaching out to shake the woman, her arm fell over the edge of the bed. Startled, he jumped backward. His heart was beating so hard he could hardly breathe; waiting a few seconds, he walked back over to the woman and, this time, placed his finger under her nose to see if she was breathing. Just as he placed his finger under her nostrils, he felt just a hint of warm air. At this point, his hand was shaking so hard that he accidentally touched the woman's nose, but she didn't move. Reaching for his two-way, he called Keri, "Hey, I believe this woman is really sick or very drunk. What do you want me to do?" Keri then instructed Ray, asking, "Is she dressed?" Keri gasped, "What? You want me to look to see if she's dressed?" Keri, sounding annoyed, asked, "Do you have a better idea of getting her out of the bed and out of the room fully clothed?"

I Saw Her from a Distance

At this point, Ray was trembling, breathless, and nervously asking, "What, do you want me to dress her?" Keri was now thinking about how to get this done. He then said, "Look, we still have time before the hallway is crowded with people. Take her out of the bed with covers wrapped around her and take her to the room at the end of the hallway." Kerri then added, "I checked that room earlier when I saw the maid's cart outside the door, and housekeeping hasn't made up that particular room. Also, make sure you are not seen. Once you've got her in bed, contact the front desk to call 911. We must not compromise the integrity of this hotel." Now moving quickly to follow Keri's instructions, Ray noticed that the woman was fully dressed and breathed a sigh of relief and proceeded to wake her up, but she was unresponsive, so he sat her up. But she fell backward onto the bed. He then decided to get her out of the bed and stand her up, but that didn't work either. Finally, he decided to carry her out with the sheet tightly wrapped around her shoulders and head before checking the hallway for traffic.

Occasionally checking for breathing and thankful the servers had not arrived with the breakfast trays, he now focused on the room near the end of the hallway, at the same time concentrating on how long it would take him to reach the nearby room. After several near drops and the woman's arms being exposed, Ray finally reached the room at the end of the hallway. Now he attempted to sit the woman upright. He removed the sheet from her head and unwrapped her, placing her back against the wall. Turning to the nearby maid's cart, he quickly threw the sheets into the cart. Rushing back to unlock the door, noticing the lady had fallen over on the floor. He then kneeled next to her, ready to sit her up against the wall, just as he bent over, and before he set her up, the elevator doors opened, and someone screamed, "Oh, my!" Ray quickly looked up, asking, "Can you help me?" Following the woman's response to what she'd witnessed, Ray instructed the lady getting off the elevator to quiet down before turning his attention back to the woman on the floor.

It was then the woman quickly ran off the elevator, followed by a man. The lady now kneeling beside Ray, asked, "What on earth has happened?" Ray ignored the question and continued to shake the woman, urgently repeating, "Miss, Miss," attempting to wake her. In the meantime, the man is also kneeling down by Ray, saying, "I'm a doctor. Let me examine her." Afterward, Ray began to explain, "From the other end of the hallway, I saw her from a distance lying on the floor," Then the woman introduced herself and her husband, "My name is Mrs. Paul, and this is my husband, Dr. Paul, and he can help." Meanwhile, Dr. Paul is instructing Ray to use his Two Way to call 911. Afterward, Dr. Paul pointed to the nearby room, asking, "Is this her room?" Ray quickly responded, "Yes, I think it is, and I can call 911 once we get her inside!" Dr. Paul instructed Ray and his wife, asking, "Help me get her inside." The first thing Ray noticed was the unmade bed, now signing, "Thank goodness!"

Dangerously Low Heart Rate

At that very moment, Dr. Paul responded, "Don't thank goodness yet. I still need to examine her." Nodding frantically, thinking, *No, sir, the thank goodness was because the maid hadn't cleaned,* but pretended saying, "No, sir, I'm thanking goodness for you." Shortly afterward, the residents coming from the continental breakfast began to emerge from the elevators while others headed to the restaurant. Ray breathed a sigh of relief, thinking, *Thank goodness for the doctor because we had to literally drag this woman into the vacant room.* Shortly after hearing the chatter of voices, Sevella cracked her door to see what was happening, only to see a group standing at the elevator and another rushing to catch the elevator. In the meantime, the doctor began to shake her, asking, "Ma'am, ma'am, can you hear me?" He then listened for her heartbeat and, looking very concerned, turned toward his wife and Ray, saying, "Her heart rate is beating at a dangerously low rate. We need to get her to the hospital right away!"

Once the EMV arrived, the doctor had a list of instructions for the paramedics. Ray questioned the doctor concerning the woman's condition, but the doctor responded, "This woman is in serious condition, and if you hadn't found her when you did, I'm sure by now she would be dead." Moreover, after the commotion, Sevella opens the door again, speaking to herself, *What could have happened to Mr. Clark?* Her first thought was to knock on his door.

After the third group flooded the elevators, the hallway was once again empty and quiet, so she decided to knock on Mr. Clark's door; suddenly, the elevator door opened, and she rushed back into her room, leaving the door cracked; to her surprise, she noticed the Paramedic getting off the elevator and rushing to a nearby room. Meanwhile, Ray quickly excused himself from the doctor and focused on contacting Keri to give him a report on the situation. Before calling, he walked over near the front door to complete the call, just as his two-way buzzed. Due to the distance between the couple and himself, Ray began to whisper, "Everything is fine, and the young lady is now in the doctor's care."

Now glancing over his shoulder at the doctor, Ray eventually decided to leave the room and quickly entered the elevator hoping for privacy. It was then that Sevella noticed the custodian rushing out of the room onto the elevator. She was now asking herself, *What's going on in the room down the hall, and when will they find out what's going on in Mr. Clark's room?* Not realizing the situations were one and the same. Soon after stepping off the elevator, Ray rushed into the room where he had left Mr. Clark. Once inside, his two-way buzzes, "Yes," Ray answered nervously. Keri began speaking, "I forgot to ask you if the doctor was nearby or in hearing range when you were giving me details of the incident." In all the confusion, Ray couldn't remember; suddenly, he remembered he was about to leave the room, now explaining, "No, I was leaving, so I was at the door, and I know I was speaking in a very low tone," Kerri interrupted, asking, "What happened?" Ray turned again to get on the elevator hoping for privacy, before he began to explain the incident.

She Was Still Dressed

"To begin with," now speaking in a much slower tone, "we, Dr. and Mrs. Paul and I successfully remove the woman from the floor, and in the room, without any other witnesses. Also, after a brief assessment, the doctor instructed me to call the Paramedics, and the rest is history." Right after that, the warning buzzer in the elevator went off, drowning out Ray's next statement; therefore, Ray waited until the crowd exited on the next floor before continuing, "I'm getting off in just a second to check on Mr. Clark, but I forgot one small detail." At this point, people were getting on the elevator. Therefore, Ray stepped off the elevator and walked over to the room where he had left Mr. Clark; just as Mr. Clark was turning over, he heard the door open but remained very still as he listened to the custodian's explanation of what just took place. Ray didn't realize Mr. Clark was awake; undoubtedly, Keri was thinking ahead and prompted Ray to lower his voice. Now stepping into the bathroom and whispering, Ray went on to explain, "Dr. Paul happens to be a resident and has everything under control. The woman is now headed to the hospital." Not convinced and very concerned, Kerri asked, "Where did you find a doctor?"

Periodically peeping through the partially opened bathroom door, Ray began to explain, "Once I got her to the room, I decided to set her up against the wall so I could unlock the door, only to have her fall over onto the floor. It was then the elevator door opened, and it was the doctor and his wife getting off the elevator." At this point, Keri breathed a sigh of relief, asking, "What did they say about her being wrapped in the sheets?" Momentarily, peeping out to see if Mr. Clark was moving around, Ray continued, "Before Dr. Paul and his wife exited the elevator, I removed the sheet. Oh, by the way, I noticed she was still dressed when I took her out of the bed. I just used the sheet to mummy-wrap her until I got her to her room, but eventually, took it off since I couldn't get her to sit or stand. It just so happened the maid's cart was still right outside the room, and they hadn't made the bed, so everything fell into place." Ray was then interrupted by Keri's loud tone, asking, "What? Was there a housekeeper on the floor?"

Now calmly speaking, Ray continued, "Don't worry. Like I said, it was just the cart, and they hadn't touched the room. Most likely, this would have been their first stop." At this point, Ray is peeing through the slightly opened bathroom door, looking for any movement, before walking out and over to the bed. The silence on Ray's end alarmed Keri, and he began to yell at Ray, "Ray, Ray, are you still there?" Ray was surprised at how loud Keri was now talking and quickly answered, "I had to make sure that Mr. Clark was still asleep, and he is." Furthermore, Ray is attempting to calm his own nerves as he continues to speak calmly to Keri, "Not to worry. Since the crowd cleared the hallway, I had time before the lunch group emerged to get Mr. Clark back to his room. Ray remembered seeing the door next to Mr. Clark's room slightly cracked; therefore, he asked, "Hey, we need to get this guy to his room so you can call his employee. When I rushed to the elevators, I noticed that the door next to his was cracked. Does his employee stay next door?" After a few sounds of tapping on the computer, Kerri stated, "I must be losing it; no, the call came from outside of the hotel."

Did Something Happen?

At this point, both men were breathing a sigh of relief. Shortly afterward, Ray chided in, "I'll let you know when this guy is back in his own room." Keri quickly agreed and hung up. Mr. Clark quickly closed his eyes before Ray ended his conversation and pretended to turn over. Just as Ray was peeping over Mr. Clark's shoulder, Mr. Clark jumped up, demanding, "What are you doing in my room?" Right after that display of his acting talent, Mr. Clark pretends to have a hangover and grabs his head while slowly laying back on the pillow, moaning, "I'm dizzy, maybe I need more sleep," but Ray rushed to help him to sit up, saying, "Mr. Clark let me get you into your room. Somehow you have ended up in our presidential suite; no problem, just let me help you back to your room." With that, Mr. Clark pretended to be drowsy as he stood and held tightly to Ray. At that moment, the servers with racks were knocking on the doors and delivering lunch trays. Mr. Clark stopped and clumsily straightened his tie, indicating he wanted to walk without Ray's support and to avoid the toe-dragging incident.

Also, Ray acknowledged Mr. Clark's brave attempt and congratulated him. For the most part, Mr. Clark was so convincing Ray didn't bother to assist him to his room; instead, he rushed past him while speaking loudly enough for housekeeping to hear, "I'll call for housekeeping, sir, and enjoy your lunch. Unlike in the earlier scene, instead of hiding before checking in with Keri, Ray went down the stairway, stopped between the two floors, and called Kari. Meanwhile, as soon as Mr. Clark picked up the phone to call Sevella, Housekeeping was knocking on the door. "Sir, we're here to straighten up." Now, motioning for them to come, shortly afterward, servers brought up a complimentary lunch. At this point, he was wondering, *Why didn't Sevella have it delivered to her room? Well, never mind, the hallways are crowded with onlookers. She's right to have lunch delivered to me. But how did she know I would be here?* At the same time, Sevella's lunch was also being delivered. As Sevella opened the door for the server, she noticed housekeeping coming out of Mr. Clark's room.

As the attendant placed the tray on the table, Sevella quickly handed him another tip, but he held his hand up to stop her, "Ma'am, I'm good, thank you." Sevella walked him to the door, closed the door behind him, and rushed to knock on the adjourning door hoping Mr. Clark was there. Instead of answering right away, Mr. Clark walked slowly over to the adjourning door and whispered, "Who is it?" Still knocking, Sevella didn't hear his response. Mr. Clark turns the lock just as Sevella's phone rings. Mr. Clark then turns and pushes his cart into Sevella's room, leaving the adjourning door open so he could hear any knocks on his door and listen in on Sevella's conversation. Sevella rushes to answer the phone while taking a small bite of her turkey sandwich, "Yes, hello." Now turning to see Mr. Clark seated in the chair, eyes on her as he listened to every word while sipping his coffee. "Good afternoon. We are checking to see if your lunch arrived on schedule. We understand that you are here to rest, and we have received your notice to 'Do not disturb.' Are you resting? Did the morning and noon crowd disturb you?"

A Plot to Kill

Since her door was slightly opened, Kerri was questioning Sevella, hoping she would ask about the paramedic. Playing along, Sevella responded, "Yes, yes, I am much rested. Also, your young man who has been helping informed me to remove the *do not disturb* sign before ordering breakfast and lunch; therefore, I wasn't at all disturbed by the crowd. However, while getting the newspaper, I forgot to close my door, but by then, the hallway was empty. Thank you so much for being so attentive. Excellent customer service, excellent, thank you!" Except for the sweat running down his right temple, Keri is breathing a sigh of relief. Now smiling this very huge grin, Kerri nodded, responding, "Yes, it gets pretty busy during the end of the continental and beginning of the 10 a.m. breakfast hour, not to mention during the lunch delivery. Please, let me know if we can be of further assistance." As Sevella hung up, she turned to Mr. Clark, congratulating him, "That's right, Mr. Clark; you must have been very convincing in your acting role, and hopefully, it will lead to us exposing this dirty game before another incident like yours and mines, and even worse like Naomi's turns deadly."

Mr. Clark was now looking very suspicious, at the same time asking, "Two questions. First, what was the call about? Secondly, who is Naomi? Did something happen to her?" Now feeling as though she had been caught in a trap, she confidently responded to his first question, "First question, the front desk clerk, Keri, was asking if I was disturbed by the early morning breakfast crowd or the lunch crowd. Secondly, I heard Neal discussing with someone that one of his employees had taken a job with a visiting investor. After that, Neal received a call, and I heard him say, 'missing,' but I can't put the two together because I only heard bits and pieces of the conversation." Furthermore, hoping to throw off Mr. Clark and get him to think more about their now situation and forget about her statement regarding Naomi. Sevella continued, "What's more, the custodian glanced my way as he was getting on the elevator. Most likely, he reported my door being slightly opened during the time the paramedics were arriving. Therefore, the head desk Clerk called and indirectly questioned me to find out if I saw anything."

Strangely, at that moment, Sevella began to reflect on the night Mr. Ellor came to her rescue. Thinking out loud, she said, "All this time, I have blamed him for everything." Deep in thought, Sevella then heard Mr. Clark's knife clicking against his plate as he cut into his hamburger. Conscious of the sound, she looked in his direction as he placed the piece of burger and fries into his mouth. Afterward, he replied to her statement, "Only Neal could lose an employee if that be the case." He then takes another cut off his burger. Now thinking to herself, *Thankfully,* while breathing a sigh of relief as the conversation ended without any more questions. "Not only am I confused," Mr. Clark began as he finished the last of his lunch before asking, "Well, what did he say?" Now looking around, Sevella realized that Mr. Clark was talking to her. "Well, what did he say?" insisted Mr. Clark. In that moment, Mr. Clark had a change of thought, stating, "You said I acted well, and I hope I did; it was only after the custodian found me that I pretended to be very drunk."

Not by Invitation

Despite her trembling hands, from the mere thought of having to explain Naomi's disappearance, she began to smile as she listened to Mr. Clark. "I was taken from the stairway to my room, but of course, my room was occupied, so the custodian took me to the presidential suite, and I really enjoyed the rest. I'm not sure how long it took him to get the young lady out of my room, but I heard him when he entered the room telling someone on his two-way that a doctor had examined her and immediately called 911." Now remembering his question and sitting straight up, Sevella responded, "So, that's why the paramedics were coming out of that room. Guess what? They moved her to the room at the end of the hallway." Taking a large sip to finish off his coffee, Mr. Clark continued, but Sevella was deep in thought and didn't hear a word. Consequently, Mr. Clark noticed the faraway look in Sevella's eyes, and shortly afterward, he was also silent as his thoughts reflected on his missing friend.

At the same time, Sevella also sat quietly. She began to think back to her attacker and began to compare Mr. Clark's situation to hers. "We were both victims of a break-in. Both my attacker and the woman were either employed by Ellor or at the party but not by invitation. Most importantly, both Mr. Clark and I are possible victims or suspects in what appears to be a dangerous plot to involve us or, worst—to kill us." Chills ran up and down Sevella's spine as she recalled her situation and began to question whether

Neal was aware of the danger she and Mr. Clark were facing. Now whispering, "Worst case: is he involved?" It was then Mr. Clark looked in her direction, but he was so deep in thought that he didn't really hear what she said, but noticed she still had that faraway look, but this time coupled with a look of anger. "Hey, Sevella, no need to be upset. Although none of this makes sense, we have to stay focused in order to complete this assignment ahead of time. Right? I can almost guarantee that everything will go as planned. That's something to celebrate. Right?"

Sevella began to smile, which was very hard to do because she remembered a past experience during her stay in the orphan; a time when she was very young, a time of sadness, fear, and loneliness, while comparing her feelings of that experience to the night Neal sent her to Florida with complete strangers. At this point in time, Mr. Clark couldn't help but wonder, "Is Sevella hiding something or possibly covering up some hideous secret for Neal?" Contrary to her fears, she could not shake the tremor that engulfed her. "In the same way," Sevella was thinking silently while comparing the situation at the orphanage to the time Neal sent her to Florida. She continued speaking silently, "Both attacks, one at the orphanage and the other in Florida; the only difference is at the orphanage, I couldn't fight back for fear of going without food, and I couldn't fight back in Florida, although I tried with all my might before losing consciousness. At least I didn't go down without a fight." Now speaking in a whisper, "Left alone to defend myself," after hearing the last five words spoken by Sevella.

What Did She Mean?

Obviously shocked at hearing those familiar words, Mr. Clark was startled but concealed his feelings; instead, he responded, "You are right. If we stay focused, everything will go as planned." Following the unexpected sound of Mr. Clark's voice, Sevella began to focus. Because of the sudden sound of the ringing phone, she dropped her fork and knife on her plate, and the clashing sound again startled Mr. Clark, putting his nerves on edge. In the meantime, Sevella was attempting to calm her own nerves before answering, "Hello, hello, is anyone there? I said, is anyone there?" but only silence followed by a dial tone. A cold chill ran down Sevella's spine as she called the front desk and asked, "I just missed a call, and I think it was the guest I was expecting. I was wondering if she was calling from the front desk." In the meantime, Mr. Clark is processing Sevella's statement, asking silently, "What did she mean by 'left alone to defend myself?'" After a few minutes of silence, she heard the front desk attendant respond, "No, I'm sorry, miss, but that was an outside call."

Since Mr. Clark was placing his silverware on his tray, as a result of the unexpected, Sevella again jumped. "Who was that?" asked Mr. Clark. At the same time, both burst into laughter out of sheer exhaustion as they stared in silence at their trays. As they sat in silence, Mr. Clark asked, "The caller just hung up without a word?" While clearing her throat and stalling, Sevella waited a moment before answering, "Exactly, the caller must have realized the wrong number was dialed after hearing my voice." Mr. Clark was now uncomfortably shifting in his chair as he checked for hot coffee. Finally, he asked, "If you feel comfortable enough, can you tell me exactly what happened on your first visit here, please, don't think about what you're going to say. Just tell me what happened!" nervously shifting in her chair, she spoke quickly, "If I could only tell you what I've been through, but I can't for now, I really can't trust anyone, not even you."

All of a sudden, Mr. Clark became very annoyed with Sevella, as he stood walking slowly toward her, then kneeling beside her, demanded, "Tell me everything you know, or I swear, I'll call the police and bring charges against you and that dirty company you are working for! I believe you know more than you admit!" She jumped up from her seat in total shock, stepping backward, voice trembling and yelling in defense, "What on earth are you talking about? I've told you all that I'm willing to share, and if you think you can force me, you better think again! This is the very reason I wanted you to take the trip alone!" Mr. Clark looked at Sevella as if he had seen a ghost because she was now frightened and slowly backed away from him as she moved toward the door. Mr. Clark was now holding both hands up, apologizing, "I'm sorry, please, I'm sorry," at the same time, motioning for her to stop, saying, "that sudden outburst of anger was a mistake, and please don't worry. It's just that I, too, have a secret, something that would frighten you if you knew, but like you, for now, I can't trust anyone with this information."

His Secret

Meanwhile, Sevella was slowly walking back to her chair, silently asking, "Why can't he trust anyone with his secret, and what words did I say?" Now speaking to Mr. Clark, "I'm listening," encouraging Mr. Clark to continue. "Earlier, you said something. I guess you thought I wasn't listening, and I wasn't until I heard those exact words, words spoken by someone I knew, and the identical words were, 'Left alone to defend myself.' Can I ask you a very personal question? Before I ask, please, please tell me the truth. Were you ever in a Group home? Well, what I mean is, did you live with foster parents? Please, tell me the truth." At this point, Sevella's emotions got the best of her; tears filled her eyes as she turned her face toward the window. Suddenly, there was a knock at the door. Startled, she quickly turned to Mr. Clark with questioning eyes but couldn't speak. Mr. Clark then motioned for her to answer the door. "Yes?' she asked, wiping the tears from her eyes as she walked over to the door, carefully looking thru the peephole and recognizing the smiling face of the concierge as he explained, "I know you are having lunch, but I wanted to ask whether or not if you wanted to order in or go to the dining room." Sevella glanced over her shoulder at Mr. Clark, mouthing, "Would you like to order dinner, or would you rather go out?" Mr. Clark mouthed back, "I'll go down for dinner." Turning to the door, Sevella told the concierge, "I'll have dinner sent up, thank you!" Then the concierge informed her, "For your convenience, the dinner menu is there on your nightstand, and I'm glad to be of service!" From that moment on, they both knew that there was something going on, and it wasn't all about their careers, shared expectations for advancement, or prominent positions. At that very moment, Sevella knew what happened on the first trip was no accident. Furthermore, the memory of that night caused the hair to stand up on her arms.

Immediately, she spoke up, "Something very sinister is unfolding, and we are right in the middle, and worst of all, one or both of these companies could possibly be involved." After pouring another cup of coffee, Mr. Clark sat looking at Sevella but said nothing. He continued to sip his coffee in silence. Finally, Mr. Clark motioned for Sevella to pass the sugar as she prepared to question him, choosing her words carefully, wanting to avoid setting a trap for herself to be questioned by him. However, before she could get the words out of her mouth, Mr. Clark asked, "Well are you going to answer my question?" While passing the sugar, Sevella answered, "Question? What question?" Mr. Clark raised his right brow as Sevella searched her memory; suddenly, she recalled but wasn't ready to talk; instead, looking from left to right, hoping she didn't end up telling him too much. After a long pause, Sevella decided to answer his question with a question.

We Both Know More

"Furthermore," she began, stopping long enough to sip her now cold coffee while attempting to control her emotions; voice quivering, she explained, "You asked me a question about my past and mentioned that you've heard the remark 'defending myself,' however, once I answer you, I insist that there will be no more questions on this subject! Understand?" Gradually sitting on the edge of his seat, Mr. Clark motioned for Sevella to continue. "First, I have two questions, and I promise to answer yours. First question, why didn't you hide when we heard the knock on the door? Second question, why do you associate that statement with fostering?" Looking intently into her eyes, Mr. Clark responded, "Answer to the first question; in your condition, I knew you wouldn't open the door. Second question, I wasn't insinuating anything, it's just that the first time I heard those words, I was talking to a very close friend of mine, and her life consisted of living in and out of different foster homes." Once again, both sat in silence, staring at each other without speaking.

Finally, Sevella broke the silence, "I was a teenager by then, but not old enough to age out of the system. My last foster parents were preparing to adopt me, but an emergency happened, and some of their family members were burned out of their homes. Following that call, they made a choice. Of course, family came first. In other words, there were good times, but there were also bad times. In addition, since you ask for the truth, well, I was orphaned, and I also lived in several foster homes for as long as I can remember, and there is more." Immediately holding up both hands, Mr. Clark insisted, "I'm not trying to bring up your past or indict you. Most importantly, I know that you understand the seriousness of this situation. From this point on, I believe we can be more open with one another. Also, I believe something has happened that may be evidence of a case that I am investigating." Quickly jumping up from her seat, falling backward over her chair as she attempted to gain her balance, Mr. Clark jumped up and caught her before she fell.

Seconds later, Sevella was shaking from head to toe but managed to ask, "Are you a police investigator? Why didn't you tell me?" Sevella yelled. Waving his hand, he motioned for her to quiet down and take a seat. "No, I am not. It's just a figure of speech. All the same, I believe we both know more than we are willing to admit." Mr. Clark remembered while preparing for the trip back to Boston, keeping a close eye on a frequent visitor coming in and out of the office, mainly paying attention to the receptionist. Also, the stranger would make his rounds, asking the receptionist questions relating to investing. Periodically recalling several strange moments, Mr. Clark also noticed this same man coming and leaving the investors' meetings, only this time, he wasn't alone but joined by a young lady. Mr. Clark provided Sevella with a list of names that Ellor insisted he learned before the final meeting. Of course, Sevella knew them all.

Suspicion Is Suspicion

However, these two strangers were not on the investors' guest list. On one occasion, Ellor expressed concern as he shared his thoughts regarding a particular man that hadn't missed an investors' meeting. Stating, "He always makes his rounds to each investors' meeting with tons of questions, appearing to be very interested in becoming a potential investor." Ellor was now looking from one staff member to another, "Don't get me wrong, many of our clients bring their own investors, and that's a good thing, but suspicion is suspicion, and with that being said, and suspicion happens for a reason; therefore, I'm acting upon mine. In other words, from this point on, I will be bringing in security to survey any unusual activity for this upcoming and final meeting." On the following day, during a visit to Mr. Clark's office, Ellor shared some shocking information, stating, "Listen, several of my clients have been approached and solicited during our gathering after the investors' meetings." Curiosity was now motivating Mr. Clark to drill Ellor regarding a missing staff member.

Not only was this Mr. Clark's opportunity to report his unfortunate incident, but also cleared his own name. Ellor went on to say, "I have also noticed several suspicious visitors looking into these gatherings and then leaving. The purpose of these investors' meetings is to interact with our clients and their investors, answer questions regarding our business portfolio, and just network before calling it a day. It's an event Neal introduced to me. I've incorporated it, and my clientele has tripled. Besides that, my regular staff loves this form of networking, a time of interacting and socializing." Mr. Clark is now leaning forward, hoping to share his awful experience at the first opportunity, but Ellor didn't seem to notice; therefore, he continued, "What's more disturbing, another client informed me of his experience with a guest who offered him an escort. Naturally, the client thought he was joking. Only later did the guy return with an escort."

"After being introduced to the young lady, my client no longer thought it was a laughing matter, seeing that his daughter was about the same age. Being insulted, he angrily refused and was very upset that the stranger would assume he would be interested." After several weeks passed, Mr. Clark made several attempts to share his incident with Ellor, but there were always interruptions. Consequently, his calls to share Ellor's confession with Sevella were also interrupted by a stranger standing within hearing range; therefore, he pretended to give instruction to the recipient, afterward whispering, "I'll call you back when it is more convenient.". However, on one particular evening, after leaving the office and entering the elevator, Mr. Clark contacted Sevella, suggesting, "I really don't think I should attend this upcoming banquet; you see, Ellor has expressed some concerns; apparently, a client attending one of the investors' meetings was approached by a couple, essentially the man offered to trade the female for cash. Undoubtedly, our client was enraged and offended, resulting in the couple rushing out of the room."

Something Is Just Not Right

"Moreover, Ellor later shared his concerns with me regarding several strangers, at the same time instructing me to be on the alert; therefore, as your acting boss, I insist that you pack and prepare for a quick exit." Sevella quickly retaliated, "Not just me. I don't think you should stay either." Feeling very nervous and not wanting Mr. Clark to know it, she spoke in a more upbeat tone, "Well, boss, do you agree?" Mr. Clark's gut feeling agreed with Sevella, but he decided to attend the banquet to distract anyone who may be watching him and allow Sevella to leave first; therefore, he spoke more forcefully, "This is no joking matter, most importantly, if Ellor is concerned, than I'm going to follow his instinct; something is just not right, and I'm determined to find out who this man is that's trading young women for money!" During their conversation, the elevator doors opened. Immediately, Mr. Clark rushed to his hotel room, at the same time reaching into his pockets for his hotel key. Glancing to the left, he noticed a man at the opposite end of the hallway standing in front of the hotel door, but his back was to the elevator.

Next, Mr. Clark quickly opened his door before the man could turn around. At this point, Sevella heard the rustling as Mr. Clark rushed to get into his room. Afterward, she heard a door open and close, "Mr. Clark, are you still there?" Mr. Clark was now peeping to see if he could get a better look at the man before he entered the hotel room. However, he was already inside and closing the door behind him. Frowns in his brow, Mr. Clark began to think out loud, "The back of that man's head looks familiar, but—" Suddenly, Sevella was alarmed at Mr. Clark's statement, demanding to know, "Who are you talking to? Is someone with you? Do I need to hang up?" Soon after closing his door, Mr. Clark could hear Sevella's frantic voice, but instead of responding to her questions, he continued his prior conversation stating, "If Ellor and Neal are involved in some kind of conspiracy, then they both are aware of the young lady in my room, but if not we are back to square one."

Sitting silently as she considered Mr. Clark's words, she wondered, *What did he mean by "back to square one?"* The sound of Mr. Clark clearing his throat caused her to focus; she leaned forward, glancing at the adjoining door and then back to the phone, listening carefully but unable to understand a word he was saying. Finally, she began to explain, "Mr. Clark, I should have shared this information earlier, and although much time has passed, I still need to share it; remember the night you found that girl in your room, and I received that called, after I answered, and didn't get a response I was so frightened that I was out of my mind with fear, at that point I was ready to spill all, I could no longer keep it to myself." Mr. Clark quickly interrupted, warning her, "Look, I don't want you to say anything else until you are safely out of this hotel. I want you to choose one of the local inns, and afterward, I'll join you before we board the plane."

Note in Her Napkin

Following the final office meeting with Ellor and his staff, Mr. Clark informed Sevella, "I'll tell Ellor that before I head back to Boston, I'll be looking at some office buildings for Neal." In the meantime, Sevella was pacing back and forth. "What if he calls and questions Neal?" At the same time, Mr. Clark is shaking his head from left to right. "Doesn't matter," argued Mr. Clark. "You know Neal; he'll lead Ellor on to think that he's aware of the project just to appear it was his idea. If Neal confronts us, we'll have an answer by then. Who knows, maybe the prospect of looking at some available properties will also appear as a suitable investment for Ellor. Overall, I need to get us out of here before anyone is aware of your identity and my fake position. Listen, this is your assignment, and once you have chosen a good place, reserve two rooms; afterward, reserve tickets for our flight back to Boston."

In addition to the sudden changes, as she researched the local inns, Sevella was somewhat excited, so to speak. After completing her list, she narrowed it down to one particular inn. Moreover, Sevella began to plan her exit. She was opening her suitcase and pulling out her disguises, a big floppy hat, dark shades, and larger-than-normal clothes. Excitement filled her heart as she remembered a particular Christmas season and sitting with other children watching a TV commercial; the little girl put on her mother's too-big shoes, then her too-large and long dress, and finally her mother's big floppy hat, accessorizing it all with her mother's dark shades. Sevella began to laugh out loud as she reflected on one of the happier moments in her life. Meanwhile, she couldn't wait to see the world from the other side of her hotel window. Moments later, Sevella's mood changed as she recalled Mr. Clark's call from the banquet. Without a doubt, their situation has turned from mysterious to dangerous.

Although Sevella agreed with Mr. Clark's plan of escape, she wasn't convinced. Speaking to herself, *Yes, his plan seems sensible. Obviously, the stranger knows his way around; otherwise, the persons responsible for the young woman in Mr. Clark's bed and the man that attacked me would have been apprehended and arrested by now.* However, as she stood looking out her window, she remembered him saying to her, "Hey, a young lady named Francis Hall, an assistant of a guest at the banquet who just happened to drop her napkin on top of my napkin, and in her napkin was a note. After retrieving the napkin, I held the note with the hand I held my spoon. Anyway, I need to get back; we'll talk later." In the meantime, knots are forming in Sevella's stomach. *What was that all about?* Sevella asked, speaking to herself, *It doesn't make sense for Ellor to have someone totally independent of his meetings interacting with his staff. At this point, I don't believe Mr. Clark has told me the whole story.*

Plan of Escape

While those questions were fresh on her mind, she decided to call Mr. Clark, but at the last minute, she changed her mind. As she waited for Mr. Clark to call, she dosed off; she dreamed she was still holding the receiver, waiting for Mr. Clark to answer. Then she began to speak to the receiver, "First, I'll inform him that I have chosen an inn, then I'll work on the questions." Fear suddenly gripped Sevella's heart as she tossed and tuned in her sleep; it was then she heard that familiar voice. Now turning and attempting to run, but a hand caught her by the wrist, she turned to look at the person, but he was faceless; at that moment, she was waving her arms so erratically that the movements woke her. Rarely did Sevella succumb to fear; she never wanted her foster brothers and sisters to know just how frightened she really was and how traumatized she felt after arriving at a new foster home. She clearly remembered always putting on a brave face and a fake smile, eventually deceiving everyone, including herself.

At this time, she was slowly sitting up in bed, whispering, "I can't and will not dismiss these horrible feelings; I can't! I know that something horrible is going on. Otherwise, that person would have never slipped that note to Mr. Clark, a complete stranger!" Suddenly, the ringing of the phone startled her. She quickly answered, "Yes!" The aftereffect of the dream caused her to tremble from head to toe. "Are you okay?" asked Mr. Clark, now sounding more concerned than ever. Sevella tried to sound cheerful, "I'm multitasking and can't seem to keep up with myself. I apologize for that jacked-up greeting, but my suspicions have gotten the best of me, and I have questions, lots of questions." After a brief moment of silence, Mr. Clark responded, "I agree, and so do I, but for now, let's just stay focused and concentrate on our plan of escape, and hopefully, Ellor will not come up with a last-minute schedule change." By now, Sevella's mind was on the note and what was on it, but she was hesitant to ask.

At this point in time, her thoughts went from the note to calling and making a report to Neal, knowing he was subject to call at any given moment. Sevella was considering whether or not to keep quiet about contacting Neal but decided to be open; therefore, clearing her throat, breaking the silence, "I, well I, I mean, I considered calling Neal to let him know that we were changing locations," cutting her off and sounding very agitated, speaking in a tone unfamiliar to Sevella, Mr. Clark demanded, "No, tell me you didn't! Remember, it was your idea to travel incognita." Sevella, in turn, defensively interrupted Mr. Clark's rude response, arguing, "You didn't let me finish! I changed my mind; however, I know Neal, and he will expect to get an update from me or suspect something is wrong, and in return, call Ellor for an update." After breathing a sigh of relief, Mr. Clark whispered, "We can't risk him calling Ellor, so you may have a point, but wait until we've change hotels."

Keeping My Identity Hidden

"In conclusion," stated Mr. Clark, "we need to stay focused and hope that this idea of property hunting will not cause any confusion. I am still shaken by what happened the morning I woke up and discovered the young woman in my bed. Incidentally, did I tell you that I never saw her face?" In that instance, Sevella was visualizing her attack and staring aimlessly out of the window. Mr. Clark, now sounding more confused than ever, whispered, "I've got to meet with Ellor, but get back with me as soon as you have assessed the inn and made your move." Meanwhile, both Mr. Clark and Sevella suspected foul play, but neither shared their deep-rooted suspicion of the other nor did Mr. Clark share the contents of the note, which read, "PLEASE HELP ME!!!" Instead, he decided to remain quiet until he made contact with the couple again. The following day as Mr. Clark prepared for the office, Sevella looked over the photos of her chosen inn before making her choice.

Gradually she scrolled from one picture to the other. The first thing that caught her eye was the building's historic beauty. Secondly, its architectural designs appeared to be out of the Victorian age. She remembered the last foster home and how she loved sitting around the table with Miss Timothy and looking through family photos at all the beautiful places Miss Timothy had visited over the years. Most of all, she would sit and listen for hours as Miss Timothy explained the history of each photo.

As a result of their conversation the night before, Sevella found herself repeating Mr. Clark's last words, "We need to stay focused and hope that this idea of property hunting will not cause any confusion." Now shaking to rid herself of the intruding fear brought on by Mr. Clark's strange and unexplained behavior, she decided to concentrate on the beauty of the Inn, once again thinking back to happier times with foster parents, and of course, it worked.

Although Sevella didn't really understand why she enjoyed Miss Timothy's stories so much but eventually decided that it must have been because she could travel and see the world through Miss Timothy's eyes. In most of her foster homes, getting attention was not always a good idea; "Likewise," whispered Sevella, "as I prepare for my exit, being discrete and keeping my identity hidden out of sight is a wise decision; hopefully, my disguises will not bring too much attention to me." Subsequently, just as Sevella completed packing her bags, bending over to latch the suitcase, her earring fell from her ear, bounced, and rolled on the floor under the bedside chair. Bending down to look for the earring, she noticed a small briefcase. She stood up, moved the chair, and immediately spotted her earring right next to the case. She slowly picked up the earring and finished packing without taking her eyes off the case.

My Only Real Friend

Afterward, her curiosity got the best of her as she sat in the chair with both hands folded in her lap, staring at the case. For a moment, she stood up, still staring at the case as she walked back and forth. She then asked herself, *What if it's stolen? Well, that would mean I should report it, and if it is stolen, I shouldn't touch it; instead, I should turn it in and be done with it. If I turn it in before taking a peep, I will not sleep a wink wondering what was in it. I know I can put my gloves on and take a peep. I know, I can say that I thought it was mine when I accidentally opened it.* At the same time, taking her gloves out of her purse and before reaching for the latch, she slowly wiped where her hands had previously touched the case. As she pushed the latch, the case popped open. "Oh, my!" she exclaimed, throwing her hands over her mouth to silence her voice. At first sight, she saw the tip of a photo, and a cashier's check, eventually concluding, "Probably a client of Ellor left his case by accident."

As she prepared to close the case, she couldn't resist taking a peep but pausing, "Look, it's none of your business, so just finish packing and mind your business," she scolded herself as she closed the case, placed it under the chair and headed for the door. "In the first place," convincing herself of a reason to take a look as she waited for the elevator, "if I'm going to report the case, I need to make sure all the contents are accounted for. Afterward, I'll come back with the desk clerk, and together, we can examine the contents, but first, I'm going to take a picture to cover myself. Turning back as the elevator door opened and she rushed toward her room, taking her phone from her purse, accessing the camera mode as she hurriedly unlocked the door. Once inside, she pushed the chair backward, revealing the case. She placed her gloves on her hands, raised the lid all the way up, and began to take pictures of the cashier's checks, then the photo.

For the most part, her imagination of discovering evidence that would solve a mysterious case and discover the story of the century. As she took one picture after the other, slowly spreading the rest of the document, thinking, *This is my evidence that all the contents were there when I turned it in."* Momentarily, looking into an inside compartment, Sevella continued explaining to herself, *Apart from this amazing discovery, there may just be a reward. Therefore, I will also share these photos with the desk clerk as my witness. Well, maybe not. Matter of fact, I'll come back up with her, and we will assess the contents together.* As she took one photo after the other, suddenly she screamed, dropping the phone to the floor as she quickly covered her mouth to muffle the sound. Slowly moving her hands from her mouth, she began to stare at the photo; looking closely in unbelief, she held that photo with hands trembling, recognizing the person to be her only real friend she met in the orphanage.

I Know That Voice

Moreover, she remembered they were sitting and listening to another girl trying to convince her friend of the dangers of running away. How some have ended up forced to sell themselves and others... Sevella began to whisper, "Dannie, Dannie, I always wondered why you listened to the girl that ran away, Dannie, oh, Dannie!" She cried through fingers that covered her mouth. "Dannie, you look as though you are asleep or...." Her voice trailed off as tears ran down her face. Apprehended by fear and confusion, Sevella quickly closed the case, placed the chair over it, grabbed her bags, and ran out as tears filled her eyes. Oftentimes she had been warned, "Crying in public was a sign of defeat," the person who warned her wasn't any older than her, so she told herself, *Nor was the girl who tried to warn Dannie not to run away. Crying may be a sign of defeat. I agree because right now, I feel totally defeated.* Speaking to her reflection as she entered the elevator, "Today, it seems inappropriate to hold back my tears because I now know what could have happened to Dannie."

As the elevator doors closed behind her, Sevella didn't bother to wipe the stream of tears showing from her reflection, and it was at that moment that she remembered her first trip. "During my first trip to Florida, I remember exiting the elevators and almost running into a man who had a similar case." She also remembered the case. Most importantly, she now vividly remembered the voice, "The elevator incident happened before the attack; that's him. Oh, my God, and he's the man that was in my room! I know that voice anywhere." Startled by the opening of the elevator doors, and as her voice echoed, she quickly placed her phone up to her mouth, smiling and nodding to the ladies getting on the elevator. "Is anything wrong, dear?" asked one of the ladies, noticing Sevella's tears. Still holding her phone to her mouth, she held her phone up to the ladies, explaining, "Oh, just a girl talk moment."

Nonetheless, as the elevator's doors closed, the ladies continued chattering. Although they were speaking English to Sevella, it sounded like a foreign language due to her own confusion. Finally, the doors opened again on the next floor. The ladies resumed their chatter as they exited the elevator. While smiling and saying goodbye to the ladies, contrary to her calm tone, Sevella's stomach was in knots as the tears filled her eyes. At that moment, she began to recall the incident with the man. "What a time to reflect on that first trip. In addition to finding that case, now I'm a total mess. Yes, I know that voice, and I know that case! It's either that case, or he had a case similar to the one left in the room. It was when his case bumped into my handbag and that's when I looked down to notice that very distinctive engraving. I saw him at least twice, once getting on the elevator and another time getting off the elevator, but much too busy to notice anything else."

One and the Same

Noticeably shaking, Sevella decided to get off on the same floor as the ladies.. but take the stairs to the lobby. After accessing the stairway, she began to take very deep breaths as she walked slowly the four flights down, hoping to look calmer before exiting the stairway. After reaching the first floor, before opening the door, she waited, standing very still and listening for any sound. After several minutes had passed, she waited five minutes more before exiting the stairway. Faking a smile and looking around as if expecting to meet someone, although, at this point, her actions weren't very convincing because she struggled to hold back the tears. "I wonder did he recognized me. Impossible. At that time, we were both rushing, and, as a habit, I learned in the orphanage when walking to look at my feet; therefore, I was surely looking down. Of course, on that first trip, I was too busy to notice anyone on the elevators, but why on earth didn't I even look the guy in his face? At least I would have a face to go with that voice."

Meanwhile, stopping at the nearest elevator as if to get on but quickly turned and headed for the lobby, speaking silently, "I need to play it safe; just maybe the man on the elevator and the person that hung up are one and the same, and checking to see if I was occupying that room." In that moment, she reflected back to the whiteness of the walls on the stairway, as she remembered, "I'm reminded of a time in the orphanage; I was very young, but I remember someone placing a suitcase on the floor, but my attention was on the very large room with the very white walls. As

I grew older, scrubbing that wall was one of my primary chores, and I scrubbed over and over even when there wasn't a single spot on the wall. Now since the attack, I have spots on my life that cannot be wiped away." Briefly surveying her surrounding as she looked to see if anyone was looking suspiciously in her direction, thinking, *I didn't want to be seen getting off the elevators. Oh, my! Maybe I've already been spotted exiting the stairway! Well, if he had followed me down the stairs, I would have caught him red-handed.*

After that, she pretended to stop near a phone to make a call, just to calm her nerves, thinking, *What if he's been following me this whole trip? No, not possible. This disguise looks nothing like me!* Still observing her surroundings. *Nothing seemed suspicious,* she thought to herself as she walked over to the front desk, *this may not be a good idea; I may just leave the case for someone else to find. What if I said that I thought something was under the chair, but I wasn't sure?* After turning in the key, Sevella decided against reporting the case. Instead, she simply closed her account with a debit bankcard bearing the company's name. At the same time, she looked around, observing each man entering and exiting the hotel. Once her taxi arrived, and the attendant placed her luggage in the trunk of the car, Sevella took one last look over her shoulder, looking for any suspicious movement. She looked toward the large picture windows and again at the entranceway to see if anyone was watching her getting into the taxi. After getting into the taxi and closing the door, she continued to look back for any rush movement or suspicious behavior as her heart raced uncontrollably.

The Perfect Hideout

For a brief moment, Sevella thought she noticed someone ducking behind the dining room door. Frightened, she ordered the taxi driver to stop: Staring carefully, focusing on the entrance to the dining room, she continued to watch for that person, waiting patiently, "Excuse me, ma'am," the driver spoke politely. Sevella briefly turned her focus to the driver. "Yes," responded Sevella. The driver continued, "Were you expecting someone else?" Embarrassed, Sevella smiled, turning back to the window, "No, I thought I saw someone waving to me." The driver turned around, awaiting instructions to drive on. After a while, she saw him, and that's when she noticed a young man and a friend joking around. She apologized as she informed the driver of her destination. As she settled back into the back seat, she began to visualize the Victorian architecture of the inn as she imagined being born into a family in that era, the peaceful feeling of excitement made her smile while looking forward to visiting the inn.

Despite the trauma caused by her earlier discovery, thinking to herself, *Yes, I think it will be the perfect hideout.* At that moment, Sevella wondered what she could have done if it had been the stranger hiding behind the dining room door. A few minutes later, just as the driver announced their arrival, looking surprised, she asked, "Here already?" The taxi driver nodded as he walked to the trunk for her luggage. Sevella slowly turned to observe her surroundings; as she walked toward the inn, she noticed the antiquated but very attractive front door, as though it was something out of a movie. Breathing a sigh of relief, she said, "Good riddance to the stranger and his briefcase, and welcome peace; second mission accomplished!" Earlier, Sevella had decided to call Neal to give him an update and inform him of their early departure, but memories invaded her peace of mind as the thought of Dannie's picture serviced. Moreover, the opening of the driver's door broke her train of thought.

"After all," whispered Sevella as she observed the building. "Maybe I should wait and talk to Mr. Clark before I contact Neal, just in case he has more information to share and just in case my nerves give way about the briefcase. Not to mention, it would be awful if Neal accidentally shared my whereabouts with Ellor or his staff." Despite her concerns, Sevella once again began to smile as she thought about the quaint little inn and how excited she was to visit. After surveying the premises, Sevella went inside. Right away, she noticed the warm and inviting decorated entryway. Slowly she observed every painting on the wall, every tastefully placed piece of furniture, and matching floor rug until the desk clerk greeted her. "Hello, and welcome to my House Inn! How can I be of service?" Smiling as she walked slowly toward the clerk, still admiring the decoration. Finally, she responded graciously, "Thank you!" At the same time, Sevella was so distracted that she blurted out, "My name is Sevella Thorn, and I have booked two rooms for me and my employer," extending a courteous hand and suddenly remembering she had given her true name.

Spilling the Truth

Obviously panic-stricken as the truth of her identity is revealed, the clerk asked, "Miss Thorn, are you okay?" Now trembling as she sought desperately trying to think of a way to make the correction when the clerk responded, "Well, ma'am, I only show two other bookings, but not for a Sevella Thorn." Now focused, Sevella waited a moment to answer, then apologized. "I'm so sorry, but the executive name is Miss Thorn. The booking should be in her assistant's name Mr. Clark, and quest, but in separate rooms." Now smiling, showing his very white teeth, the clerk responded, "Welcome, Miss James! May I call you Miss or Mrs.?" Again extending her hand and giving the gentleman a hearty hand shack, and cheerfully responded, "No, please, 'miss' will be fine. What is your name?" Again displaying his huge friendly smile before pointing to his name badge, "Stanley Adams, ma'am, but you may call me Stanley." From across the hallway, she could hear music. Looking in the direction of the music, noticing the sound was coming from the dining room.

Now she turned completely around as she admired the table setting, and every table was occupied by one or more couples. Glancing from one side of the room to the other, she noticed the dance floor and the couples displaying their skillful dance moves. In was then the voice of the clerk instructing the porter interrupted her, "Miss James, I hope you find everything agreeable, and if I can be of any assistant, please feel free to call." Still focused on the dining room and all the couples, it was at that moment she heard the clerk say, "Here is your key; by the way, both rooms are identical in floor plane, but you are welcome to preview your employer's room for your approval." As she took the key, Sevella responded, "No, I will only be looking at my room, and if it is agreeable, then that settles it!" Both were now laughing as Sevella headed toward the elevators, still looking into the dining room. "In order to keep a very low profile, I think this place will serve our purpose well."

However, just as she turned the key, the first night in Florida, remembering Dannie's photo became so very vivid and real, so much so that Sevella hesitated before entering the room. "Come on, girl, snap out of it! If I don't pull it together, I will end up spilling the truth about that whole sordid, horrible night. Most of all, Mr. Clark will suspect something if I'm looking' timid or sounding concerned." Sevella quickly opened the door and instantly stopped in her tracks, mesmerized by the beauty of the view through the large bay window overlooking the city. "Breathless!" she exclaimed as she walked slowly over to the window and just stood there in awe before opening it and letting the cool breeze blow into her face. For a brief moment, she forgot all about the horrible night in Florida and began to think about Samuel. The ringing of the phone startled her as she quickly grabbed her purse to retrieve her phone, "Hello, hello."

Sudden Change

All of a sudden, only a muffled sound could be heard. However, moments later, Mr. Clark responded, asking, "I'm assuming that 'secluded' means we will be hidden out of sight until we leave this place?" Sevella waited for Mr. Clark to continue, alternatively nodding her head but deep in thought, imagining living in peace without a care in the world. Finally, without thinking, she whispered, "It's enchanting! I have the most perfect view of the city from my balcony." Laughing sarcastically, Mr. Clark responded, "Sounds expensive." Despite Mr. Clark's cynicism, Sevella refused to let his tone spoil the wonderful feeling she experienced when she walked into the room, nor her thoughts of Samuel. "Hum," she murmured. "So very wonderful." The sound of more rustling before Mr. Clark asked. "What does that mean?" But Sevella didn't answer, so Mr. Clark spoke louder, demanding, "Do I need to repeat myself?" Shaking her head as she responded, "Now look who's concerned with expenses; besides, I've checked out of the hotel."

In a more serious tone, Mr. Clark said firmly, "No, it's not so much the expenses, but you must remember that the hotel we booked is the only accommodation that Future Ventures has agreed to cover; therefore, and with that being said, it would be best if we pay the expenses in order to keep this sudden change in accommodations our little secret. Furthermore, coupled with all we have to deal with, and in spite of the nostalgia, just keep looking until you find something more reasonable." Before hearing the word "secret," Sevella's thoughts had drifted off again; therefore, she wasn't aware that Mr. Clark had finished his statement, so, for a brief moment, she attempted to recall what was said before "secret." She then heard the rustling sound and decided to make a comment, "Don't worry, it's not expensive at all, although I think it should be. Not only is it secluded, but not the easiest place to find. Isn't that what you wanted?" Now sounding more like himself, Mr. Clark chided in, "Perfect! Cheap and secluded, that is exactly what we need to keep out of sight?"

"Furthermore," stated Mr. Clark, but stopped short of completing his sentence. Moments later, he continued, "I hope you didn't call Neal to inform him of this sudden change in accommodation; I need to add more data to your follow-up call." It appears Ellor wants us to remain a day or two longer but insisted on following up with Neal's suggestion to spy out some real estate that would be primed for New Venture's headquarters. Obviously, not calling Neal was the right decision. After speaking to Mr. Clark, Sevella decided to contact Neal to give him an update. All of a sudden, fear gripped her heart as she was about to call from the Inn. Now laughing to herself, she said, "Oh yes, that's right. Neal would have noticed the caller ID, and I would be in hot water with both Neal and Mr. Clark, not to mention extra fees and calling expenses. That's right. I must be sure to follow all instructions."

What Kind of Game Are You Playing?

Even then, she felt an uneasiness as she remembered an incident at one of the foster homes and how that same uneasiness warned her not to go to the restroom but stay in her room. As it turned out, someone spilled something on the floor of the restroom, and without a doubt, she would have been blamed; learning to listen to that gut feeling saved her many horrible moments and tears. Moments later, her cell ranged, but she didn't answer right away, thinking, *If it's Mr. Clark, he'll speak first,* but the suspense building up inside of her caused her to speak first; finally, she answered, "Hello," but no answer, moments later she heard Mr. Clark say, "Hello." Breathing a sigh of relief and complaining, "What kind of game are you playing, and why did you wait so long to answer?" Mr. Clark was unable to answer right away, but after a while, he whispered, "I'll call you back," and suddenly, he hung up. Fear once again gripped her heart as she sat on the bed, wondering if Mr. Clark had been discovered trying to leave the hotel.

As a result of the ringing of her cell, Sevella jumped up, at the same time dropping the phone on the floor, quickly stopping, picking it up with shacking hands, while attempting to disguise her trembling voice, "Yes, hello!" At this point, Mr. Clark was very concerned after hearing the constant movement in the background, "Are you okay?" asked Mr. Clark. "I'm okay and safely in the hotel," now sounding more relaxed. After a long period of silence, Mr. Clark asked, "What is going on? Are you okay? Has something happened?" At this point, Sevella was sitting to avoid fainting, voice trembling, and she nervously responded, "No, everything is not okay, but what about you, and why did you hang up on me?" Instead of an answer, she heard a ruffling sound as if there was a scuffle. At this point, she felt as if her heart had stopped as she waited for what seemed like forever.

Finally, Mr. Clark answered, "I was just putting my luggage in the cab, but earlier, when I called, Eller dropped by; I answered the door thinking it was the porter for my luggage, and that's why I had to hang up so abruptly. Evidently, something was wrong, but for now, everything is fine. What about you?" Mr. Clark asked rhetorically before continuing, "Sorry for the scare, but we can't be too careful. So, what is it like?" Now laughing, Sevella had to catch her breath as she explained, "The resident here seemed to be paired off in couples or in groups, so you will be singled out and greeted the moment you walk through the door. Besides that, I was greeted over and over by the residents as I walked from the taxi to my room." After getting into the cab, Mr. Clark promised to call once he was in the inn. Sevella spoke to herself, *Without a doubt, I would love to go walking, enjoy some outdoor activity, and maybe some sightseeing and just enjoy myself.*

Is She Dead or Asleep?

Instead, she decided to take out her phone to examine the photos. *What is this picture of Dannie doing in that case? Is she dead or asleep?* Speaking to herself, in total shock as she sat staring at the photo of her childhood friend, unable to understand, as her eyes filled with tears, she looked closely at the photo, "I can't tell if she is dead or asleep." Sevella began to slide from one picture to the other, saying, "I should have looked through the entire case; I have no doubt that there were more photos underneath those documents." She looked even closer at all the photos to see if she recognized anyone else. As she glanced at each photo, she felt that her heart had stopped beating. Not only was Dannie's photo in the case, but there were other women also. "What is going on?" It was then she noticed another photo, and it was Tramishia Ram; jumping to her feet, she rushed to turn on the table lamp to get a better look; it appeared Tramishia was sitting to the right of a man, and only the right side of his face was visible. *Again,* speaking to herself, *incognita or not, coming on this trip was not a good idea after all.*

At that moment, the ringing of her cell made her jump, dropping the phone onto the bed. Slowly she picked it up, but before she could say hello, she heard someone saying, "Hey, are you still there?" Now breathing as she was unaware that she was holding her breath, Sevella finally answered, "You can't guess what I found?" Mr. Clark was now sounding relieved; he asked, "Did you hear me, Sevella?" Unable to respond properly, she answered, "I hear you. I was just trying to clear my throat. What did you just find?" asked Mr. Clark. Sevella's continued, "A case, I found a briefcase in my hotel room, and there were cashier's checks and photos inside." After a long while, Mr. Clark whispered, "What! You're telling me that you opened it? Why didn't you just turn it in?" Sevella waited patiently for Mr. Clark to calm down, then she said, "But that's not all." After a moment of silence, Mr. Clark asked nervously, "Well, what!" Speaking very calmly, she said, "There are photos, one of an old friend and an employee who worked for Neal and Ellor; her name is Tramishia Ram, but the others I didn't recognize."

Meanwhile, the wheels in Mr. Clark's mind were turning like a windmill as he struggled to speak; finally, in a breathless tone, he asked, "What did you say?" As she prepared to repeat everything, Mr. Clark interrupted her, "No, don't repeat it, just listen, and listen very carefully. The reason I called was to get my room number and give you instructions on where to meet me. Since the resident there appeared to be social, I decided the bar would be indiscrete enough to meet in public. We may appear to have bumped into each other." Sevella quickly interrupted Mr. Clark, "Bar, I don't drink, and I don't agree." It took Mr. Clark a few seconds to respond, saying, "The bar is more visible, and I can easily spot you there without having to look around." Sevella still disagreed but gave in and agreed to go down at the appointed time. Instead, she took her time picking through her different disguises. After changing her outfit four times and before putting on her shoes, she picked up her camera and began to scroll through the photos, at the same time wondering about the man she bumped into in the elevator carrying the identical briefcase.

Speechless

Finally dressed and ready to meet Mr. Clark, she waited an extra thirty minutes just to avoid sitting at the bar for any length of time. As she headed for the elevator, she remembered she had forgotten her phone, turned quickly, and almost ran into one of the hotel porters as he greeted her, "Hello, ma'am; are you finding everything satisfactory?" Backing away and apologizing, "Great, I mean, oh, yes! My room has a beautiful view overlooking the city, and I love it!" Sevella was breathless; rushing away, Sevella remarked, "No problems at all!" Once inside her room, Sevella decided to contact Mr. Clark and let him know that she was headed to the bar just as her phone began to ring. Startled, she answered, "Hello?" Sevella remained quiet, listening for any unwelcome sound as she held the phone without saying a word. Mr. Clark began to speak, "I'll be headed that way in about forty-five minutes or as soon as the taxi drops me off." Still shaking from the unexpected ringing, she remained silent as she reflected back on the pictures of her old friend and co-worker.

Coupled with fear and excitement, otherwise considering the photos until Mr. Clark's voice interrupted her thoughts, "Did you hear what I said?" Then, realizing that Mr. Clark was still talking, she pretended to be distracted just as the hotel porter tapped on her door. "Just a minute. The attendant is here. Yes, the bar. I am headed that way." Opening the door to the attendant's smiling face informing her of the dinner schedule, Sevella then asked, "Would you mind escorting me to the bar and helping find a seat while I wait for my guest to arrive?" The attendant responded, but Sevella was distracted with her own thoughts, thinking silently, *I rather wait in the dining area.* As they entered the elevator, she began to mentally separate the items in the case just to have her information ready for Mr. Clark. The elevator door opened, interrupting her train of thought. She followed the attendant through the dining room to the bar while still holding the phone to her ear.

Once inside, she continued her conversation with Mr. Clark but stopped near a table at the entrance, at the same time pointing to her phone and the table near the entrance of the bar. "That was really nice of the attendant to come to my room instead of returning my call. The place is so welcoming, and the staff is very proficient." Sevella excused herself from their conversation, now speaking to the attendant, "Excuse me; I know I said the bar, but I rather sit here, near the entrance." After listening to Sevella's conversation with the attendant, Mr. Clark disagreeably informed Sevella, "Fine. I'll see you there, near the entrance." Finally, in the space of an hour, Mr. Clark eventually found the hotel; first, he went to his room, dropped off his luggage, and made some phone calls before heading to the dining room. Once there, he stood for several minutes glancing from one table to another before Sevella spotted him. She raised her hand but not above her head, hoping to get only Mr. Clark's attention. After seeing the hand, he remained standing at the entrance of the dining room until Sevella raised her hand a little higher and beckoned for him to come to her.

I Need to Tell You Something

Finally, Mr. Clark walked slowly toward the strange lady, wondering, *Do I know her?* Once he was close enough to the entrance of the Bar, he pretended to walk past Sevella until he heard her voice. Now beckoning for her to follow him into the bar, after sitting, he said without hesitating, "I didn't recognize you but listen. I want you to get on the next plane and head home, but don't let Neal know you are returning. I want him to think we are still covering this business venture together." Meanwhile, Sevella was looking toward the dining area as the aroma of the dinner being served caused her stomach to growl. On the other hand, Mr. Clark was waiting for the bar clerk and ordered two large ice teas before concluding, "After all, they have only seen me and my Florida assistant, so to speak; therefore, we should be able to make this work. Also, there is something I need to tell you, but not until we get safely back to Boston. Still reflecting on the dinner being served, Sevella realized that Mr. Clark was no longer talking, so she pretended to be listening, "Oh, okay."

In the same way, Mr. Clark is speaking his thoughts as he briskly waives his hand back and forth, insisting, "I know you don't agree with going back home alone, but trust me, I know what I'm doing." All of a sudden, Sevella remembered Mr. Clark, saying he needed to tell her something, so she said, "So, tell me." Now shaking his head back and forth, Mr. Clark replied, "I said I'll tell you when we get back to Boston." Momentarily, she kept quiet but believed whatever Mr. Clark had to say was less important than that briefcase of checks and photos. Sevella felt a surge of concern as she wondered about Mr. Clark's secret, now thinking to herself, *Concerns, concerns.* Moreover, Mr. Clark also recalled one of Sevella's earlier statements, "Excuse me." After looking in his direction, she noticed he was speaking to the bartender. Still distracted, she realized Mr. Clark wasn't paying any attention to her but was deep in thought as he sipped on his ice tea. She also remembered that she hadn't answered his question regarding contacting Neal. Although she knew Neal, he would expect her to call.

Subsequently, she cleared her throat, "You asked earlier about Neal, and no, I haven't contacted him yet." At that moment, she could see Mr. Clark was listening, so she continued, "First, I'll tell him that everything is on schedule, and if he asks to talk to you, well, you'll be in a meeting. Next, I'll ask how things are going. Either the phone will ring, or he'll brush me off to eliminate the small talk." In that moment, she could see Mr. Clark relaxing. As she looked around the restaurant, Sevella began to remember Samuel and Sam. On one occasion, she wanted to tell Sam about the baby's name and how she chose the name and eagerly wanted to share her new position as an executive assistant and her amazing trip to France. Once again, her thoughts were on that couch and opening the blind to watch for Samuel. After a period of endless silence, Sevella again cleared her throat, but Mr. Clark spoke first, "Sevella, you're right. Call Neal, especially if he's expecting your call: you know him better, and it may be just the thing to keep him from calling Ellor and asking questions."

Fading Away

After taking a long sip of his tea, Mr. Clark continued, "I know you may have questions; and I may or may not have the answers, but I believe in safety first, and your returning home will keep us both safe. "Of course," agreed Sevella as she nodded her head before asking, "Can we please get away from this bar and head to the dining room." Mr. Clark nodded and said, "You must have read my mind because I'm starving." In spite of the mysterious phone call, and the distinctively marked case, she remained quiet throughout the meal, but her insides were overloaded with fear and questions that she believed Mr. Clark could answer. The following morning Sevella had no problem rushing through breakfast in order to pack and catch the next plane to Boston. At the same time calling Mr. Clark while taking her last bite, "Mr. Clark, I am prepared to leave Florida as soon as possible. Also, I will call Neal before I leave the hotel. Furthermore, is there anything else you need to tell me?" Mr. Clark was now taking a spoon full of oatmeal, so he spoke in a muffle, "No, nothing else. We'll talk later."

Now she reasoned with herself, *I really believe Mr. Clark is holding back on me,* as she called for a taxi. *Maybe he already knows about the case and the pictures. No, that's not possible, or could it be possible, and he's trying to throw me off?* After packing and checking out, she climbed into the taxi. *Obviously, he's hiding something.* Her thoughts continued until the driver's voice interrupted her, "Ma'am, where are you headed?" Sevella stared for a moment in silence, "Oh, please forgive me. I'm headed to Northwest International." Glancing from side to side as the taxi drove away from the inn, she began to reason with herself, "Unlike my first trip to Florida, on this trip, I was more observant and determined to watch my back. My lack of suspicion on the first trip made me prey to those guests or uninvited guests who were mistaken for Ellor's clients. Firstly, Mr. Clark's frightening discovery. Secondly, Dannie and Tramishia's photos all may be tied to Miss Cu'Dull's odd behavior."

Later, as she boarded the plane, she sat purposely in first class, knowing that every passenger could be recognized and within voice range. Once safely seated on the plane, she signed a breath of relief as she hesitantly dozed off to sleep. Her dream was instant; as she was leaving for work, she waved at Samuel, and he waved back. Sevella began to smile in her sleep. Suddenly Samuel's image became smaller and smaller as he appeared to be fading away. Sevella tossed and turned in her seat as Samuel's image slowly began to disappear. She quickly turned and attempted to run after him. Meanwhile, the flight attendant was asking, "Ma'am, are you cold? Would you like a blanket?" Dazed and confused from being awakened by the flight attendant, Sevella quietly mumbled, "No, thank you," as she attempted to fall back to sleep. Once again, the attendant's voice could be heard in her dreams as she served a passenger across the aisle.

I Can't Hide

Despite her desperate attempt to dream of Samuel, Sevella opened her eyes. To her surprise, the attendant was talking to her, "Ma'am, I brought you a blanket. You were shivering." Realizing she was no longer dreaming, Sevella slowly nodded her head as she adjusted her seat in the upright position. The warmth of the sun shining through the window was a clear indication that she might have felt a chill. The sun also gave her a very welcoming, warm feeling inside. In that moment, she tried to recall ever having such an experienced, so warm and so wonderful. As the flight attendant walked away, Sevella looked out of the window and whispered, "For once in my life, I feel warm and wonderful." In addition to feeling warm and wonderful, Sevella felt safe. Still, she spoke silently, "I've never felt safe. There was never a time in my life when I felt safe. No matter where I lived, and now…"

In addition to pulling the blanket to cover her nose, Sevella spoke audibly, "Whatever the reason, I'm going to enjoy this feeling for the duration of this trip." Reclining her seat and turning to face the window, looking at the clouds as they take on various shapes, she laughed out loud at the cloud shaped like a duck's bib. Now dozing off, Sevella remembered her stay at the third foster home and how her foster parents were so protective of her. Of course, they would be because they had no other children. During her stay, she dreamed of parents who were not just foster parents but her parents and her protectors. In that moment, Sevella opened her eyes as she heard the sound of her own voice. Obviously embarrassed, she looked around to see who was looking in her direction before turning her head to face the window, then whispering, "Each time I imagine that I would get adopted, I would always feel this strange, wonderful feeling deep down in the pit of my stomach. Oh my, I'd forgotten about that particular time in my life."

"Furthermore," Sevella concluded, "each time there was an opportunity to believe, for parents I would wait, and because of that wonderful feeling, I waited, and I had hope, but the hope soon faded as disappointment eventually replaced my wonderful feelings." Sevella sat staring at the clouds as she remembered Mr. Clark's instructions to leave Florida right away. Now her concerns were for Mr. Clark's safety as she desperately wanted to hear from him. As she focused on her reflection in the window, Sevella whispered, "There was a time in my life when there was just me; now there is Samuel. Oh, my! How could I possibly love that baby in this way?" She couldn't control the flowing tears that sprung up from nowhere and ran down her face. "I hate the man that did this to me; I'm so confused. I love the baby and hate my attacker. What does this mean? Am I crazy? Is something like this possible? I carried him, and he is a part of me. Maybe that's why I love him."

I Don't Understand This Love

Clearly, the reality of loving Samuel, or loving anyone, was a new experience for Sevella, an experience she could have never imagined could be possible for her. As the flight attendant walked past her, Sevella turned and made eye contact with the child across the aisle sitting in her mother's lap; all of a sudden, Sevella remembered how she waited to be adopted by the childless family, but in the end, they chose a much younger child. As she stared at the little girl resting so peacefully on her mother's chest, Sevella whispered, "I don't understand this love; loving Samuel like this, and probably never will, but it is important to me that he is well taken care of." At that moment, her phone rang because she hadn't turned it off. Quickly answering it, "Yes, hello." Right away. Mr. Clark began to speak, "Are you settled on the plane, and have you spoken to Neal?" At that moment, Neal was the furthest thing from her mind. "Yes, I am settled and having a good talk with myself. What's going on with you?" she asked spontaneously to distract any more questions regarding Neal.

As a result of Sevella's spontaneity, Mr. Clark was quickly thrown off; he intended to question her but decided, for now, to put his questioning aside. "That's great. Also, I'm preparing to leave, and I wanted to make sure you were safely on the plane." "Feeling very grateful," she responded. "Yes, thanks to you, I am safely on the plane." After giving instructions to the taxi, Mr. Clark returned, but before he could speak, Sevella answered, "By the way, I haven't contacted Neal, but I promise to do so. Just being curious, how are things going with you?" Now sitting comfortably in the taxi, Mr. Clark said, "Just fine. We'll talk later." Since Samuel's arrival, watching out for him has been her primary focus, and she was now bubbling up inside with excitement. Sevella looked forward to keeping a watchful eye on Samuel, not wasting a minute of his growing days, and hoping for an opportunity to see her dear friend Sam. Momentarily, the flight attendant was standing next to Sevella, attempting to get her attention.

Finally, Sevella looked up at the attendant, but not really listening, while deciding whether she should visit Sam after dropping off her luggage. Furthermore, the flight attendant was now shaking Sevella, asking, "Ma'am, ma'am," now focusing on the attendant, she looked up, and the flight attendant was holding a ticket stub. Feeling very embarrassed, Sevella apologized, "I'm sorry. I was distracted." Now smiling, the attendant again asked, "Is this your stub?" Sevella glanced at the ticket and saw her name and the words *First Class*, now smiling at the attendant, "Yes, I must have dropped it when I put my case in the overhead compartment. However, I assume I'm in my right seat." After placing the stub in her purse, Sevella noticed the folded note, reminding her to discuss the mysterious phone call with Mr. Clark.

Look, The Plane

Moreover, David was now three years old and climbed down the stairs with minimal assistance as he maneuvered through the den, into the kitchen, and headed straight to the refrigerator for his cookies and milk. In this instance, and for the first time without Lawrence's help, he reached his pudgy little hands up, opened the refrigerator door, and on the lower shelf, Lawrence conveniently placed his small pitcher, and next to it was his spill-proof cup already filled with milk. After taking a sip of his milk, David went over to the table, climbed upon his father's chair, and took two cookies conveniently placed in a sandwich bag in the jar. Before tiptoeing up the stairs, David paused at the top of the stairs and listened for any movement coming from his parents' room before rushing past their slightly opened door. Once safely inside his bedroom, David closed his door. He climbed into the chair near the window, waiting patiently for the first plane to fly across the sky. At that moment, David's father sneaked a peep and watched David as he sat drinking his milk and eating his cookies while remembering playing with friends at the center.

Once again, focused while waiting for the plans to fly overhead; for a brief moment, David's thoughts reflected on his cookies, but he was distracted when he could see the large plane silhouetting the sky, wings covered with lights as it flew closer, it grew larger. Excited, David pointed and squealed, "Look at the plane, see?" As a result of the excitement, David's voice could be heard from his parent's room. As the plane climbed higher into the sky, flying overhead until the lights seemed close enough to touch. What's more, Lawrence was laughing so hard that he ran into his bedroom to keep David from hearing the laughter. Muffling his sound as Catheryn sat up, asking, "What happened?" Still attempting to muffle his sound, Lawrence said, "I'll tell you later." Once his laughter was controlled, he slowly walked back to David's door. Not ten minutes later, David is already in bed but not quite asleep.

As the days grew into weeks and weeks into months, David's routine was consistent when it came to his night for cookies and milk. Although, Lawrence would pretend to go to bed early so David could learn to get his own milk and cookies. Now David is confident; he has become a pro at going up and down the stairs and getting his milk and cookies without any assistance from his dad. Nonetheless, Lawrence was always watching, only to run up the stairs into his bedroom before David turned and noticed him watching. However, on this particular night, it wasn't just the planes that would entertain David; another figure would capture David's attention. As David watched the plane disappear into the clouds, suddenly on the ground, another figure appeared as a shadow in the street. He stared intently as he watched the ghostly image moving swiftly but carefully. Frightened, he quickly ran and jumped into his bed, covered his head, and did not come out until morning.

Home Sweet Home

Following her arrival, after being dropped off by the cab a block from her home just after 8 p.m., Sevella unlocked her door while looking over her right shoulder, noticing across the street a dim light in the upstairs bedroom. Suddenly, she saw something move, so she didn't bother to unpack or dress for bed; instead, she positioned herself on the couch so she could get a better look, but no one was there. Therefore, she sat on the couch and positioned herself so that she would wake up in time to see Samuel and his parents leave for the day. Overwhelmed by the trials of the travel, as soon as her head touched the pillow, Sevella began to doze, but clearly determined to be in the right position, she sat up, laying her face on the back of the couch, afterward taking one final peep across the street at the upstairs window before falling into a deep sleep. Soon after, she began to toss and turn in her sleep, seeking a more comfortable position before falling back to sleep. Now turning into the pain in her neck, she woke, holding her neck.

However, as it happens, just in time to see the couple getting into the car. She was startled. It seemed as though she had just laid her head on the couch. As Samuel's mother helped him into a car, Samuel looked so much taller for his age, "Almost four years," she whispered. Suddenly Samuel did something very strange. He turned and looked toward her window; Sevella quickly ducked to hide her head from Samuel. After hearing the car drive away, she sat holding her neck, whispering, "That was so unexpected; wow, he looked directly at me!" Obviously still shaken by Samuel's peculiar reaction and hoping he hadn't spotted her, she began to doubt herself. "Nonsense," she said as she sat up straight, slowly standing while holding her back and neck. As she walked toward the kitchen, she looked around her home as she squealed, "Home sweet home!" a sense of deep joy replaced the heavy concern brought on by Samuel's unexpected behavior.

Next, she noticed her handbag on the floor next to her luggage, "I was in such a hurry to see Samuel that I didn't think twice about taking out my notes or preparing for today's meeting." At that moment, she began to wonder about Mr. Clark, so she picked up her handbag and took out her cellphone to call Mr. Clark. After he answered, her first question was, "How are you doing?" The next sound she heard was steady movement and ruffling. Concerned, she quickly asked, "Hello, are you there?" In the meantime, Sevella was nervous as she waited. Shortly afterward, Mr. Clark answered, "You sound much more relaxed since you left Florida," but his words were muffled. Soon afterward, he dropped his phone. Sevella laughs as she listens to his mumbling. Now picking up his phone, at the same time, Mr. Clark is whispering, "This is no laughing matter, and I could tell you some things that will make your hair stand on edge!" After a moment of silence, he spoke more clearly and calmly, "Most importantly, you're home safely. Or are you?"

Could Someone Be Watching Me?

She spoke more urgently, "Please tell me you are not still in Florida." Peeking through the kitchen window, Sevella asked, "If I were, would it be okay?" There was silence on Mr. Clark's end; now laughing, Sevella responded, "Calm down, I'm home, but would it be okay if I go out?" Silently breathing a sigh of relief, Mr. Clark responded, sounding very concerned, "Sure. Just don't run into Neal until I get there. I'll be leaving at noon, but I'll probably stop by the hotel and freshen up before meeting you around four-ish. Until then, please stay out of sight until we can go into the office together. Therefore, we will have to meet somewhere near the office. Any suggestion?" Sevella thought for a moment before saying, "Yes, there is a breakfast diner a few miles away from the office, and I think that would be the perfect spot." She then gave him the address, and they agreed to meet upon his return and from the diner to the office. On the other hand, after Samuel looked toward her home earlier that morning, Sevella couldn't shake the reoccurring fear that surfaced occasionally.

Momentarily rubbing her hurting neck, she turned her head from left to right while looking at her luggage and handbag. She picked up her briefcase and took out her notebook to check her list. "Even stranger," she whispered, "did I see someone move from that upstairs window?" Obviously unable to shake off the uneasiness from that experience, she quickly turned, looking from the kitchen toward the living room window. "Could someone be watching me, and even worse, have I been discovered? Have they discovered my terrible secret and now have hired someone to investigate me?" The prospect of being spied on left her feeling more embarrassed than frightened. After standing for those few minutes, the uncomfortable pain in her neck and back returned; at the same time, she realized that it was a mistake to raise her blinds to get a better view. "Oh, boy! What's wrong with me? To raise that blind that high, or even raise it at all, and then fall asleep with my head in the window? Hopefully, if anyone noticed me, they might think I was just looking out of my window."

Not only were those words consoling, but she quickly turned her attention to the refrigerator. At that point, her cell phone rang, but she refused to answer, thinking, *I can't talk; I'm too upset from being spied on by my neighbor!* Now laughing out loud, she covered her mouth to muffle the joyful outburst, also realizing that she was home alone. "In spite of the spying incident, somehow, I still feel a sense of peace. Is it because I made it home safely or because Mr. Clark has become more of a friend than a colleague? No doubt I needed that laugh to get a grip, plus I'm an executive now, and no phone call should go unanswered." Before returning the call, she listened to her voicemail. And it was Mr. Clark. "Good morning Sevella, my schedule has changed, and I need to leave earlier than planned. Don't worry, but Neal just called, and he needs us to return earlier than scheduled, so I told him we will leave right away, but our original plan has not changed."

The Little Chatterbox

"Overall, things were getting back to normal until I was seen spying, and now Neal's request for an early arrival," Mr. Clark's voice broke her train of thought, as he explained, "I'll just drop off my luggage and head straight for the diner." After hanging up the phone, Sevella scolded herself, *Still, I haven't called Neal! Well, just maybe things worked out because, for some reason, he wants us back in Boston and pronto.* She then planned her day. Afterward, she rushed to shower and get dressed while thinking, *What now? Great!* She mused as concern replaced her peace. "I'm going to be wondering why the sudden change." In the meantime, she dressed and gathered the things she needed for the meeting. All of a sudden, her thoughts were on the strangers that invaded their bedrooms. Anxiety replaced her curiosity, leaving her overwhelmed. "I know. I'll call Neal and insist he explains this sudden change in schedule." Up until that time, Sevella thought she had discovered a way to escape the drama raging on the inside. "Just maybe Neal's explanation will calm my nerves."

At that moment, she remembered Neal had already spoken to Mr. Clark; therefore, she changed her mind saying, "No, I can't get Neal involved, not just yet, no matter how much he may know." Now laughing and saying, "That would be drama added to drama. After all, I'm still upset at being spotted while peeping on the couple across the street. Besides, I must be careful; I wonder if someone is watching me? I know what will calm me down. I'll call Sam and hang around with her until Mr. Clark shows up." Fear again grips her heart, knowing if she spends that much time with Sam, the truth about the baby will eventually come out. "I know at some point I will l have to tell Sam everything, but I don't want to risk losing her friendship, not now, and certainly not today."

In spite of David's early dismissal day, he was neither frightened nor excited. As it happens, David was distracted the whole day. On his early dismissal day, he would be taken to the center for his first ride in the school van. David was consumed with thoughts of the ghost. After his parents arrived at the center, the director met them and informed them of David's peculiar mood. "A little chatterbox," his parents lovingly called him, except for this particular day. After leaving the center, as they drove home, David's mother noticed the chatterbox was unusually quiet. "David, sweetheart, is everything okay? This was your special day, your 'Early Day,' to ride on the joy van from school to the Center. Did you enjoy your ride?" David waited a moment and finally answered. "Yes, Mommy." David's father then asked, "Son, are you feeling okay?" As he looked at his father's reflection in the review mirror, David quickly moved his head in an up-and-down motion, indicating a yes answer. Lawrence then glanced over at Catheryn, and shrugging his shoulders, Catheryn raised both hands in front of her, palms up as she spoke, moving only her lips, "I wonder what happened?"

Early Arrival

In the meantime, Sevella prepared her notes for the meeting. She also took her briefcase and began to organize the documents for PowerPoint. Glancing at the wall clock, she realized that she needed to grab a bite before meeting Mr. Clark at the breakfast diner. At the same time, David's parents arrived home earlier than normal. Sevella rushed to the couch after hearing the sound of the tires pulling into the driveway across the street. Both parents get out at the same time. The man reached into the backseat and brought out a very large colorful bag while the woman opened the back door on the passenger's side of the car but remained bending in the backseat for several minutes. Suddenly Samuel was standing at the door on the driver's side facing Lawrence as he held out his arms; Sevella pulled the blinds all the way up but closed the lace curtain just as Samuel jumped from the car to the ground, landing on both feet. Simultaneously, Sevella and Catheryn clapped their hands, celebrating his ability to jump down without falling.

As each parent took a hand, they began to lift Samuel up and swing him forward as they walked up the sidewalk. However, when his parents opened the front gate, Samuel looked back toward Sevella and then ran ahead of his parents, waiting at the door, never again looking behind him. Meanwhile, David was still thinking about the ghost; therefore, after his snack, he asked to go upstairs to play. On this particular evening, instead of playing with toys, he pulled his chair up to the window. Afterward, he hid behind the curtain, occasionally peeping from the side of the window. First, sitting down, then standing, then from beside the window, glancing back toward his bedroom door. It was then the plane from afar that distracted him. Now focused on the plane, David was no longer frightened. Still looking upward, he pulled up his chair and waited for the plane to fly over to his house. All the fear of the ghostly figure had been chased away by the excitement of the new and larger plane flying in the daylight. "Look," said David out loud as he jumped up, pointing and standing on the window seat to get a closer look at the plane.

All of a sudden, the fear of the ghost was replaced by clapping hands loud enough for his parents to hear, but David was too excited to realize how loudly he was clapping. As the plane quickly flew over David's house, he stood on the window seal, with face against the windowpane, eyes headed upward, attempting to see more of the new big plan before it disappeared. Next, he climbs down from the window seat into his chair, with his head lying on the back of the chair in case another plane appears. At this point, his heart was racing from all the excitement of the new bigger plane, so he closed his eyes and pretended to see the big plane take off and fly right over his house. As David began to fall asleep, he remembered the movie he and his daddy watched and how his father explained, "Son, please understand that everything you see on television is a game and not real." David's father warned him not to try any of those flying stunts from the top of the stairs.

A Very Small Image

Suddenly David sat up and began to talk to himself, *I'm not scared of the ghost shadow. Daddy said it's a game.* Slowly lying backward, still very excited, David began singing his favorite nursery song until he eventually fell asleep. After getting her things together, Sevella made up her mind to visit the diner earlier and hoped to come up with an excuse to avoid telling Sam the truth. As she rehearsed her story about Samuel, she felt as though she was going before a judge, found guilty, indicted, and sentenced for abandonment. "How I hated that man and the baby! But something has changed, and I don't know when, but it has. Why am I putting myself through this? Enough is enough! I don't owe an explanation to anyone but the authorities and to report that horrible man who attacked me, and I can't even do that." That's when she glanced at the wall clock and noticed the time. She quickly grabbed her purse and rushed out of the door; at that moment, she looked across the street toward the upstairs window and saw a very small image standing in the window, but he moved quickly before she could get a better look.

Almost in shock, Sevella stopped without realizing it, staring across the street at the upstairs window. Realizing the taxi would soon drive by, she slowly started walking toward her front gate, being careful to stay behind the shrubbery while still looking up at the window, suddenly realizing she had not locked her door. "Oh, no, I forgot to lock my door!" After locking her door, she turned again, looking up at the window, but no one was there. Once she was out of eyesight, and after rounding the corner, she could see the taxi pull up at the appointed location. She realized that her uneasiness from the morning's escapade left her with mixed feelings. One minute she was excited; the other, afraid of being accused of spying. "I don't care if I have been discovered!" she argued as she rushed for the taxi. "I know without a doubt, it was Samuel; he's now almost four years old and watching for me; he had to be," she said silently as she approached the taxi.

She was now thinking, *Why else would he hide when I looked up at him?* Joy filled her heart as she imagined Samuel looking out for her. Tears began to fill Sevella's eyes as she remembered feeling that same pain the morning she walked away, leaving him boxed up on her neighbor's front steps. Her heart began to break as she remembered the hatred she projected on her unborn child, hatred brought on by her attacker. "Ma'am, where will you be going?" Asked the driver as he glanced at Sevella through his review mirror. Startled, then she realized she had gotten into the taxi in a daze, apologizing before giving him the diner's address. Consequently, the terror of facing Sam has also overshadowed her to the point her hands are shaking. Sevella imagined the now unplanned meeting with Sam as she desperately tried to make up excuses not to talk about Samuel. Sevella began to speak silently, "With all that has happened, I can't imagine what it would be like when Sam finds out that I have given him away."

Too Painful to Bear

Periodically glancing at the driver, hoping her expression didn't reflect the trauma she felt on the inside, again she spoke silently, "The outcome is too painful to bear." Tears filled her eyes as she looked away toward the window and didn't care if the taxi saw her tears; "This pain is real, as real as my tears," she whispered, realizing the problem was much too big to hide. Unlike Samuel hiding, and her from the neighbors, yet, she could no longer hide from her problems. *Problems,* she thought, *yes, problems, I would surely lose Sam's friendship by telling her that I gave Samuel up for adoption. No, I don't have to tell her: I can tell her that I gave him to his dad because I couldn't take care of him. After all, the couple across the street is technically his Mom and Dad.* Although she was very excited to see Sam, there was a mixture of sadness accompanied by joy, causing an uneasiness she could not shake. In an instance, another thought began to surface as she remembered looking in the briefcase and finding those photos and the conversation with Mr. Clark that followed.

At that point, she struggled to remember everything Mr. Clark said, only to recall the statement, "Something I need to tell you." She wondered if Mr. Clark already knew who owned that briefcase or if she would ever know the truth. Now speaking in a whisper, "Oh, my!" she almost cried out. "Did I forget my phone?" Frantically looking through her purse, she located her phone. "Ma'am, is something wrong?" Looking up in his direction, she calmly answered, "Oh, no, I just thought I'd forgotten something, but everything is fine." Now thinking to herself, *While that may be true, he probably thinks I was looking for some money.* Sevella then glanced at the street sign and noticed that there were only a few blocks left before reaching the Diner, so she pulled out the fair, plus a crispy twenty-dollar bill, from her wallet and closed her purse. *Better still,* she thought, *before it is all over with, Mr. Clark will tell me whatever he's keeping secret.* At that moment, the taxi pulled in front of the diner, and she felt as though her heart had stopped beating.

Unable to move, she sat staring at the reflection of the cab from the diner's large glass window. "Ma'am, ma'am!" the driver was now sounding very annoyed, so she turned, smiling, and said, "You know it has been such a long time since I've visited my friend who works here, and I can't wait to finally see here!" She handed him the fair before giving the twenty dollars tip, saying, "Keep the change." The annoyed look on the driver's face quickly disappeared, turning into a very large smile as he politely said, "Thank you!" Sevella slowly opened the back door and stepped onto the sidewalk, imagining the worst as she moved toward the diner's entrance. She stopped abruptly, turning as the taxi drove away. At that moment, everything inside her screamed, "Run!" Now whispering, "I would… except I'm here, first to meet up with Mr. Clark, secondly to see my friend Sam." Now hearing the diner's door open, Sevella turned only to stare at the face of a customer as he held the door open for her. "Thank you," she whispered.

I Just Gave Up

Before long, she became aware of the traffic as the tires of each vehicle seemed to call her name. Then realizing that she was frozen, but managed to walk blindly toward the diner while memories raced through her mind. "Welcome to Toni's Diner. May I help you?" Turning quickly in the direction of the unfamiliar voice, Sevella stood staring at the strange young lady standing where Sam should be but wasn't. Clearly shaken by all the changes, Sevella was attempting to gather her thoughts until she finally managed to say, "Yes, I am meeting someone here. May I please have a table for two?" The young lady led her to the exact booth she sat in the first night she visited the diner. As the waitress walked away, she glanced around and noticed that nothing was the same. The place had been totally remolded, and there was no sign of Sam. "Toni's, who is Toni, and where is Sam?" She wanted so badly to ask the waitress. "Well, maybe it's for the best," she concluded as she turned toward the large picture window once again, remembering almost four years earlier and the reason she found herself in that diner, sitting in that booth.

Moreover, as she looked out of the same very large window, Sevella remembered that dark and rainy night; and how that night mirrored her own personal darkness, a darkness that has since shadowed every moment of her life. Again tears ran down Sevella's cheeks as anger filled her heart, "Sevella, Sevella!" Astonished at the very familiar voice, turning and seeing this very thin, very well-dressed lady standing with her arms held out in front of her. Suddenly she realized that it was Sam. "Sam, oh my, it is you! You look great! What on earth have you done to yourself?" Sam was now doing a complete turn, showing off her very slim body as she rushed toward Sevella, explaining, "When I first met you, I was so impressed by your appearance; the clothes you wore were so flattering and so attractive, not to mention your beautiful home. I was encouraged by all of that, so I went back to school to get an associate's degree in business, and I recently graduated! By the way, Jack is semi-retired. I am now manager of Toni's Diner!"

Occasionally wiping tears from her eyes, Sevella braced herself for the worse as Sam continued, "That's not all! Guess what? Jack has also made me co-owner and allowed me to name it after a dear friend that went missing two years ago!" At that moment, Sevella looked out of the window and noticed a taxi slowing down and quickly driving off. Breathing a sigh of relief, she felt somewhat relieved and glad that it wasn't Mr. Clark. By now, Sam was standing at the table with his arms extended; therefore, Sevella stood and wrapped her arms around Sam while congratulating her on her achievements and promotion. "Sam, I am so proud of you, and I can't believe how great you look. What did you do?" Now motioning for Sam to sit, both sitting at the same time as Sam began to explain, "I've missed you so much, but every time I called, I didn't get an answer. After a while, I just gave up. I was so heartbroken from missing you and the baby, so I decided that if I didn't pull myself together, I would lose my job."

Do You Know Him?

"After that, one night, a young lady came in, and she was studying for an exam. After taking her order, I noticed she had several books, so I asked her what she was studying, and the next thing I knew, she was sharing her ambitions, goals, and dreams of someday owning her own business. After that conversation, she," now pointing toward the waitress, "Becky became a regular customer, and we became good friends." While stopping to catch her breath, Sam and Sevella burst into laughter while holding hands across the table. "Another time, one evening, Becky came by just as I was closing the diner and invited me out with some of her friends; I almost said no, but decided that I was tired of all work and no play, but much to my surprise, I had a great time, and I fell in love with the whole group. Therefore, I became a regular in the group, and that decision eventually changed my whole course of life." Just then, the diner's door opened, and in walked Mr. Clark. He quickly spotted Sevella and noticed she was sitting with someone, so he sat at a different booth.

Immediately Sam noticed Sevella's distraction. Leaning forward, she asked, "Do you know him?" Now shaking her head up and down while signaling for Mr. Clark to come over, at the same time pointing to Sam, saying, "Mr. Clark, this is Sam, well, Samantha, my best friend, Sam, this is Mr. Clark, my co-worker." Reaching to shake Sam's hand, and at the same time, Sam stood up to shake Mr. Clark's hand while excusing herself, "I'll take your order, Sevella, and we can talk later, and nice to meet you, Mr. Clark." As Sam walked away, both Mr. Clark and Sevella watched her in silence until she disappeared behind the double doors. Mr. Clark moves to the seat facing Sevella, asking her, "Your best friend? You never talked about her… ah, forgive me, there I go again, prying; after all, you don't have to share anything else with me, especially things about your personal life."

Shortly afterward, as the young lady from the register headed their way, the double doors opened just as the phone rang, she quickly turned to answer the phone, and for a moment, Sevella stared at the young lady but was in deep thought so much so, she didn't hear Mr. Clark speaking to her. "Sevella, Sevella, did you hear me? Never mind. How long have you known her?" At that point, Sevella was looking blindly at Mr. Clark while her thoughts were on getting out of there before Sam would have the opportunity to ask about Samuel. "I'm sorry. I know we have to leave, and I haven't had a chance to talk to my friend." Mr. Clark, pointing toward the restrooms, stated, "No, we don't have to leave right away. Besides, I'm starving, and I need to wash my hands. By the way, is the food any good?" Before she could answer, he got up and walked to the restrooms. Without thinking twice, Sevella rushed over to the counter and asked for Sam. Becky then went through the double doors and quickly came out with Sam. Sevella nervously pulled Sam to the side, at the same time looking toward the bathroom's door.

Calm Down

In turn, Sam grabbed hold of Sevella's hands, asking, "Are you okay? You look like you've seen a ghost." Laughing to shake off the nerves, Sevella quietly explained, "This has been a very busy morning, and I have so much to tell you, but we have to eat and get to the office for a meeting. Would you be offended if we talked later?" Now placing her hands on Sevella's shoulders, Sam knew her friend very well; she whispered, "Calm down," before asking, "is something wrong?" Now looking relieved, Sevella smiled shyly as she explained, "He's more than my co-worker. He's my boss." Obviously shocked at Sevella's confession, Sam began to laugh out loud, saying, "Is that all?" Sevella then threw her arms around Sam, "No, that's not all! The truth is I'm supposed to be his boss." Now, laughing that very familiar laugh while returning Sevella's hug, "Hey, do you remember Jack? I was always giving him orders, so I know exactly how you feel."

At that moment, Sam suddenly stopped laughing, and her expression changed from laughter to concern while glancing in Mr. Clark's direction, saying, "You know, Mr. Clark looks familiar, but so many people come in and out of this place they're beginning to look alike." They both laugh as Mr. Clark takes his seat. "Before you go, how is the baby?" Smiling and forgetting her fears, Sevella says enthusiastically, "Growing, and he is so very tall for his almost four years!" Looking over Sevella's shoulder, Sam motioned with her eyes toward Mr. Clark, saying, "The boss is waiting, and don't worry. I believe you will someday have that position." As Sevella walked toward the booth, her heart was leaping for joy! She has seen Sam and discussed Samuel, and she still has Sam as a best friend. As she reached the booth, she knew that someday she would eventually tell Sam the truth about Samuel. "Did you place an order?" asked Mr. Clark.

In that moment, Sevella sat across from him, about to answer, but before she could, the waitress walked up with her pad. Despite his question, Mr. Clark didn't wait for an answer but turned to Becky, saying, "Great. I'll have a BLT with a glass of orange juice and a blueberry muffin." Now turning toward Sevella, Becky held up her pencil and flipped the page, asking, "And would these be separate orders?" Sevella chided in. "No, I'll have your breakfast special with bacon, eggs, scrambled please, with two blueberry pancakes, oh, and a cup of coffee." After confirming their order, Becky rushed to answer the phone. Mr. Clark looked away from Sevella toward the busy street and said, "We may be in serious trouble." He then turned toward her and continued, "I don't know how to say this, but to come right out and say it, I believed my friend who worked for Ellor is missing or, even worse—dead." Sevella jumped up but quickly sat down before she was noticed. "What do you mean missing or dead, and what makes you think that?"

What Does This Mean?

First clearing his throat, he was then whispering, "Now, you said there was a briefcase under the chair in your hotel room; before checking out, I had an idea to approach the desk clerk and pretend to have missed an old friend staying at the hotel; I gave him your room number and a fictitious arrival date. After checking his records, the desk clerk said, "That person checked out at midnight, the day before you arrived." Then I apologized, "Oh, I'm sorry, I gave the wrong room number: I then turned the number around." The clerk then said, "Oh, that person is still here." After a long period of silence, Mr. Clark looked back toward the large window and said, "I got into this business after my friend went missing. It has been almost two years, and not a sign of her anywhere or any records of her ever working for Ellor. I tried to get information without being too obvious by pretending to be a distant relative, but no one remembered her." Sevella's excitement turned into fear as she sat staring at the passing cars and wondering, *What does this mean?*

Now turning to look at Mr. Clark, she said, "One question; why did you change the number?" Looking confused, then realizing, "Oh, I guess I just lost my train of thought. Well, I did that just in case the person came back for the suitcase, and the clerk told him I was asking questions." Mr. Clark sat staring blindly at Sevella. Finally, she said, "Thanks, okay. Go on." Mr. Clark took out his wallet and showed her a picture of his friend, and asked, "Have you seen this person before?" Shaking her head left to right, suddenly she remembered the photos; she quickly took her camera out of her purse and pulled up recent photos as Mr. Clark scrolled through the pictures. Suddenly, he dropped the phone and quickly picked it up, and stared in unbelief. For several minutes, they both sat without speaking before Mr. Clark dropped his head into his hands, cupping them over his face. At first, Sevella thought he was crying, but he raised his head while shaking it from left to right, speaking in an angry tone, "I don't know what's going on, but I have a gut feeling that none of this is what it seems to be."

It was at that moment, just as he finished speaking, the waitress walked up with their order. Due to Mr. Clark's confession and their horrific discovery, they both sat in silence. After several sips of his orange juice, Mr. Clark took a deep breath, looked out of the window, and without turning to Sevella, began to speak, "It's probably best if you would not go back home; maybe you could visit a relative or friend. Just in case we've been followed, maybe, and I just suppose that the owner of that case followed us or you. That's why I don't believe you should go back to your place, not tonight anyway." At that moment, Sevella was about to take another sip of her coffee but stopped abruptly, disagreeing, "No, no, if he retrieved his case, why should he follow us or me, and what do you mean not go home? I don't have any family, remember, and the only real friend I have is Sam, and if there is danger lurking, I certainly don't want to put her in harm's way." Mr. Clark placed his face into his hands, slowly raising his face halfway, looking in Sevella's direction but not at her. He then pointed to her pancake and asked, "Are you going to eat that one?"

In Walks Neal

Meanwhile, Sevella was now looking totally confused and wondering why the sudden change of conversation. It was then a sound from behind her that caused her to turn around, and there stood Sam. "Excuse me," Sam said apologetically, "for interrupting your meeting, but Sevella, I wanted you to have my new phone number," reaching for the note and at the same time clasping Sam's hand between hers as Sam placed the note into Sevella's hand's, in addition, Sam is looking in Mr. Clark direction, asking, "Don't I know you? You look so familiar." Mr. Clark hesitated, carefully choosing his words before responding, "Well, maybe, but I can't recall where we could have met." Sam then turned toward the sound of the ringing phone to see Becky beckoning for her; she excused herself and rushed to the counter. Sam couldn't remember, but two years after meeting Toni, she saw Mr. Clark in a photo with some of Becky's friends. Meanwhile, Sevella placed the note from Sam into her handbag, then leaned forward and spoke in a whisper, "Mr. Clark, do you know my friend, and keeping it a secret, if so? Why?" Mr. Clark, now looking puzzled, then he said, "I don't know her. Like she said, 'After a while, all customers began to look alike.'"

Now following Mr. Clark's gaze, she turned around to look toward the counter, and her focus fell on the man walking in the door. Sevella quickly turns as Neal walks in. He walked straight to the counter and began a conversation with Becky; Becky's smile indicated that Neal was someone she knew. After several minutes of chatting, Neal turns toward the door and, without a word or glance in their direction, walks out of the diner. "Didn't he even see us?" whispered Sevella; as they watched Neal until he got into the taxi. With coffee cup held up to her lips, Sevella and Mr. Clark watched in amazement as the taxi drove off. Sevella waited patiently for Mr. Clark to respond; instead, he nonchalantly pointed in the direction of the saucer and the untouched pancake. Therefore, Sevella pushes the saucer over to him. Contrary to their conversation, Sevella watched in silence as Mr. Clark took the pancake, poured syrup on the now cold pancake, and without another word, began to eat as he sipped the remainder of his orange juice.

"In that case," breaking the silence, Sevella spoke calmly, "have you seen her before, here at the diner?" Now holding both hands up as if to surrender, Mr. Clark began to question Sevella, "Have you and Neal ever come here together?" As she stared at the picture on the wall behind Mr. Clark, she whispered, "No, but I worked here for almost a year, and Neal was never a customer, but it appears that Neal knows Becky. Sam just became co-owner, and Becky is a new employee." Mr. Clark asked suspiciously, "You worked here?" She nodded and said, "Yes." At the same time, Mr. Clark was pointing behind her in Becky's direction; afterward, Mr. Clark changed the subject and asked, "I wonder if Neal's visit was personnel or business-related?" Sevella turned and signaled for Becky to come over, asking Becky, "That man you were talking to, he looks familiar." "Oh, that's my dad, Ned. Do you know him?" Sevella was now smiling, saying, "No, but he really looks familiar." Becky turned to walk back to the counter but suddenly stopped, turned, looked back, and asked Mr. Clark, "Oh, by the way, are you Toni's friend?"

How Do You Know Toni?

At that time, Mr. Clark was taking a sip of his orange juice and was now choking and looking at Becky as if she had two heads. "Ah, what? I mean, yes, I am. How do you know Toni?" he finally asked while attempting to clear his throat. Both Sevella and Becky couldn't hold back the laughter; finally, Becky responded between giggles, "She was my sociology instructor, and Toni was not only my instructor but my friend. We were the same age, but Toni graduated college before I did. However, a couple of years ago, we took a photo together before she went on vacation, and you were in that photo." Becky paused before continuing, "Long story short, and I'm so sorry. I hate to be the bearer of bad news." Nevertheless, Mr. Clark played his role well as he sat quietly, cutting his cold pancake into small pieces. Becky continued, "I really don't know how well you knew her, and I really don't expect you to remember, but I guess you haven't heard that she disappeared while on vacation and was never found." Now turning to Sevella, Becky said, "Consequently, you may have seen my dad's twin, my Uncle Neal, and thought it was my dad."

At that moment, another customer walks into the diner, and Becky heads for the counter. "On the other hand," whispered Mr. Clark. "One of Neal's secrets has been discovered." At this point, Sevella interrupted him, almost shouting, "Twin, twin!" Now lowering her voice, "What does she mean, twin? I have known Neal at least ten years, and I have never heard him speak of a niece or twin brother or family in any conversation." At that moment, Sevella looked out of the window but didn't notice rushing traffic, but her eyes fell on a man standing on the corner across the street staring at the diner. Of course, she didn't think twice about it since everyone loved the diner, but before turning away from the man, a taxi stopped right in front of the man, and then he was gone. "What are you looking at?" asked Mr. Clark. "Daydreaming, I guess," said Sevella. Not convinced, Mr. Clark turned to look, but the cab was driving off. "Did you see someone you know?" asked Mr. Clark. "No, just a man who looked like he was headed this way, but no doubt he was waiting for a cab," whispered Sevella.

Still not convinced, Mr. Clark leaned forward and asked suspiciously, "Did he look familiar?" Now feeling very nauseated Sevella excuses herself and rushes to the bathroom. Once in the bathroom, she realized that the man's form brought back memories since all she could see of her attacker was a shape in the dark. Furthermore, Sevella began to scold herself, "Stop it! Mr. Clark is just being careful, but he is causing me to fear, and probably for no reason." She turned on the faucet and wet her hand, then dried them as anger filled her heart. "It could have been the man, and he recognizes me, but I have no idea who he is or what he looks like. However, if he speaks, then I can put a face to that voice." Before leaving the bathroom, she looked at her reflection, saying, "How dare he follow me? Who does he think he is?" At that moment, the door to one of the bathroom stalls opened, and the person coming out of the stall said, "Don't worry, honey, if he really loves you, believe me, he will follow you wherever you go." With that being said, the lady washed her hands and was gone.

Mistaken Identity

Before she went back to the table, she made several attempts to pull herself together. She anticipated Mr. Clark's continual questioning about the man; therefore, she prepared an answer. She realized that Mr. Clark was observing her expression as she watched the man. She then remembered that night in Florida. She had later learned she had mistaken a man for someone else when getting on one of the elevators, or was it a mistake? In spite of her cheerful smile, fear gripped her heart as she walked out of the restroom and realized that Mr. Clark's suggestion for her to go somewhere else other than home wasn't such a bad idea. "The problem," she whispered, "I don't know where to go. Maybe I can sleep in the office. After all, it's under security watch." She again changed her expression to a smile as she sat down at the booth. Mr. Clark was looking out of the window and didn't notice her sitting down. Without turning toward her, Mr. Clark said, "Can you imagine Ned and Neal swapping identities and Ned knowing everything about you, but you know nothing about Ned or his existence."

Right after that, Mr. Clark asked, "Are you thinking the same thing I'm thinking? Are you thinking that Ned and Neal have switched identities and know everything about us, but we know nothing about them?" Now nodding her head, Sevella answered, "Exactly." Meanwhile, Mr. Clark is motioning to get Becky's attention. After Becky walked over to their table, Mr. Clark asked, "Do you mind giving my number to Samantha, I don't want to disturb her, and if you don't mind, I can pay now, or do I pay at the counter?" Placing her attention on the ringing phone, "Oh, please pay at the counter when you are ready," said Becky as she rushed to answer the phone. Now insisting, Mr. Clark continued, "Are you sure there is no place you can go other than back to your home? I just feel that finding the briefcase and being in the same place as the owner of that briefcase places you in a more dangerous situation than before this trip." Now sitting up straight, she replied, "Maybe the person getting in the cab and the person in Florida are one of the same; I thought about what you said about not going home, but where would I go? Besides, how much time do we have before we have to be back at the office?"

Now looking at his watch, Mr. Clark jumped up, heading for the counter, "Twenty minutes, let's go!" In addition to all the confusion, on the drive to the office, Sevella kept wondering about the owner of that briefcase and how he would get her information. Now speaking silently, "The only information the hotel has is my fake name. Oh no!" said Sevella as she jumped forward. "What's the matter?" Ask Mr. Clark as he reached to catch her. "I paid with the company's credit card, I can be traced back to the office by whoever occupied that room, and just maybe as we speak, he is trying to locate me, and if that's the case, I am not hard to find. I guess I'll just have to make it difficult for him to locate me just in case he plans on coming after me." Mr. Clark was now motioning for her to sit back just as the taxi driver asked, "Is there a problem?" Waving his hand, Mr. Clark said, "No, not at all, she just remembered something important."

Strange Occurrences
in Florida

After what appeared to be only minutes, the taxi pulled in front of the office. As they exited the cab, neither spoke, walking in silence, speaking only with their eyes, knowing everything had changed and nothing would ever be the same. As they walked into the building, neither spoke nor made eye contact. Sevella's thoughts are on the twin, and Mr. Clark is wondering, *What's next? First, the briefcase, then Becky's confession about Toni's disappearance, and finally, Ned, Neal's twin.* As the elevator doors opened, they both walked slowly toward the office. Ringing phones, then an unfamiliar voice answered, "Hello, New Ventures. May I help you?" Neal's door swung open, and like a gust of wind, he rushed to pass the front desk as the Temp beckoned for him to stop. As they walked into the office toward the receptionist's area, Neal turned and greeted them. "Well, welcome back! How was the trip, and did we accomplish all that we set out to do, or do we need to go back and finish up?"

After that, Mr. Clark carefully chooses his words, but speaking excitedly while walking toward Neal's right hand extended, Mr. Clark said, "No, sir, there is no need to go back. We have done above and beyond the call of duty. By the way, I ran into a guy that looked just like you. Actually, I wondered why you were ignoring me." Looking puzzled, then laughing, Neal asked, "Where was this?" Quickly glancing in Sevella's direction before answering, "I saw him leaving a building I'm not sure where." Now, nodding his head, "Yes, I never talk about family, but I do have a twin brother. We usually see each other during the holidays. By the way, they call me the black sheep of the family because my idea of success is not what they would call 'family business,' anyway, I'm too busy these days to be concerned about what other people think. Our business is booming. We have new clients coming in and more expected in the future. When do I have time for family?"

Meanwhile, Neal was fingering through documents on the receptionist's desk before saying, "After all, Ned knows where I work, and I know where he works." Now pointing toward his office, he beckoned for Mr. Clark and Sevella to follow him. As they walk into the office, Neal closes the door just as Mr. Clark turns, saying, "You know, Neal, something is terribly wrong." Neal responded, "Wrong; what on earth went wrong? You just said you accomplish every task!" Simultaneously waving his hand in the air, Mr. Clark quickly interrupted, saying, "No, nothing went wrong with our plan, and I didn't mean to even insinuate that. What I said is, something is wrong." Mr. Clark took a seat and continued, "There is this briefcase, and somehow a lady turns up in my bed apparently drugged. Most importantly, your newly discovered twin brother; just maybe you can explain some of these strange occurrences we have encountered in Florida."

Just Tell the Truth

"First of all," Neal began as he wiped away the apparent sweat that had formed on his forehead, at the same time reaching for his chair. "First of all…" Mr. Clark then interrupted Neal by jumping up from his chair, "Neal, don't try to play us! We've experienced too much, not to mention what we have already seen. Please, just tell us the truth!" From that point on, Neal stood up and began to pace the floor. Mr. Clark continued, "Please sit down! We are not saying it's wrong for you to have a twin brother, but it does seem strange that in all the years working for you that Sevella doesn't know anything about him or any of your family. Secondly, well, what I want to know is, how much do you know about Ellor and his so call company?" Looking a little agitated, Neal finally answered, "What is all this about, and why on earth am I being interrogated as if I drugged the girl and placed her in your bed? By the way, do I look like a drug pusher? Now I need to know what has happened and don't leave anything out. I need to know what has bought about this suspicion against Ellor and me."

"Coincidently," Mr. Clark began…. at the same time, Neal waved his hands, but before he could utter a word, Sevella suddenly spoke up, "Neal, no one is accusing you of any wrongdoing, but you may be in business with someone shady or running a shady business. Apart from our successful trip, what I am about to say has been my dark secret for the past four years, and I never told a soul because I knew no one would believe me. Remember when I took my first trip to Florida?" Neal is swiftly moving his head up and down while at the same time motioning with his hand for Sevella to go on. "Well, I… I was attacked and raped in my hotel room." In total shock, Neal jumped up, and Mr. Clark opened his mouth without speaking. Neal stumbled backward only to fall into his chair, placing his face into the palm of his hands as if to shield his eyes from the scene he was now visualizing. Sevella slowly stood as she walked slowly toward Neal with tears running down her cheeks. She stopped a few feet from his chair, voice quivering. She said, "But I believe the man who attacked me may have been at one of Ellor's investment meetings and could possibly have been one of his clients."

Neal was now on his feet, looking into Sevella's eyes, demanding, "Who did it, and why on earth did you keep it a secret? Did you at all call and report the attack to the Florida Police Department?" Engulfed in tears, Sevella spoke in a whisper, "Would anyone have believed me, an orphaned nobody? That's right. I was orphaned at the age of three, and I know what it's like to take the blame for something I didn't do. Furthermore, I just wanted to impress you and be treated as an equal, to belong. Instead, I felt more like an escort. Neal, would you have believed me, or would you have believed the attacker? Tell me, Neal, what would have influenced your decision more, my rape or the advancement of New Ventures?" Often when Neal is backed into a corner or at a loss for words, he becomes evasive and simply refuses to answer questions. Being true to his nature, he walked blindly toward his chair, looking totally astounded, at the same time wiping sweat from his forehead, and eventually, over the top of his bald head, hesitated before speaking, "Sevella, I'm very upset at you, after working with me almost ten years now."

A Bad Judgment Call

After her confession, no one spoke for several minutes. Finally, Neal cleared his throat, saying, "For some reason, Sevella, and I don't understand why, but you don't hold me in the highest regard. When have I ever treated you as an escort, on even given you that impression? Have I ever done or said anything to that effect? Have you witnessed me being dishonest in any aspect of my business or disrespectful toward you? Sevella, have I ever been disrespectful or acted in any way to make you feel uncomfortable or threatened by me, ever? If so, you should have spoken up. You should have said something!" Sevella has always believed that she was a good judge of character; she knew that Neal was greedy for money, but he had never been disrespectful, just not protective. "Sevella, do you hear me talking to you? Have I ever been disrespectful toward you?" At this point, she slowly turned and walked toward her chair, sitting down as she adjusted her sitting position. Speaking softly, she whispered, "No, no, Neal, I have never felt disrespected, but I have felt threatened."

At this point, Neal gasped but remained silent while Sevella continued, "Allow me to quote your famous phrase, especially when it comes to making more money; and I quote, 'Doing whatever it takes,' and it took me going to Florida all alone with strangers, getting raped, and I quote, 'do whatever it takes.'" Neal began to speak, but Sevella interrupted him by standing and rushing up to him, placing her right palm near his face, almost touching his nose, before continuing, "Neal, I know your pride; sometimes that pride clouds your judgment, and sending me out of town all alone with strangers was truly a bad judgment call." Meanwhile, Mr. Clark is looking back and forth from Neal to Sevella, observing each of their reactions to the unfortunate circumstances that have exposed a very dark secret. At the same time, while hoping one of them will lead the other to say something, anything, that would help him find out what happened to his now missing friend, Toni."

Sevella continued, "I know you don't know very much about me, and, like you, I don't talk about my past to anyone. It just so happens, Mr. Clark guessed upon it, not the rape, but about me being an orphan." "Anyway," Neal quickly interrupted her, "that's why my brother couldn't find any background on you. Do we even have your correct information?" Sevella was shaking her head from left to right, saying, "Never mind, what's important now is staying safe or even alive. Because we, we meaning—" Mr. Clark quickly interjected, "What she means is, well, we believe that she is being followed. There was this guy in Florida that made it his business to ask about Sevella on more than one occasion. He may be the man that raped her, or he may just be an admirer, we don't know, but if someone believes she can expose his identity to the authorities, he is going to try to find her." At that moment, Sevella continued, "Yes, Neal, there have been times when I wondered if it was more about the money than my safety."

Let's Dig a Little Deeper

After a brief moment of silence, Sevella spoke up, "On the other hand and on a brighter note, I appreciate you for allowing me to stay in your investment property; after the purchase, you could have sold or leased it within days, but you allowed me to stay as a house sitter. Otherwise, I would have been living in a motel." Neal was now slowly sitting down as he placed both hands on the arms of his chair as if to support himself, but he remained quiet. Sevella continued, "Of course, after being employed for a few months, I moved from the homeless shelter into the motel. You never knew that. Nevertheless, when I accidentally discovered the Deed of Trust, and receipts revealing that you used money from my little earnings toward my down payment, I could not believe it." Sevella turned and walked slowly back to her seat but remained standing. "Neal, believe me when I say that your act of kindness placed you in an entirely different light, plus it made a significant impact on me. You see, I never really had a place of my own. I had my own bed and space in the homeless shelter, and believe me when I say that was my first real home."

Neal was now looking down to conceal the pain he felt deep down inside, "Please, understand why I'm a little confused with the whole idea of you and Ellor. Neal, I really hope you were not mixed up in whatever is going on with Ellor." Again Mr. Clark interrupted, "Remember, Ellor had security on-site at his last meeting because of that one soliciting occasion." Sevella nodded her head up and down but didn't speak. After what seemed like countless seconds of silence, Neal looked at Sevella and smiled, then he said, "When I first hired you, I observed your attitude, character, and how thorough and efficient you were; I also noticed a toughness about you that assured me that you were more than capable of taking care of yourself, that's why I sent you alone to Florida. First of all, I trusted Ellor as a friend and business associate to take care of you. Secondly, I knew that you could take care of yourself and represent the company with the highest integrity. By the way, I am also a good judge of character, and that's why I teamed you with Ellor."

By this time, Mr. Clark stood up, looking at Sevella and then Neal, saying, "I can tell that you both are in a state of shock over our recent discoveries, and you, Sevella, being the most vulnerable, has been forced to share your deepest, darkest, not to mention shocking secret. Now it's time to dig a little deeper and find out what's going on in Florida before someone gets hurt. Sevella, you mentioned at one time that Ellor was trying to help you; now I have to ask you one important thing, and you don't have to answer, but I hope you will, and that is to tell us everything that happened in Florida up until the time you arrived and until the time you left." Apprehensive, Sevella began pacing the floor. Finally, she felt a strong sense of confidence before saying, "Well, one important thing I have to mention; first of all, on this very last trip, I remembered something Mr. Clark said, and that was Ellor's attitude toward the strangers coming in and out of the investors' meetings, which completely cleared him of my suspicions of being responsible for my attack.»

No, I Will Not Go

"In the past, I began to blame Ellor, his clients, and Neal because I knew nothing about Neal's friends and wasn't properly informed. Other than that, I have told you everything. By the way, except for the time I received a call from Tramishia, she was not her usual joking, kidding-around self. Actually, she said something to me that struck me strangely. She said something to the effect, 'like you don't know,' and as talkative as you knew her to be, well, those four words were the jest of her conversation. Eventually, she was interrupted when someone came into the office, and suddenly she perked up." Now standing, Mr. Clark asked, "What happened after that?" As though he could perceive her thoughts. Sevella answered, "Nothing. I never heard from her again." In that instance, silence covered the room like a thick dark cloud as everyone blindly looked toward the window. Just as Neal was getting ready to speak, the phone ranged. Shortly afterward, the receptionist announced, "Mr. Ellor Fisher is holding Mr. Nest."

In contrast to all the shocking revelations, Neal straightened his tie as if to meet Ellor in person and slowly picked up the receiver, "Yes." After a brief moment of silence, Neal finally answered, "By the way, I was wondering about getting Tramishia back down here to help Mr. Clark and Sevella with this next Venture." Again silence, then Neal continued, "Sevella, oh, she is fine. Why do you ask? Oh, I see. Well, she's working hard as ever and very busy with another very important assignment, and I really need all hands on deck." Shortly after his response, Neal's facial expression changed from coy to shocking. "What do you mean disappeared? When did this happen, and was it reported to the authorities?" Neal is now looking in Mr. Clark's direction and beckoning him to come closer as he places the phone to Mr. Clark's ear. Ellor continued, "That is why I need both Sevella and Mr. Clark back up here; I am working short-staffed…tell me you will send them both?"

As soon as Ellor spoke those words, Mr. Clark was now looking very angry as he quickly pushed the phone back to Neal while whispering, "Say yes." Neal quickly took the phone and responded, "Yes, of course." After hanging up, Neal asked Mr. Clark, "What did I just agree to?" Now looking in Sevella's direction, Mr. Clark repeated, "He wants another meeting with me and Sevella, but this time in France." Finally, Neal admitted, "I haven't told you everything I know." At the same time, Sevella jumped up from her seat, literally screaming, "No, no, I will not go, no, I will not go!" Now standing, both men were now rushing toward her, attempting to calm her down. "Please, Sevella, get a hold of yourself," said Mr. Clark, at the same time placing a tissue in her hand. Mr. Clark continued, "Sevella, you said yourself that Ellor was very helpful during your first trip: now, tell me, how was your visit to France?" Sevella looked blindly in Neal's direction before responding to Mr. Clark's question, "Well," she started, then stopped and started again, "well, we actually had a wonderful time." Mr. Clark interrupted, "What has changed?"

Just Keep Me Out of It

Eventually, Sevella looked up, staring out of the window, now looking in Mr. Clark's direction, then looking downward at the floor, "I guess finding the pictures." Now turning toward Neal, Mr. Clark said, "Ellor wants us to meet him in Florida and then fly to France. Therefore, we will meet him at the airport to fly out together." Shaking her head frantically, Sevella was determined, speaking more forcefully, "No, I said!" Neal quickly chided in, "No, is right, you are not going. Instead, I will go and find out once and for all what is going on." Apparently, from sheer exhaustion, Mr. Clark sat down with both hands in the air, saying, "Neal, if you go, you go alone. There is something that I haven't told anyone: you see, I just learned today that my friend, the one that has been missing for almost two years, was among the photos in the briefcase Sevella found. During that time, Toni was hired by Ellor to tutor French lessons to a couple of his employees." Sevella was now thinking, *Toni, that's the name chosen by Sam for the diner.* Now gasping aloud, "Are you talking Toni, my friend's diner?"

"To begin with," Mr. Clark continued, "Sevella has those pictures on her phone, and maybe you can give them to the authorities." Sevella jumped up, demanding, "Look, I have had enough! Mr. Clark, I will send you those photos, and you send them to Neal; Neal, you can give them to the authorities, but just keep me out of it." Immediately, Neal jumps up from his chair, almost screaming at Mr. Clark, "What do you mean? I don't understand what you are saying! You mean to tell me you have not even talked to her in the past two years?" All the while Neal was speaking, Mr. Clark was vigorously shaking his head from left to right. Neal sits slowly into his chair, completely speechless, while Mr. Clark is standing and pacing. Eventually, Neal spoke up, "You are right, Mr. Clark, and you both should lay low. I've changed my mind, and I'm not going, but I will contact my brother Ned and ask for his help." Momentarily puzzled by Neal's statement, both Mr. Clark and Sevella answered simultaneously, "What?"

Now looking with a slight smile on his face, Neal responded, "Yes, Ned; he is a private investigator and has been working with the authorities regarding sex trafficking locally and statewide. Oh, by the way, my brother has asked me to intervene on several occasions, like sitting in for him; therefore, I have assisted him in some of his cases." Mr. Clark was now walking toward Neal, asking, "How so?" Sevella then spoke, "Yes, Neal, how so?" Neal continued, "In addition to all the revelations of hidden information, I have something else I need to reveal." Neal took a deep breath before saying, "Many of those late-night investors' meetings were staged by Ned, and many times while I was traveling, it was Ned in the office pretending to be me. I won't bother to explain, except that my father is a private investigator; his father worked undercover in narcotics. Coincidentally, that is why I'm called the black sheep of the family. If anyone can get to the bottom of this mystery, Ned can."

Undercover Investigation

Now both Mr. Clark and Sevella were now standing, looking at one another, then at Neal. Finally, Mr. Clark asked, "Was there a time when Ned pretended to be you other than during the ongoing investigation?" Before Neal could answer, Mr. Clark continued, "What I meant, was Sevella ever in any danger and Ned knew of that danger?" Now feeling very unsure of himself, Neal finally answered, "Well, there was an investigation that led them to Florida: by the way, I encouraged Ellor to incorporate those evening meetings in order to throw off the perpetrators that were being investigated, and the perpetrators fell for it. What was not planned was the substantial increase in Ellor's clientele, which caused the investigation to last longer than anticipated. Regarding Sevella being in danger, well, I was never informed of anyone being in danger." As if Neal was speaking in a foreign language, Mr. Clark and Sevella stared at him in silence. Neal realized he hadn't answered Mr. Clark's question and could not due to the nature of the investigation.

At this point, Neal knew he had to tell the truth without telling the truth; therefore, he continued, "Since Ned's work was undercover, I couldn't tell Ellor or Sevella. By the way, Ned did and does have several leads on several suspicious characters, and that's all I can say on that subject." Of course, both Sevella and Mr. Clark began to speak at the same time. "What?" Mr. Clark continued, "He's a private investigator?" Neal didn't answer but turned to his phone, called, and instructed the receptionist, "Contact Ned." Sounding annoyed and surprised, Sevella asked, "She knows your brother?" Now looking very annoyed, Neal answered abruptly, "No, she doesn't; besides, I said to her to contact Ned and not my brother. She only knows that I have a contact named Ned. By the way, Sevella, if you stop and think, so did you." At that point, Sevella recalled the call list, and she remembered that there was a contact named Ned, but she never received instructions to call him. Apart from being in total shock, Sevella was now feeling nauseated; therefore, she stood moving slowly toward the door.

Afterward, suddenly she stopped, slowly turned to look back at Mr. Clark, then Neal saying, "Mr. Clark suggested that it may not be safe for me to go home, and based on all the information Mr. Clark has shared and the briefcase with photos I'm beginning to believe he's right," Neal interrupted Sevella, demanding, "That's right Mr. Clark you mentioned photos and a briefcase. Tell me, do you still have them?" At that moment, Sevella went into her purse and walked over to Mr. Clark, and handed him her phone. Neal rushed to pull his chair next to Mr. Clark as both began to scroll through the pictures. Sevella pointed to the images of Tina. Without warning, Neal grabbed the phone from Mr. Clark, pointing to the photos of Tremeshia and Naomi, yelling, "I know these two girls! Sevella, you see this? This can be criminal evidence. Don't you remember the call I received from Florida authorities?" Sevella was now shaking her head from left to right, saying, "There were at least two calls, but you never disclosed any of the conversations."

A Dark Time

Next, Sevella pointed to the photo of Dannie, saying, "I met Dannie in the orphanage, I knew her, but we lost contact after she ran away…." Shortly after that, her voice breaking into soft sobs, Sevella weeps uncontrollably. Meanwhile, Neal was staring at the pictures, unaware of Sevella's tears. Mr. Clark passed a tissue while attempting to comfort Sevella as Neal continued, speaking in a whisper, "Hey, I met these two ladies a few years ago, but they were not employed; however, they did attend the meeting with a prospect that never really became involved with the company." As Sevella watched in amazement before saying, "Neal!" He looked blindly at Mr. Clark and then Sevella, finally back at the photos as she continued, "Neal, I relived that horrible night in Florida every day of my life, and also the night you sent me off without warning. I was absolutely terrified. It was a very dark time for me, but what I really remembered most of all was the fear that gripped my heart as you left the meeting, leaving me alone with complete strangers."

As soon as Neal heard "dark time," he looked up, staring in amazement as Sevella walked toward the door: Sevella continued, "To this day, I remember your last words because I repeated them over and over in my mind." Sevella slowly turned the knob on the door, but before she walked out, she turned again, saying, "Enough reflecting on the good times; I'm going home, it's very late, and I'm very tired, so I'm going home." Mr. Clark jumped to his feet, attempting to persuade Sevella, but she insisted, "Look, I agree it may be dangerous, but running away will only make it worst. I've never been afraid of anything except for not being adopted or loved; look, I haven't told you everything, but if I did, you would understand why I'm going home." After Sevella left the office, she climbed into the taxi cab, feeling very tired; but she knew the tiredness she felt wasn't because of work but due to emotional stress and strain of having to share her past with Neal and Mr. Clark, a new friend but still a stranger.

Eventually, the trauma of her confession left her feeling exhausted and drained. Somehow, Mr. Clark's confession caused her to open up, exposing old but painful wounds, wounds that refused to be healed. As she recalls her brief moment of excitement, speaking audibly, "Yes, this day wasn't a total loss. As it happens, the diner was a very successful visit!" It was then the taxi driver turned to respond to her remark, "Glad to hear that, ma'am! Where would you like me to take you?" Due to that brief reminder, she gave her address. She hadn't noticed the driver; he wasn't her regular driver. "How silly! I need to pull it together," Sevella whispered. In what seemed like a few minutes, they were now approaching her address. "Oh, no!" she exclaimed, before instructing the driver, "I am so sorry, but we have passed my stop, but please just make the block, and it will bring you back to my address." However, the driver's attention was on the couple across the street.

Something Is Wrong

At that moment, Sevella turned and saw Samuel and her neighbors standing midway between their house and the driveway. It appeared that three of their car doors were left open; the man's arms cradled Samuel as the woman's hands cradled his head. Instantly, Sevella knew something was wrong as she slid over to the driver's side to get a better look as her neighbors stood looking very concerned before turning to watch the cab slowly drive by. It was then the taxi turned the corner to make the block, as Samuel's parents suddenly turned and literally ran up their walkway into their home. It was at that moment that Sevella remembered the man standing on the curb across from the diner. "What a time to remember him," she whispered. As the taxi came to a stop, an uneasiness filled her entire being; Sevella realized that her brief moment of excitement was being replaced by concerns for Samuel and fear of the stranger.

Presently, deep in thought and completely distracted, seconds later, she heard, "Ma'am, ma'am!" Suddenly Sevella realized that the voice she was hearing was no longer in her head. She threw her hand up in frustration, saying, "Oh my, I am such a workaholic; forgive me, my work follows me home." As the taxi driver turned his meter, Sevella handed him his fare plus a sizable tip while opening the back door and stepping out onto the curb. Not only feeling emotionally tired and very concerned, she questioned herself, *How on earth did I go from being concerned for Samuel to thinking about the man at the bus stop? Yes, it is possible that he is the man from Florida, but that is only a probability; clearly, something has happened to Samuel; otherwise, my neighbors would not have been standing outside and holding him like that.*

As Sevella approached her home, she stopped several yards from her home, hoping Samuel would be looking out, but she was too far away. "All I wanted was to get home and see Samuel, and I have seen him, but something is definitely wrong. Momentarily standing very still, glancing across the street at the upstairs window, saying, "For the first time, I see the couple and Samuel standing outside their home in plain view, and both looking down at Samuel, then quickly rushing inside their home?" After a moment of standing and looking toward her neighbor's home, Sevella realized that she was also standing out in plain view. She quickly maneuvered between the shrubbery to her front gate, rushing up the steps, opened her front door, and hurriedly closed the door behind her. Next, throwing her still-opened purse and keys on the end table near the door. From there, she sat on the couch, watching for any movement in the upstairs window, wondering, *What has happened to Samuel?*

Without Warning

Meanwhile, after what seemed like forever, the car was pulling into the driveway, and without waiting for his father to come to a complete stop, David unsnapped his seat belt from his car seat and opened the rear door just as his mother turned to see him grabbed his certificate, while at the same time opening the backdoor of the slowly moving vehicle. Startled at the backdoor suddenly opening, Lawrence abruptly hit the brakes, causing David to tumble out of the car onto the ground. His mother was now crying out, "David, David, are you alright?" His father quickly put the car in park and jumped out of the car as his wife quickly opened her door and ran, still crying out, "David, David, are you all right?" Catheryn and Lawrence were now kneeling down beside him as he stood looking down at the dust on his knees and then his hands before looking up at his parents. Catheryn touched his arms and knees, testing for possible broken bones before dusting him off. Now she grabbed his little hands as she examined him further for broken bones.

It was then Lawrence nervously asked, "Son, are you hurting? Did you hurt yourself?" now smiling, David pulled away from his mother and started toward the house, but his father took him up in his arms. Catheryn quickly began to do a quick assessment for possible head trauma before saying, "Except for the redness in the palms of his hands, everything seems fine." Lawrence touches the same place while insisting, "But I think we should take him to the hospital just to be on the safe side!" In that instance, Catheryn eyes filled with tears when she noticed the huge smile on David's face. At that moment, David's face turned into a look of fear as Catheryn began to scold him for what he had just done. Eyes tearing up at his mother's unexpected response to his excitement and frightened by his mother's unexpected tears; then, his father's stern voice got his attention, "David, you could have been hurt. Don't you know what you just did was very dangerous!"

At the time, David thought nothing of what he did but realized by his parent's reactions it was a very bad thing to do. As he held on to his mother's hand, he could feel his mother trembling; therefore, he became very afraid. Now, he then turned to his mother as she held him closer and began to cradle his head, at the same time scolding him softly, "David, that was a very frightening moment for Mommy and Daddy. That's why we are so upset." As his mother quietly scolded him, David was looking at the house across the street and thinking about the shadow. As his parents continued to cradle him, saying, "Sweetheart, do you understand why Daddy and I are upset?" David shook his head from left to right as tears continued to fill his eyes. Then his father said, "Son, you could have been hurt, and maybe we would have taken you to the hospital for bandages."

The Lady on the Ground

David was now looking curiously at his father and remembering the lady on the ground; he asked his father, "Like the lady on the ground?" All of a sudden, the look of unbelief replaced the concern on Lawrence's face; while looking puzzled, he turned to Catheryn and said, "Honey, do you know what he's talking about?" Catheryn looked at the house across the street as David's eyes followed her glance. Catheryn mouthed the words, moving only her lips, "Remember the commotion down the street from the community center, you know, the women on the corner?" Suddenly, Lawrence remembered. All the while, David's attention is on the house across the street. "Oh, yeah, that." Now both were looking curiously at David as they followed his gaze. Eyes fixed with an unusual expression; his mother called him twice, "David, David, what are you looking at?" Finally, Lawrence interrupted her, winking his eye, saying, "Honey, don't worry; it's a man thing, you know, tuning one out when you don't want to hear it, similar to what I do."

At the same time, Catheryn was holding up her right palm to Lawrence's face. Now laughing out loud, Lawrence took David into his arm and gave him a big hug before saying, "That's my boy!" It was then Lawrence remembered that he had only put the car in park but hadn't turned off the motor, and he had also left his doors open. He quickly passed David to Catheryn while pointing toward the car and ran quickly to turn off the motor. While he raced toward the car, she quickly looked around the neighborhood to see if anyone was watching. As Lawrence walked toward her, he took David while Catheryn ran her hand over his head. It was then she looked to see if anyone was watching just in case all the commotion had caught the attention of their neighbors. At that moment, they noticed David's mode change even though his eyes were still teary. A smile emerged on his tiny little lips as he turned to look at the house across the street.

At the same time, Catheryn and Lawrence looked away from David toward their front door and again at David as they followed his gaze to the house across the street. All of a sudden, Catheryn and Lawrence saw the taxi as he slowly drove by and finally out of sight. David watched the yellow cab, but suddenly his parent's behavior distracted him; they began to rush toward the gate, almost running to the front door, quickly opened it, and rushed inside. David was amused by the quick actions of his parents, thinking they were playing a game to make him feel better, so he started to laugh. Except for that moment of horror, both Lawrence and Catheryn finally realized that they must have looked pretty silly. Lawrence said, "Look at us running like thieves to hide from our neighbors." Again bursting into laughter, "It all seems so silly running and hiding as if we had just committed some crime!" Catheryn blurted out as she broke into laughter.

Do You Understand?

It was at that moment that Lawrence grabbed David and said, "Son, we love you so much that we must keep you safe. Do you understand? So, never again open the car door until I have stopped the car, turned off the motor, and Mommy is opening the door for you. Understand?" Now smiling and shaking his head up and down, David threw his arms around his daddy's neck and gave him a big hug and kiss. As soon as he put David down, he rushed up the stairs, happily noticing his parent's weird reaction as he continued up the stairs waving his certificate in the air. Instead of watching him go up the stairs, they turned away and started to laugh heartily at themselves while holding each other as if they kept the other from falling over. In the meantime, David rushed upstairs into his bedroom and went straight to his window, waiting patiently for the yellow car to bring the lady home. He looked toward the window and noticed the blinds were opened, but he couldn't see anything.

Now feeling very disappointed at missing the lady, he went downstairs to see if his parents were still being funny. Later, David went back upstairs to his window and sat looking out, but not for the planes. After several minutes of waiting, David jumped backward to hide as he noticed the streetlight shining through the window across the street. Now he was able to see a form. Excitement caused him to climb onto the window seat, hoping to get a closer view of the image in the window across the street. As the floor squeaked outside his bedroom door, David quickly jumped from the window into his bed. Suddenly, his mother came in to see him bouncing up and down on the bed. Amused but firmed, she demanded, "David! When did you start this game? I don't like it, and sit down right now!" David sits as he bounces up and down. "Okay, Mommy, but the bed is bouncing me up." His mother was now fighting back the laughter; she then quickly turned as she burst into silent laughter and walked out, saying, "Okay, but don't let me catch you doing that again."

Afterward, still laughing between words, this time, she managed to sound stern, repeating, "Okay? Now it's time for your bath." The same night, David would sneak downstairs to the refrigerator for milk and cookies. Catheryn made sure that his spill-proof cup of milk was on the bottom refrigerator shelf and two cookies were left in the cookie jar. He then slipped past his parents' open door, down the stairs, through the den into the kitchen, and headed straight for the refrigerator. Quietly and quickly taking his cup of milk, he quietly opened the cookie jar, grabbed the two cookies, and tipped toed up the stairs past his parent's opened door into his bedroom. Once inside his bedroom, he closed the door, pulled up a chair to the window, and watched for any movement. He could see the lights from the planes as they took off from the distant airport, but tonight his focus was on the window across the street. It was then the plane appeared. In awe, David watched as the plane climbed higher into the sky until it became smaller and smaller. After a while, it was only a shadow in the sky.

Another Shadow

However, on this particular night, across the street, another figure would catch David's eye. In the reflection from the street lights appeared another ghostly shadow, but David did not run away. Instead, he watched carefully and stared intently as he watched a man moving silently but swiftly with his head down. Now, feeling a little relaxed, Sevella took off her shoes as she looked around her home and realized that it was getting dark, but she didn't really want to turn on the lights. Also, she knew that unless she unpacked right then and there, it would not get done until morning. She quickly unpacked, placing everything neatly away, even putting things in the outside storage. Afterward, taking another glance across the street knowing that there was no remote possibility of seeing Samuel until the next day, "Or maybe not until the weekend," she whispered. At that moment, she remembered Mr. Clark's warning, "Sevella, I don't think it is safe for you to go home." Again uneasiness crept into her heart just as she remembered the man standing on the corner near the Diner. Still, she was not going to be frightened by the unknown.

"After all, he was standing at the bus stop, for goodness' sake. Even though the whole while, he stood staring at the window where I was sitting. Never again!" she said as she stared out of her window, "Once upon a time, I had allowed fear to dictate my every thought and would eventually overwhelm me, leaving me with thoughts of suicide. I promised myself that I would never, ever again be that afraid of anyone, or anything, ever again!" Opening her curtain and raising the blind higher than ever, she placed her arm on the back of the couch, using it as a prop, then placed her head on her arm. Soon, she was fast asleep. Suddenly there were several light taps on her front door, then louder and quicker. Afterward, Sevella dreamed of someone knocking but was unable to move. That's when the knocking became successively harder and louder. Sevella jumped to her feet, rushed to the door, and without asking, who it was, she opened the door and was quickly pushed to the floor. Still groggy from sleep, Sevella attempted to stand, and that is when the street light revealed the frame of a man in a long coat standing over her. "You are a sly one; you must have known I was following you. All those twists and turns."

Sevella attempted to roll underneath the coffee table, but the man grabbed her by the throat, saying, "After losing you the first two times, I literally had a cab to drop me off so I could hide behind some shrubbery to watch and wait. If it hadn't been for you opening that blind, I would have passed this house up; thanks for helping me out. Did you think I would let you get away a second time? Even though I was in the wrong room, my time or money was not wasted. Although the drink I gave you didn't finish you off, I'm here to do just that." Again, Sevella goes into protected mode, strategizing her next move. The man distracted her by asking, "Remember the following day when I bumped into you on the elevator? I was surprised that you weren't dead, and I could tell you didn't recognize me, but still, I couldn't take any chances and that you were the wrong girl, but I couldn't risk you running your mouth." Quickly, Sevella jumped to her feet and turned to run for the door but felt an unbearable pain in the back of her head. She stumbled backward, falling, head hitting the glass table before losing consciousness.

Frightening Experience

Momentarily disappearing behind the shrubbery, then reappearing at the front door. Suddenly the man pushed Sevella's door open; David quickly jumped down from the window seat, climbed into bed, and immediately covered his head and did not come out until morning. Following that frightening experience, David woke up and hurried to the window, but there was no sign of the lady. David had overslept, much too tired to get up early enough to see if the lady's head was still in the window, and since there were no planned activities for that weekend, the family slept late. David felt frightened, refusing to go back to the window; instead, he fell asleep. Only to be awakened by the morning sun shining brightly through his window. Now, remembering the following night and wondering if it would be hard to see the lady's head in the window, he immediately jumped from the bed to the window and looked to see if there were any signs of the lady. The window was open, and he could see inside her home, but he didn't see the lady.

Following a full and playful day with Mom and Dad, David wanted to go to bed early. His parents didn't question him. After all, they wanted to be sure David wasn't still disturbed by their strange behavior the day before. As David ran up the stairs, he couldn't help but remember the night before, still feeling frightened but determined to be brave; therefore, David tip-toed over to his window and looked toward the house across the street. The blinds were still open, but the lady's head was not in. Suddenly, David became very concerned and thought about the man that pushed the lady's door. David also remembered the man in handcuffs and the woman on the ground. Shortly afterward, his mother called for him to come down for a snack. On the following weekend, after his bath, David's mother would join David and his father for a bedtime snack. Once in his bedroom, and after looking at the house across the street, David lay on his bed on top of his covers, hoping he would not fall asleep.

In spite of his effort to stay awake, he fell into a deep sleep. While asleep, David dreamed that he was being attacked, and the person ran and grabbed him by his jacket. David woke up screaming, waking his parents as they came running into his room. Frightened by David's scream, both his father and mother tried to get through his bedroom door at the same time. Clearly frightened themselves, stopping, realizing the sight of them could cause David more fear; therefore, Lawrence allowed Catheryn to go in as he looked around before rushing to David's bedside. Catheryn began to question David, "Sweetheart," by then, Lawrence was next to her, still looking around, then slowly sitting on the bed, pulling David into his arms. David's body relaxed, but he was still crying hysterically, at the same time reaching for his mother's outstretched hands. Determined to comfort David, his mother asked, "What happened? What's wrong? Did you have a bad dream?" David was now looking toward the window so intently that both his parents turned and looked in the direction of his gaze.

Something Is Wrong!

Now feeling very much afraid, Lawrence surveyed the window, at the same time realizing that no one could possibly get into that window without first climbing onto the roof. Occasionally looking from the window to David's bed, Lawrence spoke softly, saying, "Okay, buddy, there, there, it's going to be alright." After realizing that it was just a dream, David still felt something was wrong; he pulled away from his father's embrace and ran over to the window, frantically pointing to the house across the street and insisting that something was wrong. Looking in his mother's direction, insisting with more emotions than ever, "Mommy, come and see!" Catheryn was now speaking in her calming tone, "Sweetheart, it is okay. See? There is nothing wrong." David refused to listen to his mother's calming voice. Finally, his father spoke up, "David, if it will make you feel better and prove to you it was just a bad dream, we will go over and knock on the door, then you will see that mom is right."

Then his mother said, "I think we should wait until morning when there is more light." David looked around, shaking his head vigorously up and down, "Okay, Mommy." Quickly, Lawrence responded, "First, I think we should all get a little more sleep, and first thing in the morning, we will get dressed and go over to visit when we think our neighbor is up and ready for company. Guess what happens after that?" As David's eyes grew bigger, beaming with expectation, David squealed, "What, Daddy?" Lawrence responded with arms spread out like wings, saying, "Tomorrow we will have your celebration breakfast, blueberry pancakes, at your mother's newly discovered restaurant." Now David was thinking about the celebration, and his mother was now tugging at David's arm to lay him down; then his mother said, "Honey, it's the breakfast diner, remember, and it has been recommended by one of my coworkers. It will be my first time visiting."

While tucking David in, Lawrence signaled for Catheryn to slip out, and he would follow. After Lawrence slipped out of Davis's bedroom, Catheryn continued to explain, "My coworker would always bring me breakfast whenever she stopped by before work. She would brag on their blueberry pancakes, and you know how David loves my blueberry pancakes, but I think theirs may be just a tad better, just being honest." Laughing out loud, then shushing Catheryn as they both tiptoed into their bedroom. The following morning, as David and his parents were walking across the street, David hesitated, and being very afraid, he grabbed onto his father's hand and held on tightly. His father said, "It is okay, buddy. Everything is alright." As they approached the front gate, they slowly opened it while feeling very apprehensive about approaching a neighbor they otherwise would have never bothered to visit. All of a sudden, they were at their neighbor's front door to investigate something or nothing.

Mommy, A Lady!

From time to time, Lawrence glanced back, signaling for Catheryn to wait, but she ignored him. Finally, Lawrence knocked on the door; instantly, the front door came open. Catheryn called out, «Hello, is anyone home?" But there was no answer. With the back of his hand, Lawrence slowly pushed the door open; immediately, he jumped backward, causing David and his mother to turn and run toward the gate. Before reaching the gate, Catheryn stopped as she turned, asking nervously, "What is it, honey?" Lawrence was now smiling at David and his mother while saying out loud, "I'm sorry, honey; just kidding, I didn't mean to startle you," then walking up to give her a kiss on the cheek but whispered, "A lady is lying on the floor, take David home and call 911." Now laughing playfully, Catheryn responded, "Honey, you really gave us a scare. Come on, David, let's go and get ready for those blueberry pancakes while Daddy leaves a note for our neighbor to come and visit us."

On the other hand, Catheryn wasn't at all sure David fell for his father's trick. After closing their front door behind them, Catheryn began to question him, "David, why do you think our neighbor is a lady?" David hesitated, looking down at his feet because he was afraid he would get in trouble for looking out of the window. Still looking down, he slowly raised his eyes, looking up into Catheryn's searching eyes; as she bent down eye level to David and took both of his hands, speaking calmly, "David, it's okay, don't worry. Mommy understands." David knew whenever

Mommy understood, everything was made better. Finally, David yelled, "Mommy, she's not a ghost but a lady! I can see her when I look for the planes. I watched for the planes and for the lady." His mother fought to control her emotions. One minute she wanted to cry, the next, she wanted to hold him and not let him go. The thought of her not being there to shield his eyes from whatever happened in that house: the idea that he had been frightened brought tears to her eyes.

Rarely did David see her cry, but today she imagined him being so very afraid and alone. At the same time, she didn't want to confuse or alarm him with her tears, so she smiled lovingly and said, "Go on." Then David said, "When I see the airplane, I see the lady in the dark. The man came in the dark." David pointed at the window, "See, Mommy? I can see the lady's head right there." Shocked at David's confession Catheryn knew David's determination, but the very thought of what he had witnessed overwhelmed her. Although they had only lived in the neighborhood a short while before David, they assumed the house across the street was empty because of the for sale sign, except for an occasional driver stopping and looking, but never ever seen any activity of any kind. Suddenly fear gripped her heart when she realized that David may have seen the attack in the process. "That would be awful!" Catheryn said as she voiced her thoughts.

Fear Grips Her Heart

At that very moment, David began to tug on his mother's arm to get her attention, saying, "Mommy, Mommy, pancakes!" Now instructing David to go upstairs and get a toy to take with him, once again, fear gripped Catheryn's heart as she hesitated, wanting so badly to call David back and ask if he saw anything that would help her to understand how much he knew of the incident. Momentarily, she stood in a daze, but the urgency to ask questions would not leave her. Unable to leave it alone, Catheryn called him downstairs, sat down, and patted the stairstep. Once David sat down, she calmly asked, "David, what did you see? I mean, sweetheart, what did you see?" Before speaking, David's smile turned into a frown, then David said, "In the night, when I looked out of the window, I saw a ghost-man, but he didn't see me because I was hiding. I ran away, Mommy! Not because of the ghost, he pushed the door and went into her house. I ran and jumped on my bed and covered my head. Then I dreamed a bad dream, and I woke up."

Catheryn patted David's little hand, smiled, and asked, "What was the dream about?" his mother asked. "The man," said David. His mother realized that David was getting tensed, so she quickly changed the subject, saying, "That old bad dream better leave my baby alone." With that, David began to laugh at the funny face his mother made when she said, "that old bad dream." David continued, "In the morning, I looked out of the window, and I didn't see the head in the window, and I didn't see the sun on her head because of the man." Then David's mother thought to herself, *that was at least sixteen hours ago; the woman might be dead.* Finally, the paramedics arrived just minutes before the police cars arrived. The neighborhood eventually resembled a crime scene right out of the movies. David was coming down the stairs with his toy just as the ambulance rushed off with the woman draped in white sheets. David rushed to the window in time to see the lights on the ambulance disappear down the street.

After speaking with the police officers and investigators, Lawrence discovered that they could not share any information with anyone other than the victims' relatives. After concluding their investigation, the officer reported, "Since there were no forcible signs of entry, the assailant might have known the victim. Apparently, your neighbor knew her assailant well enough to let him or her into the home. Also, it appears that the assailant mistakenly left her for dead; therefore, we have an eyewitness that can identify him, her, or them." Someone from inside yelled out, "Seargent, seargent! We located a cell phone. It may or may not belong to the victim." The officer spoke with Lawrence, then instructed him to remain outside as he turned and went into the home. A few minutes later, he returned, saying, "This phone will give us a lead if there are any fingerprints."

This Is Real

In the meantime, Lawrence was looking behind him across the street and noticed David's upstairs window as his attention fell on the yellow tape placed around his neighbor's home. In the background, he could hear one of the officers saying, "This phone was located underneath the couch; therefore, it may belong to the victim. The handbag was on the floor; some of its contents were also on the table, and some were on the floor between the couch and the end table. It appeared that the lights were off. What light has shown through that open curtain probably revealed enough light for the robber to see the bag, taking her identification and credit cards, before tossing the rest." Contrary to his favorite TV crime scene thriller, the real experience left Lawrence tensed as each officer performed the task of collecting evidence. Ordinarily, Lawrence could figure out the plot and come to a conclusion, guessing who the assailant was, but his real-life experience left him trembling and nauseated.

Now speaking out loud, "This is not TV. This is real." The door opened behind him as another officer walked out, stating, "No, this is far from fiction or TV, and hopefully, the handbag and phone will reveal fingerprints enough to make an arrest. Therefore, the next step is to question the other neighbors; hopefully, the victim will be okay and can help further our investigation." As the paramedics were leaving, Lawrence inquired about the hospital; he was told that she would be taken to the nearest hospital instead of the county hospital. "You say your son's curiosity led you over here. Well, that is a good thing." Finally seated at the diner, they sang happy birthday, gave him a cupcake with four candles, and clapped as he blew out the candles, making David's celebration a success. Therefore, David completely forgot all about the incident with the neighbor and talked all the way home about his crayons, his friends Sam, Becky, and his personal colored placemat. David could not stop talking about the nice lady who gave him the cupcake and balloons.

Later on that evening, Catheryn tucked David into bed, placing next to him his action figure placemat and crayons. After saying good night, David continued to talk about the lady (Sam) and how she made pancakes with the funny blueberry face. The next day, David woke up very early and went to the window. He noticed that the window was still open to where he could see inside, but now there was the yellow ribbon around the house, but the lady's head was not in the window. He crawled back into bed but quickly sat up, remembering the dream and then the man pushing into the lady's house; now he was thinking, *I know, the lady is sleeping*. He crawled into bed and quickly fell asleep. At the same time, Lawrence and Catheryn were discussing the incident while Lawrence explained, "Thanks to David; help arrived just in time." Catheryn was looking at the bedroom door as if expecting David to walk in at any time.

What Is Her Name?

Momentarily distracted, Catheryn then asked. "What do you mean?" Lawrence explained, "The investigator said, 'David's quick response to getting to the neighbor's house in time actually saved her life.' Otherwise, things could have gone all wrong. Just think, since she lost so much blood, and if David had not been watching…" Catheryn held up her hand, signaling for Lawrence to stop speaking, before saying, "Honey, don't you think we've had enough drama for one day?" Lawrence nodded, at the same time laying his head on his pillow, but he wasn't able to sleep. The following day, after dropping David off at school, Lawrence suggested, "How about we both get off early and go by the hospital? Maybe we can visit, inquire about her condition, or better still, let her doctor know that we are the neighbors that discovered her. Do you think they will allow us to visit if we insist on seeing her?" Catheryn was shaking her head left to right before responding, "Honey, what's her name? Now that the property is taped off, we are not allowed on the premises, so we can't go snooping in her mailbox."

Now in deep thought, Lawrence nodded his head and said, "Without that information, we don't stand a chance." After tapping her forehead, something Catheryn did when in deep thought, she turned to Lawrence and asked, "What did the officer say to you when you were there? Surely he mentioned something about her name." In the meantime, Lawrence was looking to his right, preparing to pull in front of Catheryn's office. He turned his entire body and placed his right arm around her shoulders, saying, "Honey, all I can think is: what if that man had come to my home instead of hers? I know I would have protected you and David with my life. At that moment, when I saw her on that floor, I actually thought she was dead. Apparently, her attacker thought so, too. The officer that investigated the place said that her fall broke a vase. Since the place was dark, her attacker must have grabbed her handbag, stolen her cards and ID, and rushed off. It could have been us."

Several hours later, Catheryn's office building was overrun with people getting on and off the elevators. Suddenly, there was a knock on Catheryn's door. "Hey, lady, are you skipping lunch?" It was then, over the intercom, a young lady announced, "Mrs. Stern, Mr. Stern is on line two." Now laughing and teasing, the lady peeped in and said, "Oh, pardon me. Hot date?" Catheryn waved while responding, "Get away, Nadine," as she pressed the blinking phone line, "Hello, honey! Are you headed my way?" She laughed before answering, "Yes, I have one more client to contact before I leave." Catheryn responded, "No problem, just come on: I'll be standing on the front steps when you drive up." She made kissing noises as she hung up. After arriving, Lawrence got out, walked around to the passenger's side, opened the door, and kissed her on the cheek, hugging her ever so tightly before walking around to the driver's side. As she buckled her seatbelt, Catheryn remembered Lawrence's promise to fill her in on the conversation with the investigator, "Remember our conversation and your promise."

Too Busy to Call

Presently shaking his head from left to right, knowing Catheryn's intolerance for secrets, Lawrence laughed loudly, causing her to laugh. "I bet you've waited all day to ask that question. However, the officer was very discreet with his information, but he did mention that there was no identification found during the investigation." Fifteen minutes after leaving Catheryn's office, they arrived at the hospital. Immediately after walking through the entrance, Lawrence recognized the police investigator coming down the hallway. At the same time, he was pointing toward the officer while grabbing Catheryn's hand and rushing toward the officer. In that instance, palm facing Lawrence and Catheryn while demanding, "STOP!" With the other hand, he placed on his holster, causing both Lawrence and Catheryn to suddenly stop. Now walking slowly toward them, it was then the officer held out his right hand to Lawrence, but Lawrence stood still as the investigator approached them. Lawrence pointed at the Officer's holster, asking, "Is that a greeting formality?"

Gradually taking Lawrence's right hand, the officer smiled, explaining, "You both were moving very fast; you must know we are trained to counterattack when threatened." Both Catheryn and Lawrence laughed nervously and then relaxed after the Investigator introduced himself, explaining, "Call me Officer Troup." Now shaking Officer Troup's hand as he removed the other hand from his holster, Lawrence continued, "We are here to visit our neighbor, and we hope the doctor will allow us to see her." Officer Troup then explained, "She can't have any visitors at this time. On the other hand, let me walk you to her room. She's in ICU. Just let them know you are her visitors and leave your names." After saying goodbye to the officers, they followed his instruction leaving their names and phone number as closest relations. As a result of Sevella's last visit, Sam had hoped to invite her out and introduce her to some of her new friends. Although her schedule was hectic, she was determined to make it happen.

Eventually, feeling overwhelmed and very upset at being too busy to call, she then scolded herself, saying, "I have to somehow plan a gathering with Sevella and Samuel very soon." However, two days had passed, and Sam was still trying to work a time to contact Sevella until finally, she called. After many rings, there was no answer. After several tries, Sam gave up, deciding to go over after work and surprise Sevella. Once she arrived at Sevella's home, the first thing Sam noticed was the yellow tape, and she screamed and quickly pressed her brakes, causing her tires to skid, and squeaked before coming to a complete stop, stopping at least 500 feet from the entrance of Sevella's home. Her heart was now beating so fast, and her thoughts were telling her that something horrible had happened. "It's okay," said Sam out loud, but her heart was troubled as she stared in shock at the yellow tape around the entrance of Sevella's home.

What Has Happened?

Gradually turning her attention to the house across the street, Sam noticed that the upstairs curtains were open. Her first impulse was to rush over and pound on that door, thinking, *Maybe they saw what happened.* Sam quickly dismissed that thought and wondered in despair, "What has happened to my friend and Samuel?" She immediately took out her phone to call the police, but her hands were shaking, and tears impaired her vision. Instead, she quickly drove away. Shortly after getting home, Sam contacted the Police Department. However, because she was not a relative, they couldn't disclose any information. But before the Officer hung up, Sam said, "I just saw her and a co-worker," and immediately, the officer said, "Hold on." After a long pause, she heard, "This is Officer Troup. Would you mind coming down to the station and answering some questions?" After agreeing, Sam was now wondering, *What can I possibly tell him?*

Soon after arriving at the station, Sam waited several minutes before getting out of the car. She kept visualizing the yellow tape around Sevella's home. After a while, she entered the station and introduced herself, thinking, *I'll just play it by ear.* The first question was by the investigator, "When did you last see the victim?" Receiving a handkerchief from the officer, Sam thanked him before explaining, "It has been a few years since we worked together, and recently she and her boss came into the diner, and she told me she had just returned from a business trip. Sevella and her co-workers were customers at my restaurant, and we exchanged numbers, but that's it." Finally, the officer said, "Sevella, Sevella is her first name, and how long have you known Sevella?" Sam said, "Yes, that is her name—Sevella Thorn."

Suddenly Sam was crying and begging the officer to tell her if Sevella was still alive. Finally, she said, "We met almost four years ago, but suddenly too busy to keep in touch until two days ago, there she was." Then, Officer Troup asked, "Ma'am, give me the address to your restaurant?" Sam was very careful to say as little as possible because she didn't really want to give too much information until she spoke to Sevella, so Sam continued to cry bitterly. Finally, the officer said, "Ma'am, can I get your full name?" Through the tears, she said, "Yes, my name is Sam Dell." The officer then asked, "Is Sam short for Samantha?" Nodding her head, Sam answered, "Yes, Samantha Dell." She also gave the name and address of the diner. Broken-hearted, she began to weep so bitterly that the officers could not console her; therefore, they dismissed her as she wept uncontrollably and believed her friend and the baby were both dead. As Catheryn stared out of the window at the home across the street, she was still in unbelief at the mere thought of a crime occurring right in front of their home.

David's Dream
and Prayer

At last, Catheryn turned to Lawrence, asking, "How this could have happened without us knowing anything about it, and even more amazing, David was the one who actually witnessed the young lady's attack. Just think, if David had not been watching for the young lady, we would not have known of her attack!" Lawrence quickly stood with a look of amazement on his face as he stumbled over his words, asking, "What, when, I mean to say what was that?" Catheryn turned with a stunned look on her face while Lawrence was gesturing for her to continue before saying, "Honey, could you repeat the part after 'if'?" Catheryn repeated, "If David had not been watching?" Suddenly, Lawrence interrupted her, "Are you saying our son saw the whole thing; when, I mean, how could he have seen everything? How long has he been watching for this young lady?" Catheryn responded, "Honey, calm down. No, I'm not saying he saw anything except the man pushing his way into the house."

In turn, Lawrence jumped to his feet as Catheryn continued, "David was so frightened by what he saw, he jumped into bed; after falling asleep, he dreamed a bad dream, the rest you know." Again turning toward the window, Catheryn shook her head, speaking in a whisper, "It breaks my heart that someone's daughter lay hurt and alone in the hospital, and we don't know enough about her to contact relatives. Finally, Lawrence walked into the den but peeped back into the living room and reminded Catheryn of the following day's schedule, then saying, "You only answered a portion of my question about David's knowledge of the attack, but you are right, it's because of David our neighbor is alive." Now sitting, both staring out of the window, Lawrence suggested, "After work, and we pick David up from school, we will head to the hospital. Now that Officer Troup has given us enough information to gain access to visit our neighbor." Catheryn responded, "After stopping for a bite to eat, and by the way, the officer told us to wait until afternoon and he would meet us there."

Yesterday, we were only supposed to get a visit with the young lady. At least today, we know now that we can visit, and most importantly, the young lady will survive." Before going to bed, they both kneeled down by their bed and prayed that everything would be okay and the young lady would heal quickly. The next morning, before starting their daily routine, David told his parents that he had a dream that something bad had happened to the lady. He dreamed the lady was crying and holding out her hands for him. Amazed and speechless. "How could?" Lawrence began to ask, but Catheryn interrupted him, saying, "Honey, it is good that David has helped our neighbor, right?" At the same time, she gestured for Lawrence to follow her upstairs while David finished his breakfast. Once in the bedroom, he continued, "How could David have possibly known the extent of this young lady's attack? You said he didn't look out of the window until the paramedics were driving off." Catheryn responded, "I made sure David was distracted with his toys before the paramedics arrived and he was completed distracted until he heard the sirens."

Don't Open That Door!

Still baffled by David's dream, they both returned to the kitchen as David was finishing his orange juice. Looking at his parents, David said, "I want to pray for the lady." His father agreed with him, and immediately, David started to pray, "Help the lady feel better and safe. Amen." Afterward, his parents thanked him for praying for the young lady. At the same time, David was once again excited about going to his class and showing off his colorful placemat. "On the other hand," said Lawrence, but Catheryn shushed him and silently walked out of the house. However, the horrible sight of the yellow tape covering the entrance of their neighbor's home was a grim reminder of the weekend's horrible experience. David was now running to catch up with Lawrence. After hearing his father make the "beep, beep" sound, David raced to open the back door and climbed into his car seat. Lawrence was hoping the distraction would keep David's focus on his happy day.

Therefore, his father rushed to the car and hurried to buckle David in as his mother opened the front hurrying to buckle in, making it appear to be a game of buckle-up. Strategically she began to distract David's attention by asking questions about his coloring mat. David's attention was completely on his mother's facial expression as she made funny faces. Finally, they were safely passed their neighbor's home as David showed off his mat, excitedly explaining, "Look, the lady is happy now because she has a color mat around her house. Mommy, see, here is that color, here and here." David pointed out each picture that matched to yellow tape.

Periodically going in and out of consciousness, Sevella dreamed of a time when she received punishment for not listening. At the time, she was only six years old. "Sevella, what have I told you about running and opening that door; are you expecting someone?" yelled Miss Timothy, "No more warning, now go and get the strap!" Slowly getting up, "Please, ma'am, I was only trying to help!" She thought to herself, *How can she spank me when she can barely get around?* At the same time, tossing and turning in her sleep, Sevella began to cry out, "Please, please, Miss Timothy. I was only trying to help by getting the door for you." As she tossed and turned, the top covers on her hospital bed slid slowly to the floor. "That may be the case, Sevella," said Miss Timothy, "but you never ever open the door without first asking who is there. Did you do that?" demanded Miss Timothy. Sevella was crying in her sleep, and the trauma of that dream transcended from her dreams to reality.

Who Are They?

At that moment, she began to talk in her sleep, "No, Miss Timothy." Now pointing in the direction of the bedroom, Miss Timothy insisted, "My point exactly is to go get the strap. The last time I gave this warning, you promised me you would never do that again. Now here we are having this same conversation." Even though she was dreaming, the reality of that experience was emotionally draining as Sevella tears ran down her cheeks onto her pillow. "Please, Miss Timothy! Next time, I'll remember." Sevella was awakened by the sound of her voice. "Miss Timothy was right," whispered Sevella as she struggled to get her body to turn to the left, away from the window. Now facing the door, she continued to wonder, *I was too anxious to help and didn't remember her last warning, But I do remember the time Miss Timothy was praying for me, more so than the whipping. I don't know why I carried on so, despite her hitting as hard as she could, her whipping was much like a pat on the hand.*

Sevella's memory of that time in her life was present in her mind; as she recalled that very emotional day, saying, "Compared to the beatings I received from others who weren't as nice as Miss Timothy." Seconds later, Sevella was experiencing excruciating pain from the back of her head to her shoulders and neck. Coupled with the soreness in her side, she ached all over while slowly shifting to lie on her left side. She remembered the last encounter with Miss Timothy. *Occasionally,* she thought, as she seemed to discover a painless position to lay her head. *The other foster parent wouldn't bother to get a belt but use whatever she could get her hands on; they said I was getting a spanking, but instead of a spanking, they would hit me wherever.* Sevella's legs began to move involuntarily. Frightened, she noticed that her legs hadn't moved when she was positioning herself on her side. "Maybe they did move, and I wasn't paying attention," she reasoned.

Afterward, Sevella began to look around the room but wasn't able to visualize, but her thoughts were still on the dream and the reality of it. Sevella's face and her pillow were soaked from her tears. Moreover, Sevella was unaware of the severity of her condition; the pain in her shoulders, the throbbing headache, the pain in her neck, side, and back, and her motionless legs were only a small portion of her injuries. The name Sevella and Miss Timothy seemed so familiar, but she had no idea who they were. "Who are they, and why am I crying over them? Are they dead? Were they relatives or dear friends? Who are they?" Furthermore, she wondered about the statement, "I remember the warning." *Oh, my! Am I the girl in the dream?* Sevella's headache worsened as she pondered the memory; eventually, she dozed off to sleep but struggled to stay awake.

Can You Hear Me?

Subsequently, the pain medication took effect as she whispered, "Miss Timothy and the little girl." Sevella again dreams, except it was Miss Timothy who answered the door asking, "Who is there?" Frowning as she attempted to understand, she was now talking in her sleep, "Miss Timothy looks so happy when she smiles, and I only wanted to make her smile." Again, confused by the familiarity of the dream but unable to understand why. Waking up, only to doze off as she fought to stay awake, she realized that there had to be a reason for this reoccurring dream. "Despite the whipping, I was trying to make her smile, and that's why I forgot the warning." Again, the sound of her voice woke her, but the room was dimly lit; therefore, she closed her eyes and fell fast asleep. However, the light appeared then faded as the sun rays became overcrowded by clouds, but not before resting upon Sevella's cheek. She turned her head from side to side in an attempt to avoid the very warm rays resting on her cheek. However, the problem wasn't a dimly lit room but her eyesight.

Still talking in her sleep, "I picked up the strap, turned, and slowly walked back to my bedroom and stood by the bed, and waited for Miss Timothy. Finally, she appeared. I knew the routine; I handed her the belt, laid across the bed…" "Ma'am, ma'am, can you hear me?" Immediately Sevella began to feel alarmed as she tossed and turned. "Ma'am, can you hear me?" Then another unfamiliar voice, "I spoke to Officer Troup, the investigating officer, and her name is Sevella; that's all we have for now." After hearing the name, she began to slowly wake up, only to a horrible throbbing in her head and a thick fog over her eyes. "Ma'am, can you hear me?" Said the second unfamiliar voice. "My name is Doctor Phelhen, and you have been unconscious for a couple of days. Can you tell me your name?" As she slowly processed the words spoken by the doctor, she then attempted to respond, but she couldn't make her mouth cooperate with her thoughts. Finally, she managed to whisper, "W…why?"

Obviously, this response was exactly what Dr. Phelhan was expecting; smiling and speaking very softly, he said, "If you don't mind, we need to know if you can remember your name?" Actually, at that moment, she wanted to say, "My name is Sevella," but she wasn't quite sure. Suddenly Sevella realized her only memory was the dream. Hearing the name Sevella apart from the dream was shocking, but she couldn't put the pieces together as she reasoned, "I think the name in the dream would be a hint, and maybe that's my name." Dr. Phelhen continued, "Also, whoever assaulted you must have stolen your identification because the police weren't able to find any information that would identify you. Can you remember what happened?" As she considered the doctor's words, she quietly asked, "W…w…wh…?" But the words would not come forth; therefore, she could only make a groaning sound.

Where Am I?

Momentarily, attempting to recall all the words of the doctor, she asked herself, *Did he say police and robbery?* She then opened her mouth, and this time, her words came but sporadically, "M… na… is…" Then her head began to throb, she stopped to place her hand on her forehead, and then she continued, "I… ha…" The doctor interrupted her by softly patting the hand on her forehead, saying, "We understand; please try to rest, and we'll talk later." At that point, Sevella realized that there was something seriously wrong with her. Suddenly, the brightness of the sunlight shining directly across her face caused her head to throb even more. Therefore, she decided that it was best to keep her eyes closed to avoid the throbbing pain as the voices, one by one, exited the room. Last but least, the pain refused to leave her. "What's happened to me?" Sevella realized that the only voice she had was in her mind because her words refused to register on her lips, all the while holding her aching head.

"On the other hand, and in spite of the disconnection between her brain and her mouth, she began to search for answers, "Where am I, what has happened to me, and is this a hospital bed and not Miss Timothy's house, and did she assault me?" Now searching her memory, hoping to make some sense of her situation." Suddenly, the door opened, and another unfamiliar voice said, "Hello, Miss! I'm Officer." The tone of his voice was stern and audible, almost too loud to bear, as Sevella moved her hand from her head and placed both hands over her ears, blotting out the words spoken by the officer; therefore, she didn't hear the following questions. The officer continued, "That's why it is important to get you to help us, maybe by telling what you know about your attacker." Dr. Phelhen recognized Sevella's attempt to drown out the officer's voice but remained silent. He wanted the Officer to see for himself the seriousness of her injuries.

As the officer concluded, "I'm here to ask you some questions. You see, we need to find whoever did this to you, and your answers may give us a clue to what actually happened. Miss, you were brought into the hospital two days ago. Apparently—" She then turned to look at the officer attempting to say, "My head," but her thoughts were her only voice. Momentarily placing her hand over her mouth and her aching head, desperately she wanted to voice her concerns about the disconnection of her thoughts and voice. Sevella made a second attempt to speak this time; she was successful, but only in a whisper, "Who…?" Suddenly, the door opened and interrupted her train of thought. The doctor spoke in a whisper to the officer just as the intercom announced another doctor's name. Once again, the room was silent, and Sevella opened her eyes but could barely make out the facial features of the person standing at her bedside.

Assault

As she stared blindly in his direction, the doctor, with his small flashlight shining it in one eye and then the other, said, "Good morning," in a very cheerful tone as he examined her eyes. Speaking slowly, she whispered, "A…ssault." Her voice was again her thoughts, but not her words, as she desperately tried to connect the two. Suddenly, there was a knock on the door of her hospital room, and at that moment, she remembered that there was a knock on the door in her dream, and just as Miss Timothy had always warned her, "Never open that door without first asking who is there!" Fear gripped her heart as she remembered, "First the knock on the door, before I jump to my feet; that's right, I thought it was Sam. Oh my, I remember; I was asleep on the couch, woke up, stumbled to the door, and opened it." Apart from the shock of her first attempt to remember, she was obviously overwhelmed by the sudden ability to recall the night of the attack.

Overwhelmed at the memory of such a horrible attack, she then remembered the street light revealing the man's form in a long coat. After that, she wasn't sure what had happened. At that point, Sevella decided to keep on complaining about her head, and maybe they will leave her alone. She then heard another knock on the door and another unfamiliar voice, "Hello, I'm sorry I was hoping to peep in on my neighbor." Shocked, she repeated, "Neighbor!" Now desperately hoping the doctor would prevent the visit. Sevella tightly closed her eyes and turned her head toward the heat that she previously avoided, the bright sunbeam shining through her window. "Hello," said the doctor cheerfully. "She's awake but having terrible headaches; I need to examine her further before allowing any visitors. I'm afraid she is in a lot of pain. She has also suffered severe trauma to the head and may have lost memory as a result of the injury; furthermore, she may not remember you."

For a brief moment, the room was very quiet, then her neighbor said, "Oh, I'm sorry, but my neighbor and I never met: you see, it was my husband and me who discovered her and called for help." "Undoubtedly, she would be grateful, or will be grateful once she can remember, whispered Dr. Phelhen. Catheryn then shared her sentiments, adding, "How awful it must be to lose one's memory. Well, actually, on the day of the attack, our four-year-old was very anxious to meet our neighbor. You see, my husband and I haven't had the opportunity to introduce ourselves since we are new to the neighborhood," the opening of the door interrupted Catheryn, and the voice asked loudly, "Mommy, can I see the lady?" Obviously, the pain in her head and her shoulder kept her from moving; therefore, she lay very still, listening to every word. Now she repeated the woman's words, "Our four-year-old wanted to meet our neighbor." Without a doubt, this little boy knew her more so than his parents.

Separating Dreams from Reality

However, she began to wonder if the little boy and the little girl in her dreams were friends. For the most part, Sevella's head trauma prevented her from separating her dreams from reality. Now looking through what appeared to be a fog, she strained to see the little boy's face. In spite of the fog, Sevella stared but couldn't make out what she was seeing; as her pain intensified and became more and more unbearable; therefore, she fell backward onto her pillow. Furthermore, since consciousness, her days and nights were filled with her last experience with Miss Timothy. During that time with Miss Timothy, she came to understand the word "orphaned." She began to scream silently at herself, "Why didn't you want her to visit? Besides, she may know something about Sevella, or Miss Timothy, and the man. What's the matter with my eyesight; does the doctor know that I can't see clearly?" As she turned her head away from the heat of the sunbeam: Dr. Phelhen, in stark coincidence, walked toward her, hoping against hope that Sevella's eyesight had improved.

Once he stood at her bedside, Dr. Phelhen began to speak to someone else, "I'm finished with my examination, and I have given her a shot for pain. You will have to wait for the effect of the medication to wear off; however, that is no guarantee you will be able to question her. Her injuries are severe, and the test results for her MRI are pending; the test will reveal the severity of her head trauma; therefore, she may or may not remember what occurred during the attack. However, if there is no damage or signs of fluid on the brain, I will allow a short interview but nothing extensive. Hopefully, she can remember some of the details, but first, she'll have to rest before." The following evening Dr. Phelhen is again by Sevella's bedside, repeating her name, "Sevella, Sevella, please wake up." She then slowly and painfully opened her eyes as she struggled to visualize the man standing near, but her throbbing head prevented her from speaking.

Still, she struggled to put the pieces of her life together, "When did he learn my name, or who could have told him my name? Oh, my!" As the doctor continued to question her, "How are you feeling, and are you still having headaches?" Sevella listened quietly to the doctor's questions while she continued to search her memory of the attack. It was then her memory began to slowly return. She realized then that the person who forced his way into her home must have broken in and robbed her. *Who was that man?* she thought, *and why did he pick me to rob? It was dark, and I could only see his image from the street lights, but not his face, and he must have covered his face because his voice sounded muffled.* Slowly, Sevella began to remember bits and pieces, but nothing made sense. As it happened from sheer exhaustion, she closed her eyes and fell asleep. Suddenly, she remembered screaming at a man, "WHO ARE YOU? AND WHAT ARE YOU TALKING ABOUT?"

Still at Large

From that moment on, she was distracted by her headache and wondering, *When will the pain medicine take effect?* Suddenly, she began to feel tired and very sleepy as she slowly dozed off, thinking, *Relief, thank goodness!* As she dozed off, she heard the doctor say to someone, "I think the pain medicine is taking effect; in an hour or two, you can start your questioning." As she drifted deeper into sleep, she heard another woman's voice, and she was talking to a nurse. Following that conversation, Sevella heard footsteps, then a door opening; at that moment, before walking out of the door, the woman turned to the nurse, saying, "By the way, my name is Samantha, but my friend Sevella calls me Sam. As Sevella dozed deeper into sleep, she then heard the nurse say, "No, Community Hospital is located..." As she attempted to respond to the nurse speaking with her, she began to wake up, only to fall back to sleep.

Obviously shaken from Sevella's condition as well as the news of her attacker still at large, Sam accidentally bumped into Dr. Phelhen, but also, a nurse was attempting to catch up with the doctor. In addition to all the confusion and, apologizing, the nurse asked, "Dr. Phelhen, did you get the call from Investigator Troup? Sir, he wants to meet with the neighbors here at the hospital, and they will be arriving by noon. Please let them know." Dr. Phelhen turned to Sam, again apologizing; at the same Sam was asking, "Are you Sevella's doctor?" Dr. Ph

"Yes, and you are?" Sam was now shaking the doctor's hand while introducing herself, "I'm your patient's friend, Sam, and I just left her, I mean—Sevella's—room; please, tell me she is going to be alright." At this time, Dr. Phelhen is receiving a call over the intercom. "Excuse me, Sam, but you are a friend. I can only give the patient's information to her closest relatives."

Undoubtedly disturbed by the unknown, tears filled Sam's eyes just as the doctor was leaving. But Dr. Phelhen turned around, winking, saying to Sam, "Don't worry," before rushing off. Afterward, the room was quiet, and Sevella dreamed that Sam was speaking to her while the nurse came and placed a medical bracelet on her right wrist. Although she was going in and out of consciousness, she struggled to remember the visitor who identified herself as Sam. She remembered Sam saying, "Okay, Sevella. I'm going to be right here, even until after you have that baby." Now tossing frantically in her sleep, Sevella attempted' to respond to Sam, but there seemed to be something covering her mouth; now attempting to calm down, she remembered Miss Timothy saying, "Never struggle in a dream: you can have a heart attack." Next, she dreamed of questioning Sam, asking, "What baby?" Shortly after that, she could see herself holding Samuel for the first time as she glanced at his ID, bracelet reading, "Baby Nix; Community Hospital."

A Good Friend

In addition, an announcement was being made on the overhead system;" "Dr. Harper, Dr. Harper, you are wanted, you are wanted…." At the sound of the intercom, Sevella slowly opened her eyes, attempting to see her arms through the fog, looking for the baby, and the wristband before frantically looking around the room, the wall chart that read, "Patient, Sevella Thorn, Central Hospital," as she thought to herself, *No, I'm not in Central Hospital, but Community.* Hours later, while recalling the dream and the baby, she wondered, *Do I have a baby? Maybe the doctor can explain everything I've heard in the dream.* Suddenly, Sevella realized that her eyesight was clearing, yet, she was still very confused. She felt overwhelmed and alarmed at the prospect of her being a mother, a mother but not able to remember her own baby. Also, the nurse in her dream said, "No, Community Hospital," but the wall chart read, "Central Hospital." Most importantly, she was not there to have a baby but because someone broke into her home and assaulted her.

Suddenly, the door opened, and footsteps filled the room as Dr. Phelhen softly spoke, asking, "Miss Thorn, while you were resting, you had a visitor, a good friend; please, can you help us out?" Dr. Phelhen was now sounding very concerned, and without warning, tears began to run down Sevella's cheeks as she slowly turned her face towards the window keeping her arm draped over her forehead, hoping Dr. Phelhen would not see her tears. In that moment, Dr. Phelhen said, "She's holding her head. She is coming around; therefore, the medication is wearing off. Only after it wears completely off you can start your investigation. Her MRI revealed no brain damage but a very serious concussion. Let's leave her to rest and try again in the morning. I don't want to wear her out. I'm pretty sure your job is to get information, and once she is conscious and without pain, I will allow it. However, at this time, she is not in any condition to answer questions after being so heavily sedated."

After Dr. Phelhen and Officer Troup left the room, Sevella's tears poured from her eyes like heavy raindrops. She promised herself that no one would ever again see her cry and never again be called a crybaby. However, it was becoming harder and harder to keep that promise, especially when it came to Dr. Phelhen. She then remembered the dream, now understanding why Miss Timothy never wanted her to answer the door. "Miss Timothy was only trying to protect me from a horrible incident like the recent one." Sevella was shocked at her voice sounding almost normal. As the tears rolled down her cheeks onto her pillow, a smile surfaced on her lips as her voice echoed throughout the empty room. "Even when Miss Timothy punished me, I refused to be a crybaby. I refused to let her see me cry. Even when she wouldn't allow me to watch TV, I would only brush it off. I knew she was getting older, and no TV became her choice of punishment for me."

Being Loved

"Later on, she would punish me by sending me to my room." As she shifted her body, the ache in her head intensified, but the pain in her heart prevailed as she continued to reflect on Miss Timothy. "The whipping was supposed to help me remember not to open the door before knowing who was there; at the time, making her smile was more important to me than remembering the warning!" It appeared that the vivid brightness of the setting sun seemed to outline the darkness caused by the trauma of her attacker. Yet, her experience paled in comparison to the splendor and beauty of the blue sky. Apparently, the shapely white clouds pressed against the colorful orange and gray horizon reminded her of her first trip to France. All of a sudden, she remembered, "Samuel." She whispered as her tears now covered her face; she tightly closed her eyes, realizing that the tears were only mirroring the reality of life's circumstances. Through her tears, she cried out, "This is all Dr. Phelhen's fault!"

In addition to the pain in her head, the pain in her heart was more severe. "If he wasn't so kind and gentle, I wouldn't be crying so! His kind words and a gentle pat on my hand have continued to break through my tough exterior." As tears continued to stream down her face, strangely enough, she felt a sense of peace as gratitude replaced the sadness that always found its way into her happy moments; nevertheless, she would always manage to hide that sadness from everyone around her. "I'm so glad that Dr.

Phelhen assumed I was asleep. Or did he? Either way, I'm just glad it worked." Now all alone to cry in peace, she recalled the kindness shown by Dr. Phelhen. "No," she said aloud, as her voice returned to a normal tone, now whispering, "No, I have never received such kindness from a total stranger; no, not anyone, not even Mrs. Timothy, that's why I can't stop crying. I believe this is similar to being loved!"

Again, the heaviness of sleep caused her to doze off. She whispered, "Another thing, Miss Timothy always prayed for me. I really didn't understand the debt of those prayers until now. On the other hand, as for Dr. Phelhen, maybe he's praying for me, too." The following morning, she heard the door open and the doctor saying, "Her identification must have been stolen." Sevella was now thinking, *The truth is, I purchased a security box at the bank and placed all my personal and confidential information in that box. I had no idea when Neal would sell the house, so I used the office address to mail a copy of the keys to myself.* Again, Sevella reflected back to a certain day and smiled as she recalled Miss Timothy taking her to the store and afterward to the bank, where Miss Timothy placed some jewelry into a security box. "That day, I swore to myself I would someday get a security box for myself. In all my life, I never owned anything except what was left by my mother, whom I never knew."

Very Dark Secret

"Despite my hopeless future, I purchased the security box and received the key. I felt as though someone had handed me a million dollars. After the security box, I knew my life would never be the same because I would now have something of my very own for the very first time." Momentarily ignoring the excruciating pain, Sevella began to smile as she relived the feeling of control after putting away her private information that no one could ever take away from her. Once again, she remembered questions she wanted to ask Dr. Phelhen about the visitor he was discussing. She didn't need to reveal her secret and avoided answering the officer's questions. Furthermore, she preferred that the nurse and Dr. Phelhen didn't know that she was listening to their conversation while pretending to be asleep, so she laid very still and avoided placing her hand on her aching head.

Now laughing, she was thinking, *That's funny, even my name is fake; ever since I heard a lady say, "we'll just make up a name for her." After that, I used one fake name after another; because I never wanted anyone poking around in my past.* In spite of all the uncertainties she experienced, she was thankful that there was no stolen identification to be retrieved. Now she whispered, "I've always kept the keys to the security box hidden inside my closet in the sole of a shoe that I made just for hiding my keys away from clients and strangers. My only fear is being found out and accused of being a liar. Oh, no!" Sevella said out loud as Dr. Phelhen and the nurse were immediately by her bedside. "Miss Thorn is waking up to the pain," said Dr. Phelhen. Now checking her eye purples while the nurse quickly checked her vital signs and IV. Dr. Phelhen explained, "Miss Thorn, everything looks fine, and your discomfort is due to the trauma you sustained to the head during an attack."

At that moment, Sevella's heart pounded at the thought of being questioned. Dr. Phelhen continued, "The officers must question you before your next dose of pain medication." She was thinking, *What if he finds out everything? First, my neighbors; secondly, the officer, whose responsibility is to help find my attacker, but at the expense of exposing my very dark secret. This is unlike anything I have ever experienced in the orphanage or any foster home; if my secret as a mother who abandoned her child gets out, I will be forced to tell the police about the monster who attacked me and thought to have overdosed me, but instead, left me alive and pregnant. Oh, my! What am I going to do?* Now she recalled her earlier thought that caused her to speak out loud, "First and foremost. I need to pull it together and strategize. I remember my neighbor telling Dr. Phelhen that her four-year-old insisted that they visit my home. No doubt, their visit led them to call the police." Sevella lay very still, fighting the temptation to lay her hand on her aching head.

Plan B

Finally, Dr. Phelhen and the nurse exited her room, and the door closed; then Sevella slowly turned to position her body to face the door relieving the numbness in her right hip while speaking in a whisper, "My neighbor's view is exactly as mine, making it easy for Samuel to watch me. Oh, no! I wonder if he could have possibly seen something and waited until the next day to tell his parents. I can't bear the thought of being discovered by Samuel's parents! Apart from this hospital confinement, they never would have found me out. Nonsense, so what if they were the ones that found me? What could they have possibly found out? Dr. Phelhen even said, 'The police found no identification.' So, that settles it. I am going to pretend that I'm still suffering from amnesia." In that moment, her thoughts were back on Sam, *Could the visitor the doctor spoke about possibly be my Sam?* At that moment, she eagerly waited for the officers, so she could get past the questions and focus on plan B—her exit from the hospital.

Later on that day, after a brief encounter with a stranger who offered to pray for her, Sevella smiled and slowly closed her eyes, signaling to the Stranger that she was feeling tired. After the lady left, Sevella again turned her face to the window as tears rolled down her cheeks onto her neck as she recalled some of the words prayed by Miss Timothy. "While my life is more complex than ever, I remember Miss Timothy sitting for hours telling her funny stories, although I pretended I wasn't amused; inside, I couldn't stop laughing. After all these years, I am now remembering the exact words of Miss Timothy's prayer. The Stranger echoed the same words in her prayer." Sevella then repeated the stranger's prayer, "Lord let no harm or danger come upon her again; instead, let your hands be upon her and keep her mind, body, and soul safe in your arms. Amen." Slowly wiping tears, she thought, *Hum, Amen; before closing their prayers, those are their last word.*

Sevella began to think about that prayer and her prayer for Samuel and realized that her first attacker could have also killed her, and if the second attack had been successful, she would be dead. She then turned to look at the IV pole and said, "If I hadn't prayed and asked for help with Samuel, I would have aborted and killed him." In that moment, her thoughts were interrupted by the door to her room opening. Thinking it was the officers coming in to question her, Sevella lay very still. However, as the door slowly opened, she heard the sound of a small child's voice asking, "Mommy, can I see the lady?" After that, a woman's voice spoke and said, "Sweetie, thanks to you, the lady is going to be alright." Sevella fought to keep her eyes closed as she lay face up, now speaking silently, *I want so much to open my eyes, hold out my arms for him to run into them, but he is no longer my tiny little bundle, and I know without a doubt—that this is Samuel.*

Today I Heard His Voice

Although everything inside her screamed, "Samuel, Samuel!" and she wanted to gaze upon that tiny little face, then jump up and take him into her arms, she knew better. *Besides,* speaking to herself, *I don't want the pain to return. For the first time since her hospital stay, the pain was subsiding.* Finally, she heard Dr. Phelhen saying, "Would you like to come in and speak to her? She was awake earlier, and I think now is a good time before the officers wear her out with questions; if you would like to wake her, it's okay." As a result of hearing Samuel's voice, Sevella's emotions were unrestrained, and she was unable to control her tears. At the same time, her neighbor spoke to the doctor, saying, "Yes, if you don't mind, because our son is eager to see her." The door opened all the way, and Sevella slowly opened her eyes, looking at the ceiling until her neighbor walked over with Samuel in her arms. Strangely enough, the tears flooded her eyes, so much so that she was looking at Samuel through a cloud of tears.

Moreover, her heart ached and longed for that baby she had abandoned. Now concerned, David patted his mother's cheek, pointing. "Mommy, the lady is crying," said David, alarmed by her tears. Catheryn handed Sevella a tissue; at the same time, Sevella placed her forearm over her eyes and said, "Thank you for helping me." By that time, Dr. Phelhen was standing near Catheryn, explaining, "She suffered severe head trauma; therefore, she's probably experiencing some pain." Catheryn turned to David and asked, "Sweetheart, did you hear that? She said thank you." David was vigorously nodding and smiling as Catheryn turned and walked toward the door, saying, "David, we'll come back when she feels better." Now turning to Dr. Phelhen, she said, "Please, let her rest; she has been through a very frightening ordeal." As the door slowly closed behind her visitors, Sevella repeated the name, "David. So, they changed his name to David."

Together with the joy of being in the same room with David, coupled with the pain of conception, she tightly closed her eyes while tears of joy ran down the side of her face; she could hear Samuel's voice in the distance, saying, "Mommy, is the lady....?" As the tiny voice eventually faded in the distance, Sevella whispered, "I never experienced his first spoken words, but today for the first time, I heard his voice." As she turned to face the window, she noticed the sun setting, and she smiled as she remembered, *Following a hard day's work, this would be the exact time of day that I would be sitting on my couch, looking out of my window, waiting for Samuel, I mean David, and his parents to come home just so I could see him. How ironic; exactly at the same time of day, David and his parents have come to see me, and no peeping is required.* At that moment, Sevella realized that David's happiness was more important to her than anything in the world.

The Life You Saved

On the other hand, Neal received a call from Ned regarding the recent arrest of one of their suspects. Apparently, the man that assaulted Sevella was under surveillance and was being followed. However, it was only after the attack that the Investigator joined forces with the local authorities to identify the perpetrator. Meanwhile, Sam and Becky finally figured out that Sevella's co-worker was actually Toni's fiancé. Afterward, they located his number among her personal contacts. Furthermore, Neal was trying to get more information on the assault; his brother gave an address where the assault took place. It was then Neal dropped the phone on his desk. At the same time, Mr. Clark's phone rang; he started not to answer but thought Sevella was using her home phone to call him; therefore, he quickly answered but did not recognize the voice. After the introduction, Becky explained, "Mr. Clark, the authorities had a lead on suspects that may be responsible for several missing persons, and Toni was on that list."

Now, Mr. Clark was listening carefully, still trying to identify the voice; therefore, he remained silent during the conversation, yet caught off guard by what he was hearing, at the same time troubled by Neal's reactions. Deep down, he knew but was hoping the news Neal received wasn't about Sevella. In addition, his suspicion concerning Toni would be confirmed, and he could not bear the thought that the same misfortune had happened to Sevella. Therefore, he politely excused himself and promised to return Becky's call, at the same time thanking her for reaching out to him. Slowly he hung up but sat staring at the receiver lying on Neal's desk, wanting desperately to pick it up and ask, "Is she alive?"

At that moment, Sevella knew she would probably never hear Samuel's voice again. Suddenly, tears of joy were replaced by tears of pain. Now crying herself to sleep, she imagined the smile on Samuel, well, David's face; she whispered, "In my life, I've only had fantasy friends, but today, I have two very wonderful friends; Sam and Samuel, and they are my very special friends, and they are very real. Well, maybe three, Mr. Clark. Oh, no! What if the truth reaches Mr. Clark…Well, it doesn't really matter because I'll probably never see him again." As Sevella turned to look at the shapely clouds and then the blueness of the sky, she began to pray, "I know it's been a while since I've talked to you for myself, well since I've asked you to help me get on with my life… Life, how strange. If it hadn't been for Samuel, I would be dead." Now she cried, rushing to compose herself with the tissue given to her by Catheryn, hoping no one would enter the room. Afterward, she began to pray, saying, "I have not been totally honest, and if anyone finds out that I am Samuel's mother, well, if I have to tell of my attacker in Florida, my life will be over. Life, I have another question to ask: How is it that the life you saved…saved me?"

Epilogue

Meanwhile, we were then informed that our presence was requested by the King and Queen of the village. The five of us were then rushed to meet our guide, who then informed us of a banquet being prepared in honor of the American Ambassador's new position. Furthermore, within forty-five minutes, the five of us were being led by the chiefs to be presented to the King and the Queen Mother (Na Na). She personally wrapped her royal shawl around my shoulders. Following that amazing display of transferring authority, I was in total shock and shaking from head to toe, along with shaking of my legs, as I attempted to stand and remain standing. After glancing toward my interpreter, who directed me to look over toward Queen Mother, she was now motioning for me to come to her. Slowly I walked over and was prepared to stand next to her, but the most amazing thing happened; she stood up, spoke to her adjectives, and sat on the seat behind her royal stool as she motioned for me to sit on her royal stool. This time I felt faint, but I kept reminding myself, *This is for the children, the hurting, and the poor.*

After returning to the States, then God's story, *Orphaned*, was downloaded into my mind, and I began to write everything down. Much to my surprise, the information kept coming, and it came effortlessly. Therefore, I'm just a steward or vessel which God used to write His story. From 2005 to the present day, the words are still being downloaded, and I will continue to write them down.

Sevella, the character in this story, is fictional. At the same time, it is someone's true-life experience, especially for many foster and adoptive children. Also, this story may apply to many or just one and may appear to be a story of someone you have known. Although fiction, it is a story that must be told. This story, "Her Story," from His heart to my heart, continues until there is nothing more to tell.

Afterword

Operation Not Forgotten

As it happens, there is no end to this story, just a beginning, and below is an example of that beginning. I would like to share excerpts from an article that addresses some of the problems I've mentioned in this book. I would like to dedicate this book not only to Sharon Matthews but also to Ms. Simms and the authorities responsible for their successful intervention of thirty-nine missing children. Instead of reading about a tragedy, we can celebrate a successful transition from danger to safety. Below is the excerpt of this amazing rescue.

By Claire Simms

Published 8/28/2020

FOX 5 Atlanta

U.S. Marshals recover 39 missing children in Georgia operation, "We will never stop looking for you. That's [the] message," said Director Washington. "Well, we're not just man hunters anymore," explained Darby Kirby, chief inspector of the U.S. Marshals Service Missing Child Unit. "We also help save and rescue children as well." According to the Marshals Service, there are more than 420,000 children currently missing in the U.S. Of those, about 91 percent are runaways believed to be in danger. The Georgia Bureau of Investigation assisted in the investigation.

FBI Atlanta @FBIAtlanta

Acting Special Agent in Charge Phil Wislar attends a press conference with our partners @USMarshalsHQ announcing the recovery of 39 missing children in Georgia during Operation "Not Forgotten." Thank you to all our partners! involved! https://usmarshals.gov/news/chron/2020/082720.htm"

I salute Ms. Simms for taking an unprecedented interest in writing this excellent article, reporting the rescue and recovery of those thirty-nine missing children. Also, our First Responders, the Officers of Georgia, and the FBI, who carried out a successful rescue and recovery mission, I salute you as well! As you can see, there is hope, but it starts with us, first, voicing our concerns, and next, talking about it to whoever will listen. This book is a memorial to some and a tribute to others. Most importantly, a tool to bring awareness to neglected and abused children. It starts when a child becomes homeless, orphaned, run away, or fostered. Many become targets of kidnappers, human trafficking, prostitution, or, worst—death. The list goes on, and no child is exempt; a child was never placed on this earth to defend themselves from abuse but to be loved, sheltered, and protected.

Organizational Support

You can help! Below is a list of organizations dedicated to helping these less fortunate by providing a "safe place to sleep," a place of refuge, a sonogram of an unborn baby's heart, and many others. I have only donated to a few, but 10 percent of the proceeds from this book will go toward supporting these and other organizations dedicated to bringing awareness to the least of these. My continued prayer is that each person that purchases this book will choose to research their local charities involved in rescuing, if not thirty-nine, maybe just one, and give hope to the hopeless.

Please make and compare notes before making a decision. With each organization, we expect to find without compromise, integrity, accountability, and trustworthiness. Below is a list of just a few of these organizations:

www.abba.jave

www.covenanthouse.org

www.casacentex.org/becomeacasa

www.davethomasfoundation.org

www.fostermore.org

www.inyourcournerministries.com

www.matressfirmfosterkids.com

www.orphanspromise.org

www.prebornministries.com

www.teensinfostercae.org

CPSIA information can be obtained
at www.ICGtesting.com
Printed in the USA
BVHW050002260423
663030BV00006B/10

9 781685 566654